Capital Accumulation and Migration

Studies in Critical Social Sciences

VOLUME 46

The titles published in this series are listed at brill.nl/scss

Capital Accumulation and Migration

By

Dennis C. Canterbury

BRILL

LEIDEN · BOSTON
2012

Cover illustration: Kromantse-Nkum Village in Ghana, West Africa in 2007. Villagers fishing in the Gulf of Guinea. Kromantse-Nkum was a site of centuries of forced African migration. © Dennis C. Canterbury.

Library of Congress Cataloging-in-Publication Data

Canterbury, Dennis C. (Dennis Compton), 1953-
  Capital accumulation and migration / by Dennis C. Canterbury.
     p. cm. -- (Studies in critical social sciences ; v. 46)
  Includes bibliographical references and index.
  ISBN 978-90-04-23038-5 (hardback : alk. paper) -- ISBN 978-90-04-23039-2 (ebk)
1. Saving and investment. 2. Neoliberalism. 3. Migration, Internal. I. Title.

  HB822.C37 2012
  332'.0415--dc23

                                                                    2012025018

This publication has been typeset in the multilingual "Brill" typeface. With over 5,100 characters covering Latin, IPA, Greek, and Cyrillic, this typeface is especially suitable for use in the humanities. For more information, please see www.brill.nl/brill-typeface.

ISSN 1573-4234
ISBN 978 90 04 23038 5 (hardback)
ISBN 978 90 04 23039-2 (e-book)

This book is printed on acid-free paper.

MIX
Paper from
responsible sources
FSC
www.fsc.org   FSC® C109576

                                                Printed by Printforce, the Netherlands

CONTENTS

PART ONE

MIGRATION THEORY: EARLY ROOTS

PART TWO

NEOLIBERAL PERSPECTIVES ON DEVELOPMENT
IMPACT OF MIGRATION

PART THREE

FAULT LINES IN NEOLIBERAL VIEWS ON MIGRATION

ABOUT THE AUTHOR

Dennis C. Canterbury was born in New Amsterdam, Guyana, grew up in East Ruimveldt in the Capital City of Georgetown, and completed his undergraduate degree in political science at the university of Guyana. Thereafter he worked as a researcher at the Institute of Development Studies at the University of Guyana and pursued graduate studies in social sciences with a specialization in economic development in the Consortium Graduate School at the University of the West Indies in Jamaica, international development studies at Saint Mary's University in Halifax, Nova Scotia, and a doctorate in sociology at the State University of New York at Binghamton. He has taught at the University of Guyana, Saint Mary's University in Halifax, Nova Scotia, the State University of New York at Binghamton, the University of Cape Coast in Ghana, West Africa, and he is presently Professor of Sociology at Eastern Connecticut State University. He has served as an alternate member of the Management Committee of the Caribbean Network for Integrated Rural Development, Treasurer of the University of Guyana Workers' Union, Project Director of the Industrial Social Welfare Benefits research project funded by the International Development Research Center in Canada, Assistant Dean of the Faculty of Social Sciences at the University of Guyana, Associate Director of the Latin American and Caribbean Area Studies Program at the State University of New York at Binghamton, President of the New York African Studies Association, Executive Member of the Canadian Association for the Study of International Development, and Visiting Professor at the University of Cape Coast. Canterbury has won the Connecticut State University System 2009 University-Level Trustees Research Award, and the Connecticut State University System 2009 System-Level Trustees Research Award, and was appointed as a Commissioner for the African American Affairs Commission for the State of Connecticut. His recent books are *European Bloc Imperialism* (2010) and *Neoliberal Democratization and New Authoritarianism* (2005). He edited *Guyana's Gold Industry: Evolution, Structure, Impacts and Non-Wage Benefits* (1998) and co-edited *Global Africa: The Challenges of Globalization, Democratization and Transition* (2001). He and his wife of 30 years in June 2013 Sandra Jennifer reside in Willimantic, Connecticut.

PREFACE

The emergence of neoliberal capitalism to global prominence in recent years has engendered a renewed and increased interest and understanding among development theorists and practitioners about how migration affects households, local economies and national, regional and international economic development. This interest is reflected by the plethora of theoretical works, studies, and national, regional and global institutional mechanisms established to promote understanding of the development impact of migration, and to formulate and influence policies for the efficient management of migration to aid in the development processes of both migrant-sender- and receiver-countries. The principal goal of this amalgamation of interests and understandings is to channel these activities on migration at the institutional, theoretical, practical, and policy levels into a single mold to stimulate and enhance economic development in the form and shape of neoliberal capitalism.

The problem with this neoliberal focus on the development impact of migration is that there is hardly anything to be gleaned from it about the process of capital accumulation the *raison d'être* of capitalist production and the social relations it produces. There are nonetheless, two discernable features of neoliberal capitalism under the hegemonic domination of financial capitalists at the current historical conjuncture. The first is the use of migration to fashion a global political economy characterized by the appropriate institutional mechanisms and policy arrangements to facilitate the smooth incorporation of migration into the operations of financial capital globally. The second feature is the harnessing of migration and the activities surrounding migration to stimulate capital accumulation. Both of these features combine to fashion an imperialist centered model of capital accumulation appropriate to financial capital's neoliberal capitalism.

What is the relationship between migration and capital accumulation? How does migration further the process of capital accumulation under neoliberal capitalism dominated by financial capital? These are the big questions that are crying out for answers to advance our knowledge about the migration phenomenon in capitalist societies. Each historical period in the evolution of capitalist society produces its own dynamics about how migration is used by the dominant capitalists of the era to further the process of capital accumulation. In the current period of neoliberal capitalism, migration processes are being subjected to financialization. Migration processes include the costs individuals incur in preparation for migration like payment of fees to middlemen, etc.; the costs associated while travelling to destination countries; the cost of socializing into their new destinations; their activities in their destination-countries such as the formation of Diaspora networks; the cost of remittances; and the creation of financial instruments and arrangements to capture monies expended by migrants in all these arenas.

A proper understanding of migration as a phenomenon of capitalist society requires much more than the concerns and issues that permeate the neoliberal literature. We need to drill down deeper to unravel the different ways in which migration is an integral component of capitalist society subscribing to the existence, survival and perpetuation of different forms of capitalism in different historical epoch. We therefore have to study migration in its role in production, the working population, and the organization of work and not merely in terms of the market forces – the buying and selling of the services of migrants. The study of migration in capitalist society must therefore be undertaken in the context of the struggle between labor and capital. This therefore is the general contextual framework of this book on capital accumulation from migration processes. This is in direct contradistinction to the neoliberal approach that utilizes migration to deepen neoliberal capitalism globally and accumulate capital for the financial capitalists.

ACKNOWLEDGEMENTS

I would like to thank the many people without whose help this book would not have become a reality. Thanks to my wife Sandra Jennifer for her patience and appreciation as I disappeared in my world of writing for many hours in the day. Also, thanks to James Petras and Henry Veltmeyer for their assistance as I struggled to give shape to the book. The ideas for this book were first presented and took shape in the Brown Bag seminar series in the Department of Sociology, Anthropology and Social Work at Eastern Connecticut State University, organized by University Professor James Russell. They were also presented, discussed and shaped further at an annual convention of the Southern Conference for African American Studies Inc. in Dallas Texas, USA, and at an annual meeting of the Canadian Association for the Study of International Development in New Brunswick, Canada. My thanks, extends to Professor Carmen Cid, Dean of the School of Arts and Sciences at Eastern Connecticut State University, for her support to attend the SCAASI convention and the CASID conference mentioned above.

CHAPTER ONE

MIGRATION AND CAPITAL ACCUMULATION

Introduction

The mobility of humans is a primary characteristic of the species in their evolution from primitive communal societies to the present. In this evolutionary process each type of human society has produced its own migration dynamics. This book is a study of only one dimension of the march of humans through space and time. It investigates key aspects of migration in the current period of neoliberal globalization, dominated by finance capital. It is concerned with the manner in which neoliberal capitalism extracts profit to accumulate capital from an age-old practice of humans – migration for whatever reason, from famine, war, drought, persecution, or in search of greener pastures – hence migration and capital accumulation.

The dominant capitalists may deliberately promote migration to line their pockets from migrant labor, although there are times that people move on their own accord. In both cases, the dominant capitalists at the time position themselves through the creation of domestic and international policies and rules to profit from migration processes, mainly the hire of migrant labor to reduce the cost of production or as is currently the case to profit from arrangements migrants are involved with to transfer money, knowledge, technologies, commodities, inter alia to their countries of origins.

Thus, what the neoliberal theorists regard as the "development impact of migration" is really about the accumulation of capital from migration processes under neoliberal capitalism. How does capital accumulation takes place from migration processes? This is the central question. Each epoch of capitalism, dominated by a given class of capitalist, produces its own migration dynamics including arrangements for capital accumulation from migration processes. In the same manner that mercantile and industrial capitalists created elaborate processes to stimulate and exploit migrant labor in order to accumulate capital for themselves, neoliberal capital is exploiting migration processes to accumulate capital in the neoliberal epoch of capitalism.

Hitherto studies on migration have overlooked this crucial aspect that is the accumulation of capital from migration processes at different historical conjunctures in the evolution of the capitalist system explored in this book. In particular, the book formulates a general critique of migration studies in the current neoliberal epoch of global capitalism, which focus on explaining the development impact of migration. In essence, the frantic search by neoliberal theorists for explanations of the development impact of migration provides the general framework for capital accumulation from migration processes. Indeed, the very areas on which neoliberal theorists focus to explain the development impact of migration are used to demonstrate how capital accumulation from migration processes takes place under neoliberal capitalism. The complex of institutional and policy arrangements, and recommendations concerning migration in the current period provide the framework for capital accumulation from migration under neoliberal capitalism.

Indeed, there is glaring evidence of this omission from the neoliberal considerations of what are considered to be the critical lessons of experimentation on migration and development in the first decade of the twenty-first century. Newland (2011)[1] identified seven critical lessons learned from experimentation on migration and development in the neoliberal period. The first is "decision-makers and policy developers have largely (although not completely) moved away from the notion that economic development is a general cure for migration."[2]

Second, in the current period the focus in migration and development discussions has been on labor migration, but "the search for work is not the only motive for migration." People who migrate "for reasons other than work make meaningful contributions to development in their countries of origins." Third, there is a "a more nuanced understanding of remittances," which has emerged "as research and observation have revealed that remittances reduce poverty but do not necessarily bring about more sustainable growth and development." Fourth, "migration and development policy has broadened its focus beyond remittances and 'brain drain.'"

Fifth, unilateral efforts alone are insufficient to "substantially reduce or redirect migration flows." This requires "collaboration among origin,

---

[1] Newland, K. (2011). Migration and Development Policy: What Have We Learned? Washington DC: Migration Policy Institute, October.
[2] Newland, K. (2011). Migration and Development Policy: What Have We Learned? Washington DC: Migration Policy Institute, October.

transit, and destination countries." Sixth, the policy discussion on migration and development "have historically been framed almost exclusively around South→North, South→South, and North→South migration, with a much smaller volume of North→South movement." However, several middle-income developing countries 'have become major immigration destinations while still remaining sources of immigrants.' Seventh, "national policy is not the only relevant locus of migration and development action."

This chapter presents the argument, method and hypotheses that underlie the study of capital accumulation from migration processes. Also, it offers a different perspective on development and globalization combining them into a single process identified as development-cum-globalization. It broaches the issue of politics, development, and migration while arguing that the role of politics is to create the framework for the extant dominant form of capital to subordinate migration process for the purposes of capital accumulation. The final section provides a synopsis of the structure and organization of the book.

Argument, Method and Hypothesis

The development impact of migration is a neoliberal idea that seeks to explain how migration promotes or hinder capitalist development. It is a phenomenon at the current historical conjuncture of capitalist society characterized as neoliberal capitalism. It is the deliberate attempt by the neoliberal capitalists to combine migration and development theories for the explicit purpose purportedly to bring about the socio-economic development of the migrant-sending developing countries. Neoliberal capitalism seeks to combine capitalist development and migration into a single global process and is in search of the appropriate theoretical analyses and policies to achieve this outcome. In the neoliberal perspective, development and migration theories should no longer be separated but combined. The same goes for development and migration policies, which should aim to achieve the varied objectives of the programs, set out by the global, regional and national institutions that concern themselves with the development impact of migration.

Taylor (2006) noted that "Recent economic studies suggest that migration and development are closely linked to one another: development shapes migration, and migration, in turn, influences development, in ways that are sometimes surprising and often not recognized by researchers and policy makers."[3] Thus, increasingly, all of the leading global institutions essentially created at Bretton Woods and the new agencies that spin-off from them are becoming immersed in issues concerning the development impact of migration.

The argument set out in this book is that the development impact of migration is the method and set of practices by which migration processes are subordinated by neoliberal capitalism – a form of capitalism dominated by financial capital, for the purposes of capital accumulation. Financial capital is rapidly bringing all aspects of economy and society under its thumb. Financial capital does not have the legs to stand on its own but needs the productive economy that migrants participate in for which it has created the framework of operation. Financial capital "writes the rules, controls its regulators and has secured license to speculate on everything, everywhere and all the time."[4]

The elites who control financial capital are only a component albeit a dominant one of the ruling class. The financial ruling class is internally stratified into three sub-groups the "big private equity bankers and hedge fund managers" who are at the top, "Wall Street chief executives" in second position, and thirdly the "senior-associates or vice-presidents of big private equity funds who are followed by their counterparts at Wall Street's public equity funds."[5]

The Marxist "historical and structural" critique of international migration theory and alternative approach advanced by Petras (2007) is the point of departure for this study of capital accumulation from migration processes under neoliberal capitalism, which neoliberal theorists identified as the development impact of migration. Petras (2007) begins with an examination of the "dynamic inequalities and exploitative relations between 'sender countries' and 'receiver countries' in order to determine

[3] J. Edward Taylor. (2006). International Migration and Economic Development. International Symposium on International Migration and Development, Population Division, Department of Economic and Social Affairs, United Nations Secretariat, Turin, Italy, 28–30 June 2006. UN/POP/MIG/SYMP/2006/09 26 June. See also Migration and Development Conference, Final Report 2006, Brussels, A joint initiative: The Government of the Kingdom of Belgium, The International Organization for Migration (IOM), The European Commission, The World Bank, March.
[4] James Petras. (2007). *Rulers and Ruled in the US Empire: Bankers, Zionists, Militants*, Atlanta, Clarity Press.
[5] James Petras. (2007). *Rulers and Ruled in the US Empire: Bankers, Zionists, Militants*, Atlanta, Clarity Press.

the socio-economic conditions which lead to individual decisions to migrate and to explain why masses of immigrants depart when they do, and why not before" (Petras 2007 40).

According to Petras (2007) "historical structural analyses provide a global map of the flows of profits, interest payments, rents and royalties." He superimposes "that map on the immigration flow to argue the hypothesis that *global flows of capital determine the direction and flows of immigration.*" This implies that capital accumulation takes place in the "receiving countries" through these flows, much of which result from the exploitation of "sending countries." Thus, the capitalist accumulate wealth in the "receiving countries," and immigrants follow the money by migrating to those centers with a high level of capital accumulation.

The principal hypothesis argued in this book however is that not only do "global flows of capital determine the direction and flows of immigration," but that dialectically the internal and global flows of immigration determine the direction and flows of capital and that these are a major source of capital accumulation from migration processes in the current period of neoliberal capitalism dominated by financial capital. The form of capital, which is dominant at every historical conjuncture in the evolution of the capitalist system of production for market exchange, creates and accumulates wealth from immigration processes. Generally, how this is done will be determined by the uses to which immigrants are put.

The productive sectors demand immigrant laborers to put them to work in productive activities, but finance capital merely seeks to profit from the money transactions in which immigrants are involved. Finance capital therefore needs the productive sectors to make money from migration processes. It subordinates migration processes through rules, regulations, and policies imposed by the state and international financial institutions to bring the associated monetary transactions under its control, while at the same time claiming that it operates best within a free market with a minimum of state rules and regulations. The tacit goal of subordinating migration practices to neoliberal capitalism is to increase capital accumulation for the existing dominant sections of capital – finance capital. However, the subordination of migration processes by the dominant form of capital is only but one avenue through which capital accumulation takes place. The central focus in arguing this hypothesis is on neoliberal capitalism under the domination of financial capital.

The arguments in support of the hypothesis will expand on the literature on financialization, considered to be less than a decade old.[6] The big
ideas contained in the Special Issue of the *Radical Review of Political
Economics* on financialization[7] include "how financialization necessitates
the re-conceptualization of Marxian categories/concepts" reconsidering
the role of labor as capital. "In addition to labor power as variable capital,
under financialization it is argued that the reproduction of labor is now a
source of surplus value transfer in the form of interest payments."[8] Another
theoretical idea is that the competition among capitals is intensified by
financialization. "New classes of financial instruments, such as securitization and derivatives, are seen as transcending the fixed/illiquid physical
form of capital into fluid competitively driven capital." This leads ultimately to an "intensification of the capital-labor conflict over the extraction of relative surplus value."[9]

While Hilferding's *Finance Capital*[10] analyses "a new phase of capitalist
accumulation associated with the concentration and centralization of
capital and the rise to power of a class of financial capitalists,"[11] the focus
here is on how the neoliberal form of capitalism at the current historical
conjuncture dominated by financial capitalists accumulate capital from
migration processes. The financialization of migration processes including the means by which migrants leave their countries of origin, function
in their countries of destination, remit resources to their home countries,
and establish business and other relations with them is a major aspect of
the capital accumulation from migration processes under neoliberal
capitalism.

---

[6] Jonathan P. Goldstein. (2009). "Introduction: The Political Economy of Financialization," *Review of Radical Political Economics*, Special Issue: The Financialization of Global
Capitalism: Analysis, Critiques, and Alternatives, Volume 41, Number 4, Fall.

[7] See *Review of Radical Political Economics*, Special Issue: The Financialization of Global
Capitalism: Analysis, Critiques, and Alternatives, Volume 41, Number 4, Fall 2009.

[8] Jonathan P. Goldstein. (2009). "Introduction: The Political Economy of Financialization," *Review of Radical Political Economics*, Special Issue: The Financialization of Global
Capitalism: Analysis, Critiques, and Alternatives, Volume 41, Number 4, Fall.

[9] Jonathan P. Goldstein. (2009). "Introduction: The Political Economy of Financialization," *Review of Radical Political Economics*, Special Issue: The Financialization of Global
Capitalism: Analysis, Critiques, and Alternatives, Volume 41, Number 4, Fall.

[10] Rudolf Hilferding. (1981). *Finance Capital: A Study of the Latest Phase of Capitalist
Development*, Ed. Tom Bottomore London, Routledge & Kegan Paul.

[11] Jonathan P. Goldstein. (2009). "Introduction: The Political Economy of Financialization," *Review of Radical Political Economics*, Special Issue: The Financialization of Global
Capitalism: Analysis, Critiques, and Alternatives, Volume 41, Number 4, Fall.

Because neoliberal capitalism is a global phenomenon its attempt to subordinate migration processes is global in nature rather than focused on a particular region or country. It would seem that the goal of neoliberal capitalism is to create a single global theoretical and policy grid on the development impact of migration attendant to the needs of all migration corridors, geographical regions, and sending and receiving countries.[12] This global theoretical and policy grid is connected with the global financial grid in terms of the flow of money to and from internal, international, regular and irregular migrations. Also, linked with the migration and financial grids are the flows of finance that result from the transfers of technologies, knowledge, and skills, and networking processes that migrants are involved with.

The development impact of migration involves the creation of theories by liberal and conservative oriented academics in combination with the formulation of socio-economic policies by bureaucrats and researchers in the global institutions controlled by the neoliberal capitalists, which are then forced on regions and countries around the globe. The primary objectives of these theories and policies are to enhance capital accumulation from migration but under the disguise of bringing socio-economic development, variously defined, to the developing countries.

A variety of global, regional and national institutions engage in this aspect of the capitalist development project now in its neoliberal phase. For example Özden and Schiff (2007) of the World Bank sought to provide "new evidence on the impact of migration and remittances on several development indicators, including innovative thinking about the nexus between migration and birth rates."[13] According to Francois J. Bourguignon, Senior Vice President and Chief Economists of the World Bank, in his Foreword to Özden and Schiff (2007)

> The growing importance of international migration as a contributor to the integration of the world economy has led to renewed interest – including analysis of institutional and policy reforms designed to ameliorate its impact – in source and destination countries, international migration, and the research community. However, the renewed policy and research interest, until recently, was not matched by the available knowledge. In order to help put migration research on a more solid footing, the World

---

[12] See for example IOM. (2003). IOM's Role in Enhancing Regional Dialogues on Migration. Eighty-Sixth Session, MC/INF/266, November 10.

[13] Çağlar Özden Özden and Maurice W. Schiff. (2007). *International Migration, Economic Development and Policy*, Washington, DC and New York, A co-publication of the World Bank and Palgrave Macmillan.

Bank initiated the Research Program on International Migration and Development in 2004, with the objective of producing and disseminating new migration data as well as rigorous conceptual and empirically based policy analysis (p xi).

To this end the World Bank's Research Program on International Migration and Development had its first major publication in 2006, "which examined the determinants and impact of migration and remittances in several developing countries as well as various aspects of the brain drain." Also, that study "provided the most extensive brain drain data base ever produced and has since become the reference in this area."[14]

Bourguignon (2007) noted that Özden and Schiff (2007), "reflects the expansion of the World Bank Research Program on International Migration and Development into new substantive and geographic areas. It presents a new global migration data base and includes studies of the determinants and impact of return and circular migration, the impact of the flow of ideas on fertility, host country policies and their impact on immigrants, and the impact of international migration and remittances on poverty and other development indicators" (pp xi–xii).

Undoubtedly, the main goal behind the World Bank's involvement in the promotion of studies on the development impact of migration is to generate data to the benefit of the global capitalists whose interests it serves. In this particular instance the research activities serve the interest of financial capital that is at the helm of global capitalism today. After decades of World Bank reform programs in the developing countries with little or no real success the Bank has a legitimacy problem, as "many developing countries see it as an extension of Western influence."[15] As a chief advocate of neoliberal capitalism the World Bank has veered from its original mandate when it was established to serve the global interest of industrial capitalism. It became a debt collector under neoliberal structural adjustment and now a generator of data and policies to centralize migration in the global capitalist system for the purposes of capital accumulation from migration processes, disguised as explaining the development impact of migration.

---

[14] Francois J. Bourguignon. (2007). "Foreword." In Çağlar Özden Özden and Maurice W. Schiff. (2007). *International Migration, Economic Development and Policy*, Washington, DC and New York, A co-publication of the World Bank and Palgrave Macmillan.

[15] Peter Lanzet. (2011). "Toothless Tiger," *The European Magazine*, January 14.

Development-cum-*Globalization*

Misguidedly, some development theorists argue that the development project is dead. They fail to correctly observe the twists and turns the capitalist development project has taken since its inception. As a consequence, they posit that the ascension of neoliberal capitalism has shifted the focus of the global institutions away from development and towards globalization.[16] McMichael (2008) for instance argues that the development project lasted from the 1940s to the 1970s, and that "its successor" is the globalization project from the 1970s to the 2000s.[17]

This mistake stems from the fact that first development is construed as something that originated as an imperialist project after the Second World War. It is regarded as a mechanism that was created especially for the former European colonies in Africa, Asia, Latin America, the Caribbean, etc. This mechanism serves to entrap the developing countries in a capitalist production system, with the illusion that they could become economically and socially like the advanced capitalist countries.

Development is therefore regarded as a "thing" that had its birth, maturity, and death. It is regarded as something that must be done to and by the countries in Africa, Asia, Latin America, the Caribbean and southern Europe. Development is something that these countries must aspire to achieve, which requires the creation of special theories and the formulation and implementation of development policies based on development theories. In retrospect, however, these development theories and policies aimed to produce the capitalist transformation of the former colonies to bring them in line with the dominant form of capitalism.

Talk about socialist development theories was also misguided because socialism is something to be radically established by socialist revolutions. However, the competition between capitalism and socialism during the cold war led both sides to generate vast literatures and policies on what could be construed as capitalist and socialist development. The Third World countries were given a choice between these two so-called development paths – capitalism or socialism.

Since the end of the cold war, this thinking has led to a second mistake, which is that capitalism has won the struggle with socialism and therefore

---

[16] Philip McMichael (2008). *Development and Social Change: A Global Perspective.* Los Angeles and London, Pine Forage Press.

[17] Philip McMichael (2008). *Development and Social Change: A Global Perspective.* Los Angeles and London, Pine Forage Press.

capitalism is now global, with no serious or credible competitor. In this connection, the belief is that globalization started with the gradual and eventual collapse of Eastern European socialism from the 1970s to the 1980s/90s. Thereafter, the former socialist countries began to "transition" from socialism to capitalism and to adopt Western-style "democratic" political systems.

Due to these developments capitalism and democracy are now said to be global being pursued by the countries that are already capitalists, the former socialist countries in Eastern Europe, authoritarian states in the Third World, and even China under its doctrine of "one country two-systems." China adopted this policy to allow certain regions in the country to pursue capitalist production for market exchange, and the return of capitalist Hong Kong to China by the British in 1999, while other regions operated under state-directed socialist policies. In this perspective therefore, globalization means that all countries at the current historical conjuncture of global capitalism have common political and economic systems – democracy and free market economies.

The fact of the matter however is that capitalist development and globalization are essentially one and the same phenomenon. They both refer to the universal spread of the capitalist system of production for market exchange. Development is the process by which the capitalist system becomes universal to all countries in the globe. Its problematic is how to bring countries into the capitalist system for them to be exploited more effectively, through the extraction of their human and natural resources, and their creation as markets for commodities and services produced by the trans-national corporations. Thus, so long as the capitalist system persists development will always be with us because the dominant form of capital will always be in expansionary mode.

Every form of dominant global capital has its specific needs and methods of accumulation and focuses on how it would go about bringing all countries into the global capitalist system it creates and dominates. The reason why dominant global capital brings countries into the global capitalist system it creates is to exploit them, to accumulate wealth from the economic activities in which they are engaged with the dominant capitalist. Thus, although a country is already in the capitalist system, there will always be the need to bring it into the capitalist system depending on which section of capital is dominant at the time. In other words, a country already in the capitalist system could be outside of the system of global capital dominant at the time. Thus, there was the need to integrate countries into the global mercantile and industrial capitalist systems, as there is the need today to integrate them into the neoliberal capitalist system.

For example in the current period of neoliberal capitalism in which finance capital is dominant, there is still a need for countries to be brought into the neoliberal capitalist system. The talk now is about integrating the developing countries into the global capitalist system, which means in essence making these countries, which are already in the capitalist system, more amenable to exploitation by finance capital, which dominates the capitalist system today. This means that the developing countries are to be integrated into the dominant form of global capitalism, and not into capitalism, as such, since they were already drawn into the capitalist system by different forms of historical capital.

The developing countries were already in the capitalist system historically dominated by mercantile capital and industrial capital. Yet, today we hear that the developing countries are still to be integrated into the capitalist system. If they are still to be integrated into the global capitalist system, a system that they are already in, it must be that they are required to integrate into the current neoliberal capitalist system dominated by finance capital. The observation is that each form of dominant capital requires countries to be integrated into it, for that form of dominant capital to become global.

As more countries become integrated into the neoliberal capitalist system the extant form of dominant capitalism becomes more global. Thus, globalization is not merely about the integration of a country into the capitalist system, but rather it is their incorporation into the dominant form of capitalism. It is therefore more apposite to talk about a series of globalizations appropriate to the form of dominant capital rather that to identify globalization as something that had its birth in the collapse of Eastern European socialism. Globalization is the processes by which different forms of dominant capitalisms are spread to incorporate all countries in the globe. Nonetheless, it is inherently a process of the global advancement of the capitalist system or the development of the capitalist system.

Mercantile capital and its critique by the classical political economists laid the foundations for this process, which may be described as capitalist development-*cum*-globalization. The classical political economists held the view that people the world-over will be better off if the protective walls around the economy were broken down and the free trade mantra was sung in every corner of the globe. From since the time of the classical political economists, coinciding with the collapse of mercantilism and the institution of the industrial capitalist development process, the theoretical and policy foundations were laid for development-*cum*-globalization as the way forward for the socio-economic system that

Marx labeled capitalism. Migration played a central role in capital accumulation in each of these historical forms of the advance of development-*cum*-capitalism.

Politics, Development and Migration

The political dimension of development-*cum*-globalization embraced by the ideologues of neoliberal capitalism is problematic. The ideologues of neoliberal capitalism are of the view that neoliberal capitalist economic development works best with Western-styled democratic traditions. Thus, neoliberal capitalism favors Western-styled democracy as the political superstructure to be erected on the neoliberal capitalist economic system. But, the reality is that neoliberal politics has produced authoritarian rather than Western-styled democratic states. Thus, authoritarian political arrangements reign supreme under neoliberal capitalism. The Latin American dictatorship of General Pinochet, the Chilean dictator was for many years the poster-child for politics under the hegemony of neoliberal capitalism in Chile and globally. Indeed, neoliberal democratization, that is the attempt to spread Western-styled democracy to the former socialist countries in Eastern Europe and the authoritarian states in the developing world, has produced instead new forms of authoritarian states, founded on "free" elections in places as diverse as Guyana and Iraq.[18]

As a general rule capitalism does not need any particular form of political superstructure – liberal democratic, authoritarian, fascist, etc. for its success. This is because the capitalists typically exert sufficient influence and power over the political system to bring it in line with the interests of capital accumulation of the dominant form of capital. The Bonapartist state, nonetheless that dictates to the capitalists who control the economy is a notable exception to this general rule. In such a situation the political elites who control the state are not merely executives in the employ of the capitalists. Instead, they exercise power in their own right and in the process subordinates the capitalists to their power, thus bringing about a separation of state and economy.

The development of industrial capitalism in Germany and Italy for example, was once associated with fascism. Authoritarian states in Latin America have brought about peripheral capitalist development in that

---

[18] Dennis C. Canterbury. (2005). *Neoliberal Democratization and New Authoritarianism.* Aldershot, Ashgate Publishers.

region. The UK and the US, bastions of Western-styled democracy, in their fight against communism promoted and supported authoritarian states as the political model to accompany capitalist development in the developing countries. The Churchill administration in Britain for example overthrew the democratically elected government of Cheddi Jagan seen to be communist by the British and Americans, as a means to combat the perceived communist threat in the Caribbean and Latin America.

However, neoliberal capitalism dominated by finance capital advocates a shift in the politics of capitalism in the developing countries towards Western-styled democracy as a political condition for the capitalist development of these states. The financial capitalists figured that Western-styled democracy would be the easiest way for them to accumulate wealth from the developing countries. Thus, in order to bring about political change to suit its modus operandi, neoliberal capitalism promoted "free" elections in the former Eastern European socialist countries and authoritarian states in the developing world to elect governments that would implement neoliberal economic policies.

While the old politics favored productive capital neoliberal democratization favors finance capital. Observe the global swing in politics in the neoliberal era – even former socialist political parties ran for office on neoliberal economic platforms that would strengthen the domination of finance capital. In Brazil for example political leaders such as Fernando Henrique Cardoso and Luiz Ignácio Lula da Silva, purportedly on the left, implement the deepest neoliberal reforms to fortify the power of finance capital in that country. Now, Brazil is considered as an emerging economy in the neoliberal capitalist system recording one of the fastest rates of economic growth globally. However, to the vast majority of Brazilians the social cost associated with the rapid growth is exorbitant as they see their social benefits reduced dramatically. It is only a small section of the Brazilian population that enjoys the benefits of the growth as social inequality in the country becomes even more pronounced.

Also, the neoliberal capitalist embed in the developing countries political institutions through reform programs to allow finance capital to operate unhindered. To this end, laws are rewritten to regulate the new property relations that emerge under neoliberal capitalism. Members of the domestic judiciary received training in Western-styled legal arrangements to adjudicate disputes between the neoliberal capitalists and the locals in the developing countries. Civil society agencies mushroomed across the political landscape advocating different just causes while enriching their leaders in receipt of foreign monies channeled to their agencies by institutions supported by the financial capitalists in the rich countries.

Politics concern the exercise of power over the institutions of state, including the formation, implementation, adjudication and enforcement of laws. Politics serve the interests of the dominant form of capital to aid in the process of capital accumulation from migration processes. Politics in the era of neoliberal capitalism create the frameworks of laws, structures and policies for finance capital to maximize its wealth from migration processes.

Structure and Organization

The book is organized in three sections that focus on the early roots of migration theory, neoliberal perspectives on the development impact of migration, and fault lines in the neoliberal views on migration. The chapters in part one discuss migration in development theory from the classical to the neoliberal models, and poor economic performance with increased migration.

The idea in chapter one is to present an appraisal of migration in classical political economy, Marxian, neoclassical, Keynesian, development and neoliberal theories. It argues that with the exception of Marxian theory, these theoretical formulations are designed to reinforce the imperialist-centered model of accumulation, of which capital accumulation from migration processes is only but one aspect, in furtherance of the global expansion of capitalism.

Albeit he did not termed it as such, Marx explained the dire suffering associated with rural-urban migration, as agricultural workers were transformed into industrial workers in England. The human cost associated with the disintegration of the agricultural economy in Europe was horrendous, as the lives of the laboring population that migrated from agriculture to industrial cities were transformed permanently. The radical issue here was how to transform the production system that generated those horrid conditions rather than to accumulate wealth from them. The structure of the argument is organized around analyses of the classical model, development and migration; Marx' economic theory and migration; the neoclassical and Keynesian "revolutions"; development economics and migration; and neoliberal theory and migration.

The chapter that follows is a critique of a central idea, which emerged in the early migration literature and remains dominant today. It broaches the subject of "push-pull" theories of migration, which take the position that poor economic conditions is the cause why people are pushed to leave their countries, and that countries with a high level of economic growth pulls migrants from poorer countries towards them. The evidence suggests however, that although the US is experiencing its worst economic downturn since the Great Depression, migrants are still flocking to the country. This means that economic growth is not the determining factor why people migrate to the US. Alternatively, it is hypothesized that the level of capital accumulation over time, which translates into a higher quality of life is what attracts people to the US. Thus, a country with a high level of capital accumulation over time will continue to attract migrants even though it is experiencing economic decline.

The analysis here discusses economic theories of migration focusing on push-pull approaches. It presents alternative questions and counter-proposition to those advanced by push-pull theories. It engages in a descriptive analysis of the companies hiring illegal immigrants, and concentrates on US economic growth and unemployment between 2000 and 2009, US layoffs and separations between 2007 and 2009, industry distribution of 2008 mass layoffs and separations in the US, increased migration to the US during the great recession of 2007 to 2009, and Caribbean migration to the US between 2007 and 2009.

Part two focuses on neoliberal perspectives on the development impact of migration – by analyzing the liberalization and financialization of migration, the development impact of remittances and diasporas, the Millennium Development Goals' impact of migration, and the human development impact of migration. The main idea here is the elaborate on the activities of the academics and policy makers regarding the neoliberal idea about the development impact of migration. The principal point of this section is to establish a central argument in the book that neoliberal capitalism spearheaded by financial capital utilizes the global institutions they dominate to formulate top-down policies to bring migration processes under its control for the purposes of accumulating capital.

Thus, the discussion on migration and financial liberalization focuses on labor mobility and capitalist globalization, the General Agreement in Trade in Services (GATS) and Migration, the "great financialization" and the financialization of migration. Analyses are undertaken of these issues in support of the hypotheses that a principal goal of neoliberal capitalism is the exploitation of migration processes to accumulate capital through the imperialist centered model of capital accumulation.

The development impact of remittances and Diasporas are explored
by focusing on the cases argued for their roles in the economic development of sending countries. The global agencies discussed that argue these
cases are the World Bank, the International Organization for Migration
(IOM), the Global Commission on International Migration (GCIM), and
the Global Forum on Migration and Development (GFMD). There are
many other organizations however operating at the global, regional and
national levels, and other forums, programs, and agreements that focus on
the development impact of remittances and Diasporas, which are not discussed here. They are all mostly within the domain of the Breton Woods
institutions.

The argument is that remittances and Diasporas reinforce rather than
transform the capitalist power structure and its imperialist centered
model of capital accumulation. The most meaningful global impact they
could have is to participate in a genuine shift of power decidedly in favor
of working people, but this is not the case. The discussion here concentrates on Diasporas, remittances and power; the World Bank's case for
remittances; Diasporas in the development process; and a critique of the
development impact of remittances and Diasporas.

A key proposition is that neoliberal capitalism includes the Millennium
Development Goals in the discussion on migration for the simple reason
to tighten its grip on the neoliberal capitalist development process in
the developing countries. Linking migration and the Millennium Development Goals, makes it easier for finance capital and the global institutions to increase their presence in the developing countries, and for the
latter to implement migration policies formulated by the former agencies.
The developing countries have agreed to implement the Millennium
Development Goals but soon after migration policies were foisted on
them as integral components for the achievement of the Millennium
Development Goals. Highlighted here are descriptive analyses of the
Millennium Development Goals; neoliberal ideas on the impact of migration on the MDGs; and migration and the limitations of the MDGs.

The inter-relationships between human development and migration
are examined, since the elites that control the international financial institutions and other global institutions have designated migration as a factor
in the achievement of human development. Migration is presented as a
factor that corrects the imbalance in the global distribution of human
capabilities. Thus, it is regarded as something that reduces global inequalities, a primary focus of the human development approach. The problem
however is that the persistence of global capitalism is at the very core of

the human development approach. The human development approach is primarily concerned with reforming neoliberal capitalism to make it more equitable. Transformation of the capitalist power structures that make the inequalities possible is completely off the radar of human development. Its emphasis on increasing freedoms, equality, participation etc., is all about freedoms, equality and participation, etc. within the realm of neo-liberal capitalism.

The focus here is on a range of issues concerning migration and human development. The analysis begins with a discussion on the origins of the human development approach in development studies. Included in the analysis are considerations of migration and human development in theory, and the impact of migration on human development. The analysis of migration as a cost reduction device under neoliberal capitalism focuses on the reduction in the cost of production due to migration, the financial cost of moving, and the costs associated with the use of cell phones for money transfers and other forms of money transfers.

The focal points of the analysis of health and migration are low-skilled migrant workers and the migration of health professionals. The provision of human rights is regarded as an important component of human development. Migration poses a dilemma for human development because of the high incidence of violations of the human rights of migrants. The policy reforms outlined in the Human Development Report to enhance the human development impact of migration are also analyzed.

Part three spotlights key fault lines in neoliberal views on the development impact of migration. Its focus is on migration fault lines under neoliberal globalization, and the European Union and migration with an emphasis on the Africa connection. The discussion on migration fault lines under neoliberal globalization pinpoints the contradictions in the neoliberal approach to migration. It examines the Israeli separation walls with Egypt and Palestine; current US – Mexico border issues; the US – Mexico border fence also known as the "Great Wall of Mexico"; and aspects of migration policy issues in the European Union and the US primarily EU and US immigration restrictions and entry policies. Also, it highlights the ascendancy of anti-immigration movements, and pro-immigration mass movements.

The principal proposition in the discussion on the European Union and migration with respect to Africa constitutes a major fault line to the development impact of migration. The European Union's migration strategy towards Africa involves its "global Europe" approach, the Joint Africa-EU Declaration on Migration and Development (JA-EUDMD), the EU-Libya

Migration Cooperation Agreement, and the European Parliament's recommendations to the Council on the negotiations on the EU-Libya Framework Agreement.

The EU's approach to African migration does not promote democracy on the African continent, but encourages the restriction of the human rights of migrants. The point of departure of the analysis here is on the EU and migration with a focus on the EU's global Europe strategy and Libya and the EU's migration strategy. This is followed by analyses of the Joint Africa-EU Declaration on Migration and Development, the EU-Libya Migration Cooperation Agreement, and the EU-Libya Framework Agreement. The EU had full knowledge of Libya's mistreatment of North and Sub-Saharan African migrants in Libya, but did nothing about it because Libya's actions prevented the migrants from crossing in to Europe.

The concluding chapter sketches an outline of ideas for the formulation of a radical alternative framework for the analysis of human migration. The radical framework on capital accumulation from migration processes is more informative for transformative action by migrants in combination with other working peoples. The set of ideas considered include the radical treatment of the role of financial capital in migration in the current era of neoliberal globalization. Also, they comprise a redefinition of the development impact of migration for the benefit of working people.

PART ONE

MIGRATION THEORY:
EARLY ROOTS

CHAPTER TWO

CLASSICAL POLITICAL ECONOMY TO NEOLIBERAL THEORY

Introduction

Scholars and policy makers in both the North and South have focused their attention on the development of the Third World countries since the 1940s. To this effect various theories of development have emerged in the new academic discipline development studies that draw on the theoretical traditions of classical political economy, and Marxian, neoclassical, Keynesian and neoliberal theories. The study of migration is interwoven in these theoretical traditions but the focus on its development impact is concentrated more in the current period of neoliberal capitalism. There was a hiatus in the search for clarity on the relationship between migration and development until the neoliberal turn in global capitalism when interest in the problem of capital accumulation from migration became disguised as the development impact of migration. Under the hegemony of neoliberal capitalism in recent years migration has resurfaced as an agency for development. Policy makers, international organizations, and academics operating within the neoliberal tradition have deepened their search for clarity on the relationship between migration and development.

The purpose of this chapter is to provide an appraisal of migration in classical political economy, and Marxian, neoclassical, Keynesian, development and neoliberal theories. The goal here is to argue that migration is merely used in these theoretical formulations with the exception of Marxian theory to strengthen the imperialist-centered model of accumulation in furtherance of the global expansion of capitalism, thus contributing to capital accumulation from migration processes. Marx is considered within the classical political economy system in the light of the fact that he provided a critique of political economy, and like the classical political economists analyzed the entire economy albeit focusing on its revolutionary transformation based on class analysis.

Classical political economy formulated the development problematic in terms of the causes why nation-states accumulate wealth. The development problem formulated from a Marxist perspective however concerns the revolutionary transformation of the capitalist mode of production to socialism. Neoclassical theories focused on the improvement of the wellbeing of atomized individuals operating in multiple markets to accumulate wealth, which is not a concern, as did the classical political economists and Marx respectively, with capital accumulation of the nation-state and the revolutionary transformation of the capitalist mode of production.

Keynesianism represents a reformulation of neoclassical theory by inserting in it a dynamic theory of growth to extricate the Western capitalist countries from economic depression. Development theories however are specialized suppositions for Third World countries to modernize or westernize by imitating the economic, political and social advances achieved by the rich European and North American capitalist states. These theories are founded on admixtures of classical political economy, neoclassical, Keynesian and neoliberal approaches and purport to be the first, which are explicitly concerned with modernizing the Third World countries. They are considered to be outside the domain of any of those specific approaches forging a development paradigm in their own right although their effect is the same – reinforcing capitalist development and capitalist penetration of the Third World. Neoliberalism is a throwback to neoclassical free market fundamentalist individualistic theory that holds no quarter for collective behavior.

Each of these frameworks is examined in turn considering the neoliberal idea about the development impact of migration.

The Classical Model, Development and Migration

Classical political economists such as Adam Smith,[1] the Rev. Thomas Malthus,[2] and David Ricardo[3] engaged the problem of development or progress of the entire nation-state. Classical political economy and development theory are not really different in the sense that they both

---

[1] See Adam Smith. (1952). *An Inquiry Into the Nature and Causes of the Wealth of Nations*, London, Encyclopedia Britannica.

[2] See Rev. Thomas R. Malthus. (1951). *Principles of Political Economy, Consider With a View to Their Practical Application*, New York, Augustus M. Kelley.

[3] See David Ricardo. (1980). *Principles of Political Economy and Taxation*, London, George Bell and Sons. Note that Karl Marx is considered to be Classicists by some writers and he is treated in the same manner as Smith, Malthus and Ricardo. Marx is treated in a separate category, because he has formulated an entirely different explanation of the evolution of capitalism compared with that advanced by Smith, Malthus and Ricardo.

focus of the progress of the entire nations-state unlike neoclassical theory whose concern is with individual market behavior. The problem of development or progress became overtly visible with the emergence of nation-states.

Adam Smith and others concerned themselves with formulating theory and policy to bring about the industrialization or modernization of agricultural feudalistic economies in Europe. Development in the classical model seeks to move the country forward by apportioning more income to the classes considered responsible for the capital accumulation. It therefore favors the rich over working people with the pitiable view that they spend more than they save and hence should receive a smaller share of the national income. For sure therefore classical political economy is not concerned with improving the conditions of working people but with generating wealth for the rich.

Concern about transforming the lives of working people is the domain of alternative analyses of development, which the works of Marx[4] provide a good framework. Marx did not only formulated a critique of classical political economy, he gave the name capitalism to the socio-economic system it created, and developed the rudiments of an alternative in which, the direct producers are restored to the ownership of their products.

The classical political economists and Marx recognized the significance of migration to the development of capitalism. They surmised that emerging industry required the transformation of agricultural labor to new technical skills and involved the migration of people from the countryside to the budding industrial centers. Currently, there are more people engaged in rural-urban than in any other form of migration. Marx provided a succinct analysis of the brutality involved in the transformation of agricultural laborers into industrial workers. Rural-urban migration was definitely not in the interest of working people at the origins of the industrial capitalist system. The process was fraught with pitfalls as it is today. However, because of the centrality of agriculture in the entire system of classical political economy the belief then was that the movement of people from agriculture to industry was a temporary phenomenon, as land and population changes were regarded as the driving forces of economic development.

In the classical political economy system the law of diminishing returns governed the availability of fertile land for cultivation, which encouraged

---

[4] See Karl Marx. (1909). *Capital: A Critique of Political Economy*, Volume I, Chicago, Charles H. Kerr and Company.

the view that food output increased at a slower rate than the population. The combination of these factors meant that in the absence of relevant technology the economy was prone to crisis because its population was faced with starvation since it grew at a faster rate than the output of food.[5] There was no assumption of technological change to control the growth of the population and food production. It was Marx who in his critique of political economy identified the centrality of technical change in the development and evolution of capitalism.

Mistakenly, however, classical political economy is seen to be unconcerned with economic growth and development because of its focus on progress. This flaw in the development literature is the result of the failure by development theorists to make the backward leap to connect terms such as "progress," "growth," and "development." Because the words "development" and "growth" do not permeate their works, it is mistakenly believed that the classical political economy theories are not theories of "development" and economic "growth." However, development means the growth or progress of capitalist society, while alternative development is concerned with the transformation of capitalist society.

The inequalities between nation-states stimulated the classical political economists to find out what it was that a country needed to do to increase its wealth, or make progress, or grow, or develop. This concern was also a reaction to the Mercantilist view, which equated wealth with money and, which advocated that all a nation-state needed to do was to accumulate precious metals such as gold and silver to enrich itself.[6] The classical political economists rejected that view and preoccupied themselves with explaining how the systems of production, exchange, distribution and accumulation operated and interacted, to generate progress, growth, expansion, development or the wealth of nation-states.

Understandably, the terms progress, growth, expansion, and development have specific levels of meanings, even when they are considered in terms of a country. But, they could be used interchangeably to refer to the movement forward of capitalist society and individuals. The classical standpoint is that progress requires the accumulation of wealth and its productive reinvestment. However, the wealth accumulated under the

---

[5] This was the basic argument of the theory of population advanced by the Reverend Thomas Malthus who assumed that the human species has a basic passion to copulate, which is the source of population expansion. Wars were proffered as a means of controlling population growth, instead of technological change, which Malthus clearly overlooked.

[6] See Maurice Dobb. (1973). *Theories of Value and Distribution Since Adam Smith*, Cambridge, Cambridge University Press, for a discussion on this point.

feudal system was not reinvested productively, but squandered in riotous living. This was the central critique of feudalism by classical political economy.

In classical political economy if a nation were to exploit all of its natural resources to the full, it would only achieve a certain limit of wealth. Thus, the main concern was to find out how a nation could reach that limit. In other words, a country could progress only to a certain limit and then it would stagnate; hence the notion of the steady state or stationary state, in classical political economy theory. The capitalist economy is not foreseen to be expanding or growing *ad infinitum* as claimed through mathematical proof in neoclassical theory. Sir W. Arthur Lewis[7] held the view that David Ricardo, John Stuart Mill and Karl Marx all subscribed to a stationary state theory, but he pointed out that Marx was convinced that society, once liberated from the constraints of private property, would move swiftly to abundance the equivalent to a stationary state.

Now, what is the cause of this tendency towards stagnation rather than indefinite growth in the classical model? Their answer to this question is closely integrated with the problematic of the distribution of accumulated wealth, known today as the national income. What social groups are responsible for the production of wealth and how is wealth distributed? What determines the proportion of income that each class receives for its contribution to the production of a nation's wealth?

In the classical political economy system, production is the result of the application of labor and capital to the land, which is assumed as fixed in supply, and subject to the law of diminishing returns. It is assumed that as more labor and capital are applied to the land, the law of diminishing returns would assure a decrease in the marginal productivity of land, and hence to the rate of return to labor and capital. At the same time rent, the share of the national dividend that goes to the owners of land will increase as more land, albeit of a decreasing quality is put under cultivation. But, the owners of land do not spend rent productively; instead they waste it on conspicuous consumption. Institutional pressures, however, tend to keep wages constant, implying that profit and thereby investment will decrease.

In this classical scenario, the problem of distribution of the social product was considered in connection with the productivity of labor and the

---

[7] See Sir W. Arthur Lweis. (1971). "Socialism and Economic Growth," The Annual Oration, London, London School of Economics.

structure of ownership of productive resources. After the cost of production is deducted from the value of the social product the surplus which remains, is distributed to labor in the form of wages, to land in the form of rent and to capital in the form of interest (rentiers) and profit (entrepreneurs). The economic surplus is distributed according to some principle, such as wages per man-hour, rent per unit of land, interest per unit of money lent, and profit per unit of capital invested. To the classical political economists the problem of the distribution of income was integrally connected with the problem of development or the accumulation of capital.

Capital accumulation takes place through reinvestments out of profits thus the principal role of profit is to accumulate capital, while wages and rent were consumed. If, the greatest part of the national dividend goes to the land owning class as rent on an increasing ratio, and a smaller proportion goes to labor as wages at some constant ratio, then profit will grow at a decreasing ratio and at sometime in the future falls to zero. The economy is therefore headed for a "stationary state," as less profit becomes available for investment or capital accumulation. Thus, the stationary state is associated with the abundance of full employment when the economy is at its maximum, or when there is no profits to invest so the economy marks time.

Marx's law of the tendency of the rate of profit to fall may therefore be seen as similar to the classical "stationary state" in the sense that a fall in profit could place a damper on capitalist expansion, and cause the economy to "mark time," as it were. Capital accumulation, the distribution of wealth, technical change, and the labor supply, assumed to be unlimited, and influenced by population size, are regarded as the basic driving forces of progress or development under capitalism. The struggle to identify the factors that stimulate or hinder those forces of progress has ever since been the major preoccupation of social theory concerned with socio-economic development.

Migration is a critical factor that hinders or stimulates the forces of progress in the classical political economy system. The failure of labor to migrate from agriculture to industry would dampen the capitalist's ability to expand and accumulate capital. The neoliberal idea and studies on the development impact of migration have therefore not gone too far past the central idea of migration in classical political economy. The availability of labor for capitalist production whether in the classical period or at present has similar negative or positive impacts on capital accumulation. The neoliberal study of the development impact of migration is therefore an integral component of the debate on the availability of labor for capitalist exploitation in both the sending and receiving countries – a disguised study of migration and capital accumulation.

In the classical model the link between capital accumulation and income distribution is explained by the uses to which social classes put their share of the economic surplus. As was indicated above, the size of the economic surplus and the way it is consumed by the social classes that share it determines the possibility for and the rate of capital accumulation. The social classes that control interest and profit are therefore given the crucial role of shouldering the burden of development or the accumulation of wealth, in capitalist economies and *ipso facto* the size of the economic surplus to be distributed. In the long run, therefore, economic expansion, growth, development, or progress depends on the social classes that control profits and interests. The rate of profit is therefore important in two ways, first as a stimulant for investment, and second as a source of funds for investment. Thus, increasing profits stimulate the demand for labor due to expanded investments, and migration. The capitalist needs labor to migrate from all non-capitalist productive activity to produce goods and services for exchange in capitalist markets.

In classical political economy analysis the division of labor is necessary to produce use values (commodities), which are then exchanged as exchange values. In this sense, therefore, exchange is inseparably connected with the division of labor since the division of labor is an underlying condition of commodity exchange. The essential feature of production is the combined activity of labor and other factors such as land and capital, including the products of past labor embodied in productive capital and objects of nature. If the productive factors – labor, land and capital, are combined to produce use value, which are then exchanged as exchange value, the problem classical political economists faced was that of determining the principle, which explained value.

Adam Smith advanced an adding-up theory of value determination since he believed that the value of a commodity was determined by the amount of wages, interest and profit taken up in its production. David Ricardo, on the other hand, provided a labor theory of value by arguing that the value of a commodity was determined by the amount of labor involved in its production. Karl Marx also put forward a labor theory of value but he substituted labor power for labor, in the determination of the value of a commodity.

The classical political economists also identified another important role for the distribution of income. Now, the general rule of commodity exchange is that exchange value must at least be equal to the cost of production, i.e., wages, rent, interest, and profit. But, these very costs are incomes on which exchange value depends. This means that before exchange value can be determined wages, rent, interest, and profit will have to be known. In other words, theoretically the problem of distribution will have to be solved prior to the determination of exchange value.

To solve the problem of distribution it became necessary that the classical political economists formulated a theoretical measure of the size and variation of the economic surplus, which essentially reduced the surplus to a common standard of value.[8] Thus, exchange value, dependent on distribution, could not also at the same time be a measure of value. Inseparable as they are, though, exchange value and distribution were both subject to explanation by the classical theory of value. A solution to the problem of value eluded Ricardo and other economists until Piero Sraffa[9] published his work on the production of commodities by means of commodities, which provided a formal solution to the value puzzle, in the classical system.

Marx's Economic Theory and Migration

Karl Marx[10] was concerned with discovering the laws of motion of capitalism as an entire mode of production in order to determine its progress from lower to higher, or from simple to complex forms of social organization. Marx outlined a theory of capitalist development and also an alternative theory to capitalism. To accomplish that task, Marx started out with an analysis of the commodity employing a modified version of the classical labor theory of value developed by Ricardo. Marx put the labor theory of value to an entirely different use than did the classical political economists.

Ricardo's principal focus on the labor theory of value was to solve the problem of an "invariable standard of value,"[11] as a part of the solution to the distribution problem. The quantitative relationship between relative price and labor value is a main area of difference between Ricardo and

---

[8] Ricardo struggled to find such a measure of value, even in the last days of his life, as can be seen from correspondences he had with the Reverend Thomas Malthus on this matter. Piero Sraffa brought much of this information to light in his introduction to the Works and Correspondences of David Ricardo. See Maurice Dobb Ibid 1973 for more on this.

[9] See Piero Sraffa. (1960). *Production of Commodities by Means of Commodities: Prelude to a Critique of Economic Theory*, Cambridge, Cambridge University Press.

[10] See Karl Marx Ibid 1909.

[11] See David Ricardo Ibid 1980; Donald J. Harris. (1978). *Capital Accumulation and Income Distribution*, Stanford, Stanford University Press; and Maurice Dobb Ibid 1973.

Marx. Whereas Ricardo believed that price and value had a proportional relationship, Marx argued that value was transformed into price, and that the two were not proportionate "except under conditions of an equal organic composition of capital in all branches of production."[12]

Furthermore, Marx made the vital discovery of the difference between labor and labor power. The former is identified as the capacity to work, while the latter is regarded as labor set to work.[13] Through that division Marx was able to solved the problem of surplus value by applying the Ricardian labor theory of value to determine the value of labor power.

Through the separation of labor and labor power Marx was able to prove that the latter had value like any other commodity. Labor power nonetheless had a special characteristic that made it unique and different from all other commodities.[14] Labor power as the basic ingredient of all other commodities is not produced in the same way as other goods, and that is its unique feature. Labor power is the embodiment of all other commodities, and, therefore, its value could not be determined in the same way as the value of other commodities. Now, the value of the product of labor i.e., a commodity, is equal to the labor power embodied in it, while the value of labor power is measured in terms of all that was necessary – food, clothing, shelter, health, etc., to sustain that labor power by keeping the laborer alive.

This was a significant development because neither did the Physiocrats or the classical political economists Smith, Malthus, and Ricardo differentiated between the value of labor power and the value of the product of labor. And, because of the failure to differentiate between the two, Ricardo assumed that the value of a commodity was equal to the amount of labor (not labor power) taken up in its production. Thus, although there appears to be a similarity between Ricardo's Iron Law of wages, which is that wage is equal to the subsistence level, and Marx value of labor power being equal to the subsistence of the laborer they are inherently different.

For Marx, surplus value was the difference between two values – the value of labor power and the value of commodities i.e. the product of labor power. In turn, surplus value was absolute or relative, the former resulting from working the laborer harder to extract more from him in the same time period, or from the quantitative lengthening of the working day. The latter was due to changes in technology and in the organization of work.

---

[12] See Donald J. Harris Ibid 1978 for an elaboration on this point.
[13] See Karl Mark Ibid 1909 for extended definitions of labor and labor power.
[14] See Karl Marx Ibid 1909.

Due to their failure to recognize the difference between labor and labor power, the classical political economists could not have undertaken such a penetrating analysis of capitalism as Marx did, and arrived at such a convincing conclusion.

They assumed that fluctuations in production resulting from short-run variations in price and value were the guiding principles in the determination of the value of commodities. The Malthusian law of population, which assumes a positive relationship between wages and population growth, as the guiding principle for the maintenance of the wage rate, the same as the subsistence rate, governed the remuneration of labor. This rate was regarded in the classical system to be the "natural price of labor."[15]

Marx, however, put forward an entirely different perspective on the matter of the valuation of commodities, including the only commodity owned by the laborer – labor power. He argued that in the process of capital accumulation, the problem of the valuation of labor has to do with technical change that creates a "reserve army" of unemployed labor or a "relative surplus population" and heightens the class struggle.

Thus, it is possible to argue that technical change is a critical variable in the creation of the conditions for migration under capitalism through the formation of surplus labor. This is so because a large chunk of domestic and international migrant labor is surplus labor in search of better living conditions and employment in the destination countries.

According to Marx it is technical change and class struggle and not population changes or short run variations in price and value that maintained the price of labor in the progress of capital accumulation, as the classical political economists believed. Although the value of labor power is equal to the goods necessary to maintain and reproduce the laborer, the magnitude of those goods that the laborer receives had to do with technical change and class struggle, rather than with population increase and disparities in the price and value of commodities.

In the process of capitalist production labor power creates more value used to reproduce labor power in an ever-expanding circuit of commodity production. Marx regarded capital accumulation, through the quest for the production and expansion of surplus value, as the driving force of capitalism. Thus, from a Marxian perspective migrant labor, as an imbedded factor in the process of capitalist commodity production, plays a

---

[15] See Adam Smith Ibid 1952; David Ricardo Ibid 1980; Maurice Dobb Ibid 1973; and Donald J. Harris Ibid 1978 for more on the natural price of wages.

central role in capital accumulation and the imperialist-centered model of capital accumulation. Insofar as migrant labor and the economic activities involved in migration processes contribute to capital accumulation, migration is a vital part of the driving force of capitalism.

Capital accumulation takes place through the conversion of surplus value into capital in an ever-expanding circuit of capital. Capital is therefore a "self-expanding value," while the profit rate or money form of surplus value represents "the rate of self-expansion of the total capital." Although Marx and the classical political economists regarded capital accumulation as the motive force of capitalism, they diverged in that Marx saw the process as being characterized by a historically specific mode of production in which class struggle was a deciding factor.

Marx outlined some important characteristics of the process of capital accumulation in capitalist society that are worth noting. These characteristics include the perpetual changes in the level of technology, the economic and social organization of production and society, and the endless increase in the organic composition of capital. That is to say that the value composition of capital, comprising the values of constant and variable capital, in relation to the technical composition of capital, characterized by the material means of production and living labor, will rise steadily. In the process of expansion in the organic composition of capital, there is an increase in the concentration of capital and the control it exercises over the economy and state. There is also an increasing tendency for the rate of profit to fall, crises, and for the proletarianization of the workers on a world scale as capital expands globally, subjecting all hitherto forms of production to the capitalist mode.[16]

As capital expands globally it is accompanied by the migration of both skilled and unskilled labor to perform their role in the production of value in the imperialist-centered model of capital accumulation. Thus, as capital traverses the globe in search of investment opportunities labor moves in search of better employment and improved living conditions. However, labor faces more constraints on its movement than capital, as noted in chapters that follow. Capital does not only go to labor in foreign lands it

---

[16] This is a very important point to note in the light of the current debate on globalization in which its proponents behave as if the idea of capitalist domination of the globe is something new. Marx forewarned that the natural progression of capitalism is to spread to all existing societies and this is precisely the case as socialism has collapsed in Eastern Europe and the capitalist market is being extended into the former socialist countries and existing ones such as China and Cuba. Whether it is called globalization or not, Marx predicted that such was the natural tendency of capitalism.

also recruits labor from foreign lands thereby perpetuating the proletarianization of workers on a world scale and class struggle globally.

The Neoclassical "Revolution"

The break with the classical tradition engineered by Stanley Jevons,[17] Carl
Menger,[18] and Leon Walras[19] classified as the neoclassical "revolution" in
economics shifted the focus of study from the economy as a whole to individual households seeking to maximize their utility. This shift intensified
the application of mathematics to explain economic behavior, which
moved economic analyses further away from social reality into the realm
of questionable abstractions. The neoclassical assumption is that all free
market behaviors, including those of the stock exchange could be reduced
to static equilibrium conditions. Because of its focus on the utility maximizing behavior of individual households, neoclassical economics gained
special importance in the study of migration.

The works of Jevons and Menger that appeared in 1871 and Walras in
1874 led to the abandonment of the study of growth and development of
the entire economy in favor of utility analysis of the individual household.
The pursuit of individual household utility analysis has led to the view
that neoclassical economics has no basis for a theory of capital accumulation or development of the whole economy. Although there are several
versions of neoclassical economic theory, represented by economic theorists such as Jevons, Menger, Walras, Edgeworth,[20] and Marshall,[21] this tradition has shifted the debate from capital accumulation to static
equilibrium analysis.[22] It is assumed that economic resources are scarce
or limited and therefore has to be efficiently allocated in relation to consumer preferences.

Neoclassical economics borrowed Smith's notion of the "invisible hand"
of the market to solve their problem of efficient resource allocation.

---

[17] See Stanley Jevons. (1965). *The Theory of Political Economy*, 5th Edition, New York,
A.M. Kelley.

[18] See Carl Menger. (1965). *Principles of Economics*, New York, New York University Press.

[19] See Leon Walras. (1954). *Elements of Pure Economics, or the Theory of Social Wealth*,
London, Allen and Unwin.

[20] See Francis Ysidro Edgeworth. (1925). *Papers Relating to Political Economy*, London,
Macmillan and Company.

[21] See Alfred Marshall. (1910). *Principles of Economics*, London, Macmillan and Company.

[22] See John Buttrick. (1960). "Toward a Theory of Economic Growth: The Neoclassical
Contribution," in Bert F. Hoselitz, et al, *Theories of Economic Growth*, Illinois, The Free
Press.

Static equilibrium analysis therefore starts off with price and quantity being in a state of equilibrium, defined as "a constellation of selected interrelated variables so adjusted to one another that no inherent tendency to change prevails in the model, which they constitute."[23] The view is that for equilibrium to prevail "all variables in the model must simultaneously be in a state of rest."[24] The state of rest "is based only on the balancing of the internal forces of the model, while the external factors are assumed fixed," hence "parameters and exogenous variables are treated as constants."[25] Because equilibrium is "characterized by a lack of tendency to change" it is referred to as statics.

However, the neo-Keynesians Roy Forbes Harrod[26] and Evsey D. Domar[27] restored the study of growth to neoclassical economics. According to Banerjee and Duflo (2005)[28]

> The premise of neo-classical growth theory is that it is possible to do a reasonable job of explaining the broad patterns of economic change across countries, by looking at it through the lens of an aggregate production function. The aggregate production function relates the total output of an economy (a country, for example) to the aggregate amounts of labor, human capital and physical capital in the economy, and some simple measure of the level of technology in the economy as a whole ... The key assumption behind the construction of the aggregate production function is that all factor markets are perfect, in the sense that individuals can buy or sell as much as they want at a given price. With perfect factor markets (and no risk) the market must allocate the available supply of inputs to maximize total output (p 475).

In the neoclassical model therefore migration is subject to static equilibrium analysis in domestic and international labor markets. Supply and demand factors are identified as determinants of migration described as pull and push causes. The neoclassical model is built on the notion that society is classless with only atomistic individuals who are the owners of

---

[23] See Alpha C. Chiang. (1984). *Fundamental Methods of Mathematical Economics* 3rd Edition, New York, McGraw-Hill.

[24] See Alpha C. Chiang Ibid 1984.

[25] See Alpha C. Chiang Ibid 1984.

[26] See Roy Forbes Harrod. (1936). *Towards a Dynamic Economics: Some Recent Developments of Economic Theory and Their Application to Policy*, New York, St. Martin Press and (1939). "An Essay in Dynamic Theory," *Economic Journal*, Vol. 49.

[27] See Evsey D. Domar. (1946). "Capital Expansion, Rate of Growth and Employment," *Economectrica*, Vol. 14, and (1964). *Essays in the Theory of Economic Growth*, New York, Oxford University Press.

[28] Abhijit V. Banerjee and Esther Duflo. (2005). Growth Theory Through the Lens of Development Economics. In Philippe Aghion and Steven Durlauf (ed.) *Handbook of Economic Growth*, Vol. 1 Part A, Elsevier, pp 473–552.

the productive factors operating in it. The individual unit of analysis is the household, which it is assumed behaves like a single person making rational decisions.

It is therefore a rationally thinking individual household that makes migration decisions. Also since in neoclassical theory the society is perceived to be classless and the focus is on the individual, migration does not have a class bias. This emphasis on the individual led Schumpeter[29] to refer to the neoclassical approach as "methodological individualism." But, as Bukharin[30] pointed out it is impossible to separate social classes from a study of the economy.

In essence, the main economic problem the neoclassical economists are concerned with is how households exchange goods and factor services and the price arrangements concerning those exchanges. It is not concerned with economic growth and development. Neoclassical economists also believe that there could be a system of "pure exchange" without any production. Resource allocation takes place at equilibrium market price and quantity, which means that there exist certain given household preferences, states of technology, and supply of productive resources such as migrant labor.

Income distribution takes place in accordance with factor endowments and price or the marginal physical product. A change in supply or household demand changes price, and therefore influence income distribution in accordance with the marginal productivity theory. In the neoclassical model, therefore, migration is narrowly confined to supply and demand analysis in labor markets thereby overlooking the broader class forces at play under global capitalism that lie at the heart of immigration.

The Keynesian[31] "Revolution"

The standard viewpoint expressed in the literature on John Maynard Keynes[32] and his neo-Keynesian disciples such as Roy Forbes Harrod[33]

---

[29] See Joseph Schumpeter. (1954). *History of Economic Analysis*, Cambridge, Harvard University Press.

[30] See N. Bukharin. (1972). *Economic Theory of the Leisure Class*, New York, Monthly Review Press.

[31] See John Maynard Keynes. (1953). *The General Theory of Employment, Interest, and Money*, New York, Harcourt and Brace.

[32] See John Maynard Keynes Ibid 1935.

[33] See Roy Forbes Harrod. (1963). *Towards a Dynamic Economics: Some Recent Developments of Economic Theory and Their Application to Policy*, New York, St. Martin Press, and (1939). "An Essay in Dynamic Theory," *Economic Journal*, Vol. 49.

and Evsey D. Domar[34] is that they restored the study of growth to economics. But, the reality is that the so-called Keynesian "revolution" merely served to salvage neoclassical economics from its static nature and to equip it with a dynamic theory of growth. Lord Keynes, the so-called inventor of macroeconomics and his neo-Keynesian followers reformulated neoclassical economics in the light of the depression in the 1930s. Keynes recognized that at the very core of the capitalist crisis was a lack of investment. The crisis led him to postulate that government intervention in the form of increased investment spending was the key to stimulate the necessary economic recovery to take the economy out of a low-level equilibrium trap. Although Keynes was accused of being communist because of his state interventionist policies, he emerged as a savior of capitalism from the throes of the Great Depression, in the 1930s.

The basic Keynesian national income model is stated, as income is equal to consumption expenditure plus investment and government spending. Income and consumption expenditure are the endogenous variables, while investment and government spending are exogenously determined.[35] Here, the equilibrium condition is met, that is national income is equal to total expenditure. The model has a second equation, which represents the consumption function. In this case consumption is stated as being equal to the parameter for the "autonomous consumption expenditure" representing the vertical intercept of the consumption function, plus the parameter representing the "marginal propensity to consume" that is the change in consumption as income changes.[36]

The problem that Harrod[37] was concerned to address in the light of the Keynesian model as a solution to the problem of the Great Depression, was whether or not a capitalist economy in a stationary state can continue to grow indefinitely. It was already pointed out above that the classical economists believed that the economy was moving towards a stationary state. Harrod was not interested in the problems of economic expansion in the colonial or underdeveloped or socialist countries, a concern that later led to the emergence of development economics, he focused his attention on the advanced capitalist countries. Harrod believed that there was only one rate at which the economy could grow, and that there was no guarantee that that rate could be achieved and maintained.

---

[34] See Evsey D. Domar. (1946). "Capital Expansion, Rate of Growth and Employment," *Economectrica*, Vol. 14, and (1964). *Essays in the Theory of Economic Growth*, New York, Oxford University Press.

[35] See Alpha C. Chiang Ibid 1984.

[36] See Alpha C. Chiang Ibid 1984.

[37] See Roy Forbes Harrod Ibid 1939 and 1963.

Utilizing the Keynesian assumption that saving was equal to invest-ment, Harrod postulated that there is a given amount of net income that is saved per period of time. The economy will be in equilibrium when this saving is equal to the investments of firms, I = sY where I = investments, s = the proportion of net income saved and Y = net income. Thus, invest-ment has a Keynesian multiplier effect (1/s) on income and demand. Now, if the value of total capital (K) is increased at a rate say (g), and assuming that the capital-output ratio (v) is constant, then the basic Harrod growth model may be expressed as g = I/K = sY/K = sv. Thus, if firms were to grow at a rate (g), saving would be exactly equal to the level of investment, and the rate of growth in income and capital would be the same because of the constant capital-output ratio. With this Harrod growth model, firms may continue to grow indefinitely, and in this way Keynesian economics was able to develop a theory of economic growth within the neoclassical tradition.

It is on this neo-Keynesian growth theory within the neoclassical frame-work that "push-pull" migration theory depends as its theoretical home. Remittances by migrants are now considered as contributing to both sav-ings and investment capital on whose shoulders economic development resides.

Development Economics and Migration

The focus in this section is on the unique ways in which development eco-nomics while trying to find its originality albeit borrowing from the classi-cal, neoclassical and Keynesian theoretical traditions, attempted to deal with the issue of the impact of migration on development. In a fundamen-tal sense however development theory is no different from classical politi-cal economy because they both focus of progress of the entire nations-state unlike neoclassical theory, which concentrates on individual market behavior. The 1940s are generally agreed, albeit mistakenly, to be the start-ing point of development economics, however, interest in the economics of underdeveloped countries date from earlier times.

Levitt (1992)[38] pointed out that the debates in Russia between Preobrzhanski[39] and Bukhanin during the 1920s concerning the industrial

---

[38] Kari Levitt. (1992). The State of Development Studies, IDS Occasional Papers No. 92.1, Saint Mary's University, Halifax, Nova Scotia.
[39] See E.A. Preobrzhanski. (1979). *The Crisis of Soviet Industrialization: Selected Essays*, New York, Sharpe.

and agricultural strategies of the first Soviet Five Years Plan were forerunners to the current development economics literature. Also, the observations by colonial administrators such as J.H. Boeke,[40] and J.S. Furnivall[41] on development in the colonies, and even the work by H.S. Jevons[42] on the art of economic development during 1918–1922 are crucial to a comprehensive understanding of the historical evolution of development economics. Further, a number of British Royal Commissions made recommendations that address issues concerning the peculiarity of economic and social conditions in the British colonies. The wide-scale recommendations of the Moyne Commission established by the British to investigate the disturbances in the British West Indies during the 1930s fits squarely into the development economics literature.[43]

The development debate that emerged with the works of writers like Paul N. Rosenstein-Rodan,[44] Ragnar Nurkse,[45] Hla Myint,[46] Eugene Stanley,[47] Hans Singer,[48] Kurt Martin Mandelbaum,[49] Raúl Prebisch,[50] and Sir W. Arthur Lewis[51] focused on the economic problems of the

---

[40] See J.H. Boeke. (1953). *Economics and the Economic Policies of Dual Societies*, New York, Institute of Pacific Relations.

[41] See J.H. Furnivall. (1939). *Netherlands India: A Study of Plural Economy*, Cambridge, Cambridge University Press and (1948). *Colonial Policy and Practice: A Comparative Study of Burma and Netherlands India*, Cambridge, Cambridge University Press.

[42] See H.S. Jevons. (1916–1917). "The Teaching of Economics," *Indian Journal of Economics*, Vol. 1.

[43] The wide-ranging recommendations of the Moyne Commission Report (1945) led to sweeping social and economic development changes in the English-speaking West Indies. The social welfare system implemented came out of the recommendations of the Moyne Commission Report.

[44] See Paul N. Rosenstein-Rodan. (1943). "Problems of Industrialization of Eastern and South-Eastern Europe," *Economic Journal*, Vol. 53, No. 210/211.

[45] See Ragnar Nurkse. (1952). "Some Aspects of the Problem of Economic Development," *American Economic Review*, Vol. XLII, No.2, and (1953). *Problems of Capital Formation in Underdeveloped Countries*, Oxford, Blackwell.

[46] See Hla Myint. (1948). *Theories of Welfare Economics*, Cambridge, Harvard University Press, and (1954). An Interpretation of Economic Backwardness," *Oxford Economic Papers*, Vol. 6, No. 6.

[47] See Eugene Stanley. (1944). *World Economic Development: Effects of Advanced Industrialized Countries*, Montreal, International Labor Organization.

[48] See Hans Singer. (1950). "Distribution of Gains Between Investing and Borrowing Countries," *American Economic Review*, Papers and Proceedings, United Nations. (1949). *Relative Price of Exports and Imports of Underdeveloped Countries*, and (1952). *Instability in export markets of under-developed countries in relation to their ability to obtain foreign exchange from exports of primary commodities, 1901 to 1950.*

[49] See Kurt M. Mandelbaum. (1947). *Industrialization of Backward Areas*, Oxford, Basil Blackwell.

[50] See Raul Prebisch. (1950). *The Economic Development of Latin America and Its Principal Problems*, New York, United Nations.

[51] See Sir W. Arthur Lewis. (1954). "Economic Development With Unlimited Supplies of Labor," *The Manchester School*, Vol. 22, No. 2.

colonies and underdeveloped countries. Development economics was
mainly concerned with strategies that would bring about the rapid industrialization of the Third World. Industrialization would remove push factors associated with migration, primarily poverty, low economic growth,
poor living conditions, etc.

The central themes of the debate among development economists were
the terms of trade (Singer 1950 and Prebisch 1950), and balanced growth
(Rosenstein-Rodan 1943; 1957 and Nurkse 1957), versus unbalanced growth
(Hirschman 1958, and Streeten 1959). The structuralist versus the monetar-
ist approach to inflation, dependency analysis,[52] and the Lewis model of
economic development with unlimited supplies of labor, were other
themes.[53]

The Caribbean plantation dependency school[54] in large measure was a
reaction to the Lewis model about the industrialization of the British West
Indies.[55] Lewis emphasized the development of the local capitalist sector
as the engine of growth and his model of industrialization of the British
West Indies, is based on the implementation of policies that would attract
foreign investors to the Caribbean. The plantation dependence school
argued that "industrialization by invitation" would not be beneficial to the
region because of the small plantation dependent characteristics of
Caribbean economies. A plantation economy is considered a high-cost
satellite export propelled economy, specializing in the production of raw
materials for industry in the metropolis and importing from them all consumption goods.

While the main themes in development economics represented critiques of both the neo-classical and Keynesian traditions the criticisms
were of an in-house nature in the sense that their perpetrators did not

[52] Crístóbal Kay. (1989). *Latin American Theories of Development and Underdevelopment*,
London, Routledge, classified dependency theorists in two categories – reformist and
Marxist. The reformist are closely related to the UN Economic Commission for Latin
America and are referred to as structuralist or nationalists who favor reform of the capital-
ist system, and not its replacement by any other social system. The Marxist argues for
socialist revolution as the solution to dependent development.

[53] See Kari Levitt. (1992). The State of Development Studies, IDS Occasional Papers No.
92.1, Saint Mary's University, Halifax, Nova Scotia.

[54] See Lloyd Best. (1969). "Outline of a Mode of Pure Plantation Economy," *Social and
Economic Studies*, Volume 19, No. 1, and Norman Girvan. (1973). "The Development of
Dependency Economics in the Caribbean and Latin America," *Social and Economic Studies*,
Vol. 22, No.1. See also Clive Y. Thomas. (1974). *Dependency and Transformation: The
Economics of the Transition to Socialism*, New York, Monthly Review Press, for a Marxist
dependency critique of plantation economics.

[55] See Sir W. Arthur Lewis. (1950). "Industrialization of the British West Indies,"
Caribbean Economic Review, Vol. 2, No.1.

advocate an alternative social system to capitalism to address the problems of underdevelopment. Seemingly, the main position that emerged from these themes in development economics was that there was need for a special set of tools drawn from existing schools of economic analysis to explain development in Third World countries, and the concern was to develop these tools.[56]

These studies, which evolved only after the World War II,[57] coincided with the process of political decolonization in the Third World and are said to have spawned a new discipline called development economics, which is the formulation and study of theories and policies about how the former European colonies described as developing or Third World countries could achieve technological change. Development is presented as synonymous with industrialization, a pull-factor while non-industrialization is tantamount to poverty, a push factor.

Ronald Findlay[58] pointed out for example that development is concerned with "the achieving of a sustained increase in per capita incomes of the millions of people living in the so-called Third World." Massey (1988), argues that "economic development is the application of capital to raise human productivity, generate wealth, and increase national income," which is accompanied by "a constellation of social and cultural changes that scholars generally call 'modernization.' "[59] In Massey's (1988) view "economic growth depends only on amounts of labor and capital, but also

---

[56] See John Toye. (1987). *The Dilemmas of Development*, New York, Basil Blackwell, for more on this point.

[57] Kari Levitt. (1992). The State of Development Studies, IDS Occasional Papers No. 92.1, Saint Mary's University, Halifax, Nova Scotia, had this to say about the pioneers in the early literature on the economics of underdeveloped countries. "Among those in England at the time were Arndt, Bauer, Frankel, Lewis, Mandelbaum (Martin), Singer and Rosenstein-Rodan. Scitovsky also participated in early planning debates. Others at times concerned themselves with developing countries included Kaldor, Balogh and E.A.G. Robinson. Somewhat younger, but influenced by the prevailing intellectual and social climate were Seers and Streeten... No list of European pioneers of the economics of underdeveloped regions would be complete without Myrdal (Sweden), Frisch (Norway), Tinbergen (Netherlands), Perroux (France), and, among those who migrated to the United States, Hirschman and Nurkse. Frisch and Tinbergen pioneered quantitative techniques of development planning and econometrics. With the possible exception of Lord Bauer in England, all of these economists worked within the mainstream of political economy, drawing on the heritage of Smith, Ricardo, Marx, Menger, Marshall, Wicksell, Keynes, and Schumpeter."

[58] Ronald Findlay. (1982). "On W. Arthur Lewis' Contribution to Economics," in M. Gersovitz, C.F., Diaz-Alejandro, G. Ranis, and M.R. Rosenzweig, (Eds.), *The Theory and Experience of Economic Development: Essays in Honor of Sir W. Arthur Lewis*, London, Allen & Unwin.

[59] Douglas S. Massey. (1988). Economic Development and International Migration in Comparative Perspective, *Population and Development Review*, Vol 14, Issue, pp 383–413.

on institutional, cultural and technological factors that determine how labor and capital are used." Thus, "capital accumulation transforms social institutions, cultural values and technologies in ways that affect the course of subsequent development."

The essence of development economics is its search for specialized theories appropriate to Third World settings for the achievement of technical change (industrialization), even if that means shying away form Western theoretical traditions already established. Thus, the claim to originality in development theories is the degree to which they bypass classical political economy, Marxian, neoclassical and Keynesian theories in search of location specific explanations that address the specific characteristics of poor countries.

Sir W. Arthur Lewis a foremost development economist located within the classical framework because of his assumption that the supply of labor was unlimited[60] sets himself apart from other development economists by the approach he adopted, which in essence represented a break with neoclassical and Keynesian theories and a return to the classical political economy tradition. Lewis made his intervention into the debate on economic development with his seminal article in 1954. His concern was different to that of the neoclassical marginal utility individual household analysis and the Keynesian growth theories. Lewis set out to explain how the former colonies in Africa, Asia, and the Caribbean could achieve some level of economic development comparable with that of the advanced capitalist countries.

Lewis' work on "economic development with unlimited supplies of labor" is a direct extension of the body of ideas associated with the classical school and worked well to complement Keynesian economics especially from the viewpoint of the role of the state as an economic agent, which had come to dominate domestic and international economic policy until the neoliberal counter-revolution in the 1970s. Lewis presented the case for industrialization based on existing conditions in the Third World.

In a fundamental sense the model is a theory of internal migration and capital export. The Lewis model is founded on the assumption that migration takes place from the rural sector with low wages and where the marginal product of labor is below zero to the modern capitalist sector where the wage rate is much higher. Eventually, surplus labor in the traditional sector will disappear being absorbed by the modern capitalist sector.

---

[60] See Sir W. Arthur Lewis. (1954). "Economic Development With Unlimited Supplies of Labor," *The Manchester School*, Vol. 22, No. 2.

Harris and Todaro (1970) argue however "despite the existence of positive marginal products in agriculture and significant levels of urban unemployment, rural-urban labor migration not only continues to exist, but indeed, appears to be accelerating."[61]

Lewis was concerned with developing a theory of economic development that was suitable to former European colonies that emerged as new nations after they gained independence beginning in the 1940s. In the process he developed a general theory of economic development of capitalist societies. Lewis likened the socio-economic conditions in the new nations to the situation in Europe at the time of the industrial revolution. The major puzzle that confronted classical political economists in England at that time was how to explain the transition that was taking place from agriculture to industry, involving the conversion of farmers into industrial proletariats. The classical political economists believed that the transition was temporary as is evidenced from their work, which is based almost entirely on agricultural societies.

Lewis observed however that the transition from agriculture to industry was not temporary but a permanent feature in the historical evolution of capitalism. All capitalist and other advanced forms of pre-capitalist societies have developed along the same trajectory of an expanding nucleus that is a capitalist or lead sector absorbing surplus resources in the rural agricultural sector. This idea of growth was developed fully in Lewis' book on the theory of economic growth.[62] Now, if the new nations were under similar conditions to those of European states at the time of the classical political economists, then it was appropriate to apply the very theoretical framework of classical political economy to explain the transition from agriculture to industry in the newly created nation-states in the Third World. This was the general reasoning Lewis used to develop his theory of economic growth in, which he focused on the classical problems of distribution, accumulation, and growth. But, although the conditions were assumed to be the same there were sufficient differences supplied by time that caused Lewis' theory of economic development to be an advance on the classical model of development.

---

[61] John R. Harris and Michael P. Todaro. (1970). "Migration, Unemployment and Development: A Two-Sector Analysis," *The American Economic Review*, Vol. 60, No. 1, 126–142.

[62] See Sir W. Arthur Lewis. (1955). *The Theory of Economic Growth*, Illinois, Richard D. Irwin.

It follows, therefore, that Lewis believed that the major economic development problem confronting the new nations was how to transfer labor from the rural agricultural traditional sector to a modern industrial capitalist sector – in essence rural-urban migration. This is what had happened in Europe and North America as those continents became industrialized and developed. It was now time for the underdeveloped areas of the world to follow suit. The classical political economists assumed that labor was unlimited in supply at a subsistence wage rate and Lewis adopted that very assumption for the traditional agricultural sector in his model.

To this effect he parted company with the neoclassical economists who distinguished between the short and the long run and assumed that the supply of all factors were fixed in the short run and were therefore limited in supply. Lewis believed that while labor was indeed limited in supply in developed European countries this was not the case in undeveloped regions of the world where there was surplus labor. These regions had an unlimited supply of labor, which will only become limited after all surplus labor had been absorbed by the capitalist sector. He therefore rejected the Keynesian model on the grounds that it assumed that not only labor but also all other factors were unlimited in supply. The classical political economists believed however that fertile land had a limited supply subject to the law of diminishing returns, and that capital was scarce.

Economic expansion in the manner that is suggested by the Lewis model for a closed labor surplus economy could not go on *ad infinitum*. Its duration is restricted to the size of the labor surplus, which once absorbed the economy then becomes opened to a growth model fuelled by international trade. The existence of surplus labor in other economies has a significant bearing on how the now opened economy pursues its growth objectives.

When surplus labor is absorbed "wages begin to rise above the subsistence, and the capitalist surplus is adversely affected." The capitalist has two options to hold wages down and thereby augment his surplus, either "by encouraging immigration or by exporting their capital to countries where there is still abundant labor at a subsistence wage." Lewis favors the export of capital to immigration because of the social unrest that the latter may cause due to trade union opposition out of fear that immigrants will lower the wage rate. In Lewis' view small-scale immigration of skilled or unskilled labor will not lower the wage rate but large-scale immigration would. Importantly, the cause of the export of capital is not the absorption of surplus labor, but the fall in capitalist surplus due to a rise in wage locally. Capital will be exported so long as there is a greater return to be had from investing abroad.

Trade between labor surplus and labor scarce economies, is explainable by the law of comparative costs but for different reasons in the Lewis model. In the case of labor scarce economies, the law of comparative costs is a strong argument in favor of free trade. In labor surplus economies, however, the law of comparative costs provides a strong case for protectionism. This is because of the link in the terms of trade between the tropics (labor surplus economies) and the temperate-zone (labor scarce countries), in favor of the latter. Lewis supplied evidence to show that despite the growth in productivity of labor in the labor surplus economies, using sugar production as an example, these countries enjoyed only limited income benefits from international trade. He believed therefore that a rise in the productivity in agricultural exports in labor surplus economies led to the deterioration in the terms of trade of those commodities *vis-à-vis* the imports of manufactured goods from the temperate-zone.

Neoliberal Theory and Migration

The search for originality in development economics is tantamount to an exposure of the limitations of hitherto economic theories in adequately addressing the conditions of poverty in the developing countries. This search for originality nonetheless became the basis for the neoliberal critique of development economics and a restatement on the virtues of the very theoretical traditions that development economics want to supersede in order to stimulate technical change in the Third World.

The neoliberal critique of development economics reinstated two core values of the Western theoretical tradition – the positive method founded on the principles of science, and free market fundamentalism. In terms of the positive method, economics is regarded as a science whose findings are universal, which leaves no room for deviations such as development economics that seeks to discover particularistic rather than universal values; or values that are universal only to particularistic conditions. The subjection of all phenomena to scientific method and the laws of the capitalist market mean that migration and all its derivatives are market phenomena. Thus, migration, remittances, diaspora, etc., must be freed from excessive government regulations, and liberalized.

Neoliberal theory is leading the resurgence of studies on the development impact of migration. The basic idea is to bring migration policy in

line with the free market. The neoliberal theoretical debate is centered on
the development impact of migration. The global institutions such as the
International Monetary Fund (IMF) and World Bank dominated by neoliberal theorists are seeking to create the appropriate policies to bring
migration in line with the market liberalization. The focal points of neoliberal theory are inter alia financialization and liberalization, remittances, Diasporas, the millennium development goals, and human
development. The neoliberal idea is to maximize profit from migration,
which it is argued here is the primary goal for the development impact of
migration.

Conclusion

Migration and capital accumulation are inextricably linked in the schools
of thought reviewed above. As the driving force of capitalism, capital
accumulation is undertaken from all aspects of the capitalist production
and social organizational processes. The primary focus of classical political economists, neo-classical economists, Keynesians, development economists and neoliberal theorists, with the exception of Marx, is the
acquisition and hence accumulation of wealth by nation states and individuals. This involves rural-urban migration as agricultural workers are
transformed into factory workers in newly emerging cities. Rural-urban
migration also to some extent stimulated population studies as the emer-
gent cities became overcrowded. It embraces international migration and
trade as industrial capitalism expanded across national borders.

Furthermore, the focus on atomized individuals in neoclassical theory
has brought to the fore utility maximizing behavior a staple in the analysis
of migration. Migrants are said to behave in consonance with maximizing
their utility, since it is believed that it is rational individual households
that take decisions to migrate. Migration is therefore subjected to static
equilibrium analysis in domestic and international labor markets devoid
of class issues.

Additionally, Keynesian growth theory within the neoclassical framework became the foundations of push-pull migration theory. Growth
serves as a "pull" factor, which implies that the opposite is also true –
non-growth serves as a "push" factor. People will leave economies that are
experiencing no or little growth for economies with high growth.

From the perspective of development economics, therefore, migration
could be couched within the context of poor people in the Third World

wanting to catch-up with their rich neighbors in the advanced capitalist countries. The view is that people migrate to greener pastures in order to bring about an improvement in the living conditions for themselves and families. "Push-pull" migration theory therefore is also a nice fit with development economics because it satisfies the condition of low-income countries sending people to high-income countries that would through remittances lead to an increase in income and hence development in the sending countries.

Finally, neoliberal theory seeks to liberalize every facet of the human experience including migration. It financializes migration, bringing remittances under the control of financial capital for the purposes of capital accumulation.

CHAPTER THREE

POOR ECONOMIC GROWTH WITH INCREASED IMMIGRATION

Introduction

The primary purpose of this chapter is to argue a case against the idea that people are stimulated to migrate to a particular country if it is experiencing strong economic growth and to leave a country, which is undergoing poor economic growth. This idea is the hub of "push-pull" theories of migration associated with neoclassical economics discussed in the previous chapter. US official data on economic growth, unemployment, layoffs and separation, and immigration are analyzed to establish the thesis that it is not in every case an economic downturn may cause people to leave a country or to desist from migrating to that country.

Alternatively stated, economic and financial crises in a country do not always cause people not to migrate to that country. People may still queue up to migrate to a country going through hard times. A country could experience increased immigration during the period in which it is experiencing economic and financial crises. The argument is that it is the level of capital accumulation in a country and not economic growth in the immediate period, which matters most to people in taking their decisions to migrate to that country, even as the country experiences an economic crisis. With a high level of capital accumulation a country will be able to sustain its standard of living relative to other countries despite the fact that it is in economic and financial crises.

In developing the thesis and argument first there is a brief examination of economic theories of migration, with a focus on push-pull approaches, followed secondly by an outline of the question and counter-proposition being presented here. Third, there is an analysis of economic growth and unemployment in the US for the period 2000 to 2009, followed by an examination of US layoffs and separations between 2007 and 2009, and a discussion on the industry distribution of the mass layoffs and separations in 2008. The final part turns to a discussion on increased migration to the US during the great recession between 2007 and 2009, and Caribbean migration to the US between 2000 and 2009.

Economic Theories of Migration: Push-Pull Approaches

A central focus in the study of migration has been on the factors that "push" people to leave their countries to go abroad and those that "pull" them from their places of abode to other locations. The "push-pull" approach has been particularly standard from the perspective of economic theories. These include "political economy theories of rational choice, supply and demand, world system, and network" analysis.[1] According to Sirojudin (2009), "rational choice theory helps to identify the personal and household considerations for emigration by weighing the costs and the benefits," compared with "supply-and-demand theory," which "takes into account the oversupply of labor as a strong push factor and the demand for labor in advanced industrial countries as a strong pull factor." The discredited world system approach "focuses on the complex political and economic factors that lead to exploiting third-world countries and create a strong push to emigrate," while "network theory can be used to explain the dynamics of immigrant communities in both overseas countries and country of origin that can create a pull toward emigration" Sirojudin (2009).

These "push-pull" theories are collectively and individually a part of the theoretical antecedents to the neoliberal approach of the development impact of migration. They tend to support the basic idea that poor economic growth in a country will "push" people to leave, while strong economic growth in a country will "pull" people towards it. In other words, poor economic growth in a receiving nation-state is a disincentive to migration into that country.

This position is in line with the idea that if a country is experiencing economic development relative to another, then people will leave the latter to go to the former in search of greener pastures. It is conceivable also that a high level of job layoffs indicative of an economic crisis in a receiving country would place a further damper on the number of arrivals of migrants. It is anticipated that migration levels would decline in a receiving country if it experiences zero or poor economic growth and a high incidence of job layoffs.

It is noticeable however that historically, people do not always leave their country because it is experiencing economic crisis. During the Great

---

[1] Siroj Sirojudin. (2009). "Economic Theories of Emigration." *Journal of Human Behavior in the Social Environment*, 19:702–712.

Depression, for example, many workers in the US were forced to migrate from the manufacturing sector from which they were downsized, to the agricultural sectors on farms.[2] However, much of the literature on the economics of immigration focuses on three related issues, namely the determination of the size and skill composition of immigrant flows to any particular host country; the issue of the adaptation of immigrants to conditions in the host country's economy; and on the impact that immigrants have on the economy of the host country.[3]

Alternative Question and Counter-Proposition

The main position taken here however is that economic growth does not in every situation determine whether people migrate to a country or not. Based on the standards set by key proponents of neoliberal economic theory, the US economy has been experiencing low levels of economic growth for an extended period over the last decade. However, as the US economy experienced these low economic growth levels, and a high incidence of job layoffs between 2000 and 2009, Caribbean and other migrants continued to pour into the country. The question is therefore if poor economic performance and a high incidence of job layoffs have not hindered immigration to the US, then, what really is responsible for the draw the US has on immigrants?

The answer to this question leads to the counter-proposition presented here namely that because of the consistently high level of capital accumulation in the US, which translates into higher standards of living, an economic crisis and job layoffs, do not deter migrants from continuing to flow into the country. It is not always the case however that the overall standard of living will be high as a result of a high level of capital accumulation. A high level of capital accumulation and a high level of poverty may go hand-in-hand in the same country as currently witnessed in the newly emerging economies like China, Brazil and India.

There are other conditions that derive from the high level of capital accumulation that shape immigration to crisis racked imperial countries.

---

[2] Robert L. Boyd. (2002). A "Migration of Despair": Unemployment, the Search for Work, and Migration to Farms During the Great Depression, *Social Science Quarterly*, Volume 83, Number 2, June.

[3] George J. Borjas. (1989). "Economic Theory and International Migration." *International Migration Review*, Vol. 23, No. 3, Special Silver Anniversary Issue: International Migration an Assessment for the 90's (Autumn), pp. 457–485.

Although the economic crisis may be severe in both sending and receiving countries, the high level of capital accumulation in the latter may provide more opportunities for migrants. People may lose jobs in both sending and receiving countries but in the latter the social safety nets might be stronger thereby providing a greater cushion to the unemployed, compared with the situation in migrants' former countries. Thus the crisis may not be a deterrent to migration because the real effect of the crisis is felt to varying degrees in sending and receiving countries. The relativity of the effects of a global crisis or a crisis confined to the developed countries is really what matters.

Another issue is what we may call the tyranny of the exchange rate in the capitalist system. Thus, because of the relatively high exchange rate for the US dollar in sending countries, migrants to the US from countries where the US dollar exchanges at a high rate, will have the real or illusory feeling of earning much more that they did in their home countries. Real because when their US income is denominated in the currencies of their home countries it far exceeds what they earned there. Illusory, because they can barely survive on their US incomes in the US.

For example a manager in Ghana paid in Ghanaian Cedis because of the US$-Cedis exchange rate earns less than an American making US$15,000 a year, which is below the US poverty line. But, because of the purchasing power of the Cedis in Ghana, the Ghanaian manager may provide for his family reasonably well with his level of income, there. However, a migrant from Ghana to the US earning below the US poverty line will not be able to provide adequately for his family, even though his US income is much higher than what he earned in Ghana. Thus, economic crisis in the US or not, even if the Ghanaian earns US$15,000 a year he will be perceived to be in a better position in the US. Although his income in the US places him at the bottom of the US economy, in Ghana it will place him at the top. The level of capital accumulation in the US will afford such an individual better access to social services and utilities, etc., compared with in Ghana.

However, the increase in the supply of foreign products whose prices, being influenced by the exchange rate are denominated in foreign currencies, makes it difficult for the Ghanaian manager to buy imports for which he has developed a taste. The television bombards him continuously with advertisement about products, which are not produced in Ghana. This draws him to the US despite the economic crisis there. This is a case of following the foreign products in search of a better life.

Furthermore, the fact that the Ghanaian manager may occupy a lower class position in the US than in Ghana does not matter. The meager income he earns in the US for the menial job he does is sufficient to give him middle class and above status in the Ghana, where he builds his mansion over a number of years. Furthermore, just being in the US places him in a higher class position in Ghana compared with his peers who remain in the country.

Although economic crisis may be raging in both sending and receiving countries, the education system is perceived to be better in the locations where there is a high level of capital accumulation. Thus, the Ghanaian manager will want to leave Ghana for the US to secure a better education for his children. And due to, their disposition towards education his children perform well securing scholarships, and graduating with high honors.

The problem is that the exchange rate is very oppressive in the capitalist system it that it punishes the developing countries. There must be some alternative way to determine the external value of currencies in capitalist economies other than by the current oppressive exchange rate. Undoubtedly, the problem is with the currency system of capitalism developed by the powerful capitalist states not only at Bretton Woods, but also before then by the banking system in European countries such as England and Holland and adopted by the US and foisted on the rest of the globe.

The key point nonetheless is that if there is any fall-off in immigration to the US in times of economic crisis, it is not because people have stopped trying to migrate to that country. It is due partly to restrictive migration policies pursued by the US government influenced by the economic crisis. In such a situation there is a tendency for locals to blame immigrants for the crisis. Thus, during an economic crisis, politics or political factors tend to take center stage in determining the fall-off in migration in a country with a high level of capital accumulation. The political elites that constitute the ruling class will tend to implement restrictive migration policies to please their political constituents, in order to win votes in the next elections cycle. Thus, the curtailment of immigration becomes more so a matter of politics than economics.

The counteracting tendency on the part of the capitalists during an economic crisis is precisely to hire migrant labor at lower wages and hence reduce production costs in order to stimulate profit to bring the economy out of the crisis. But the capitalists may not always have the national interest at heart in that they may not utilize the increased profit that result from hiring immigrant labor at lower wages to stimulate economic recovery in the domestic economy, they may choose to horde their money and/ or to save it abroad. This seems to be the case in the US in the current economic and financial crises.

Because of the crises however the locals will mount strong opposition to immigrant labor, blame them for the crisis, and the government will resort to measures to restrict migration. Thus, the argument is that it is expected that during an economic and financial crises, there may be a tendency for the number of legal migrants to fall and for illegal migrants to increase. The crises therefore stimulate immigration rather than restrict it.

This outcome is in response respectively to the government's restrictive measures to satisfy the political objectives of elected representatives, and the demand for cheap labor by private companies. In this situation there is a disjuncture between the political elites with reelection on their minds and the business classes who finance their political campaigns. The evidence in support of this argument is provided by the US immigration data examined below, and by the increase in the number of prosecutions of companies in the US that hire illegal immigrants in the current period of crises.

Companies Hiring Illegal Immigrants

The US Immigration and Customs Enforcement (ICE), has recently brought to books several US companies for hiring illegal immigrants. According to Susan Carroll "there are some big names on the list of 220 companies" fined by the ICE for hiring illegal immigrants. In her article *Big names on the list of companies ICE fined*,[4] on September 9, 2010, Carroll states that for example

> Westex Well Service, a company headed up by Texas Tech University Regent Mickey Long, paid $60,984 to immigration officials earlier this summer (That's the 16th largest fine nationally and the third-largest in Texas since 2007.) Long was appointed to his regent position by Gov. Rick Perry in February 2009. He has contributed $135,000 to Perry's campaign over the years and is listed as his co-chair for fundraising based out of Midland (Carroll 2010).

Also, Carroll (2010) stated that "Koch Food of Cincinnati, LLC" had to pay "($536,046), Johnson Dairy LLC out of Colorado ($100,800), and American Rice Inc. of Texas ($5,486)." Furthermore, according to Carroll (2010) the businesses employing immigrant labor and fined by the ICE "ranged from remote egg and cat fish farms in the South to New York's

---

[4] Susan Carroll. (2010). "Big names on the list of companies ICE fined," *Immigration Chronicles* September 9.

Chelsea Art Museum, which was hit with a $9,770 fine in December 2009. ... In Texas, ICE busted a Mr. Gatti's Pizza Store to the tune of $18,279."

Sarah Baker's article in *Wolfsdorf Navigating Immigration* on January 28, 2011 entitled "Immigration Enforcement Against Employers of Undocumented Workers is a 'Cash Cow' for State and Local Agencies!" reinforces the argument being made here.[5] Not only is the crises pushing private capital to hire illegal immigrant labor but the government is cashing-in on the money made through fines paid by companies that are caught hiring such workers.

According to Baker (2011) Kumar Kibble, Deputy Director of ICE in his address to the US House of Representatives Committee on the Judiciary, Subcommittee on Immigration Policy and Enforcement, on January 26, 2010, "indicated that in fiscal year 2010, ICE commenced a record 2,746 worksite enforcement investigations, which represents a nearly two-fold increase from the number of cases the agency initiated in FY 2008." According to Kibble, "in FY 2010 ICE ordered employers to pay fines totaling a whopping $6,956,026, up from $675,209 in FY 2008" (Baker 2011).

The government investigated IFCO Systems, an international logistics service provider, allegedly whose undocumented workers were seen destroying W-2 forms at the company's pallet plant in Albany, NY in February 2005. The government investigated 40 of the company's pallet plants that revealed 1,181 undocumented workers in 2006. Several state and local law enforcement agencies in New York received money as a part of the record-breaking settlement of the IFCO Systems case on January 13, 2011 (Baker 2011).

According to Baker (2011), "The $2.3 million disbursement came as part of a $6,132,000 payment by IFCO, the first in a series of three shell outs totaling $20,697,317.51." The New York State Police received $2,207,520, the Albany County District Attorney received $61,320, and the Guilderland Police Department, received $61,320 (Baker 2011).

The federal prosecution of companies hiring undocumented workers is not the only political reaction. Some states are passing legislation that would curtail such hires. Chris Arsenault in his article "Migrants Decry New US Legislation,"[6] published in Aljazeera.net June 23, 2011 stated

---

[5] Sarah Baker. (2011). "Immigration Enforcement Against Employers of Undocumented Workers is a 'Cash Cow' for State and Local Agencies!" in *Wolfsdorf Navigating Immigration* January 28.

[6] Chris Arsenault. (2011). "Migrants Decry New US Legislation," *Aljazeera.net*, June 23.

> Despite the recession and high unemployment rates across the industrial-
> ized world, Pols in the UK, Turks in Germany and south Asians in the Arabian
> Gulf – who have no hope of ever getting citizenship – will take jobs that
> naturalized citizens simply don't want to do. Elements of the working class
> in these regions complain that migrants lower wages across the board, while
> business elites often support increased migration, allowing them access to
> large pools of labor with fewer rights than the native born population
> (Arsenault 2011).

Arsenault was analyzing the situation in the US in which states are
abrogating to themselves the right to make immigration laws, which
arguably is a function that constitutionally belongs only to the federal
government.

The North Carolina state congress and senate passed House Bill 36 that
will implement an "E-Verify System, demanding some employers match
social security numbers against the names of people they hire." Immigrants
oppose the bill on the grounds that "the computerized system is based
on unreliable data and its implementation will make it harder for immigrants to find work, as business won't want to risk the trouble or oversight
of hiring people of color or those whose English isn't perfect" (Arsenault
2011).

The main idea here is that there is a tendency for private entities to hire
illegal immigrants in or out of an economic crisis to lower their production cost and increase profit, while the state tends to step up its actions to
deter immigration to fulfill the political objective of elected representatives. The elected representatives are faced with a dilemma in that in their
desire to be reelected in an economic crisis they have to ride two horses
that have differing positions on migration – the electorate that want to
restrict it in the light of the economic crisis, and their financiers who want
to increase it to lower production costs.

The empirical data showed nonetheless that in order to win votes the
political elites are prepared to take the gamble to prosecute companies
that hire illegal immigrants, and use the money raised in the process, to
finance state projects. Elected representatives are affected in different
ways by this dilemma depending on whether they are up for reelection.
While those up for election in the next election cycle may vote in favor of
measures to restrict immigration to please constituencies, those not up for
reelection may vote against such measures to please the private companies. Undoubtedly, this is the story of political opportunism on the immigration issue in the US.

Foreign-Born Workers in the US Labor Force 2007 and 2010

Foreign-born workers, comprising "persons residing in the United States who were not U.S. citizens at birth," that is individuals who "were born outside the United States or one of its outlying areas such as Puerto Rico or Guam, to parents neither whom was a U.S. citizen,"[7] continue to be a central plank in the U.S. labor force. The data does not differentiate among them but the "foreign-born population includes legally admitted immigrants, refugees, temporary residents such as students and temporary workers, and undocumented immigrants."[8]

In 2007, for example, foreign-born workers outstripped their native-born counterparts in service occupations 22.8 to 15.4 percent, in natural resources, construction, and maintenance occupations 16.4 to 9.7 percent, and by 16.2 to 11.7 percent in production, transportation, and material moving occupations.[9] As the US experienced a serious recession in the 2008 – 2010 period nonetheless, there was an increase in foreign-born workers in service occupations. Foreign-born workers outstripped their native born counterparts in service occupations by 25.0 to 16.4 percent in 2010. In the same year, the ratio of foreign-born to native-born workers was of 16.1 to 10.8 percent in production, transportation, and material moving occupations, and 13.6 to 8.6 percent in natural resources, construction, and maintenance occupations.[10]

In 2007, "about 1 in 4 foreign-born men were employed in natural resources, construction, and maintenance occupations, while nearly 1 in 3 women were in service occupations." However, native-born workers outstripped foreign-born workers in management, professional, and related occupations by 37.0 to 27.2 percent in 2007,[11] and 2010 – 38.9 versus

---

[7] U.S. Department of Labor Bureau of Labor Statistics. (2011). Foreign-Born Workers: Labor Force Characteristics – 2010, News Release, USDL-11-0763, Friday, May 27.

[8] U.S. Department of Labor Bureau of Labor Statistics. (2011). Foreign-Born Workers: Labor Force Characteristics – 2010, News Release, USDL-11-0763, Friday, May 27.

[9] U.S. Department of Labor, Bureau of Labor Statistics. (2008). Foreign-Born Workers: Labor Force Characteristics in 2007, USDL 08-0409, March 26.

[10] U.S. Department of Labor Bureau of Labor Statistics. (2011). Foreign-Born Workers: Labor Force Characteristics – 2010, News Release, USDL-11-0763, Friday, May 27.

[11] U.S. Department of Labor, Bureau of Labor Statistics. (2008). Foreign-Born Workers: Labor Force Characteristics in 2007, USDL 08-0409, March 26.

28.0 percent.[12] In 2010 native-born workers outstripped foreign-born workers in sales and office occupations by a ration of 25.3 to 17.3 percent.

According to the US Department of Labor (2008), while foreign-born workers made up 15.7 percent of the US civilian labor force in 2007, their share was up from 15.3 percent in 2006. At the regional level, foreign-born workers "made up a larger share of the total labor force in the West (24.6 percent) and in the Northeast (18.3 percent) than for the nation as a whole." The US Department of Labor (2008) stated "the shares of the labor force made up by foreign-born workers in the South (13.8 percent) and Midwest (7.5 percent) regions were less than for the nation."

Between 2006 and 2007, nonetheless, the unemployment rate of foreign-born workers increased from 4.0 percent to 4.3 percent, while the jobless rate of the native born remained the same at 4.7 percent. According to the US Department of Labor (2008), in 2007 the "unemployment rate of the foreign born was lower than that of the native born for the third year in a row." However, "the unemployment rate for foreign-born men rose from 3.5 to 4.1 percent, while the rate for foreign-born women was little changed at 4.6 percent," between 2006 and 2007.

Economic Growth and Unemployment 2000–2009

Undeniably, the US economy is faced with prolonged economic crisis but still people are queuing-up to migrate to the country. According to Petras (2011) "The symptoms and structures of a deep economic crisis are readily visible to any but the most obtuse government apologist or prestigious economist." Indeed, as un- and under-employment reached "between 18 to 20 percent" the reality is that "one out of three US families is directly affected by loss of employment," and "one out of ten American family homeowners are either behind in the mortgage payments or face foreclosure" (Petras 2011).

Petras (2011) observed that, "Over half of the current unemployed (9.1 percent) have been out of work at least six months," and that there are "massive cutbacks in public expenditures and investments," which "have led to the end of health, educational and welfare programs for tens of millions of low income families, children, the disabled, the elderly pensioners," as "private firms have eliminated or reduced payments for

---

[12] U.S. Department of Labor Bureau of Labor Statistics. (2011). Foreign-Born Workers: Labor Force Characteristics – 2010, News Release, USDL-11-0763, Friday, May 27.

health insurance, leaving over 50 million working Americans without health insurance and another 30 million with inadequate medical coverage" (Petras 2011).

Compounding the hardships on working and middle class people is that the state is eroding the compact between the people and itself. Additionally, waged and salaried workers are faced with increased taxation and reduced net incomes because of tax exemptions, and reduced and regressive taxation that favor the rich. The net incomes of middle and working class employees are reduced further because they have to pay more for pensions and health care.[13]

The "environmental, workplace and leisure space living standard" have deteriorated considerably in the light of the wars in Iraq, Afghanistan, Pakistan, Libya, preparation for war with Iran, "support for the world's most militarist state (Israel) and a greatly expanded and costly domestic police state apparatus (Homeland Security alone costs $180 billion)." There has been an increase in "fear, insecurity and virtual terror among employees," as they are faced with "increased speed-ups and arbitrary elimination of any say in health and workplace safety, work schedules, over and under time workloads," which result from "corporate political power and absolute tyrannical control over the workplace."[14]

Simultaneously, there is a proliferation in "low pay service jobs," the outsourcing of high pay jobs to other countries, the relocation of manufacturing plants abroad, the importation of lower paid immigrants professionals and laborers, which combine to increase "pressure on US workers to compete for lower pay and lesser benefits." These features of the US economy reveal that the crises is embedded in the deep structure of US capitalism and is not a 'cyclical phenomenon' subject to a dynamic recovery, restoring lost jobs, homes, living standards and working conditions."[15]

Indeed, the data on US real gross domestic product, unemployment, layoffs and separations between 2000 and 2009 showed that the US economy performed well below par,[16] when measured by the very neoliberal

---

[13] James Petras. (2011). US Working and Middle Class: Solidarity or Competition in the Face of Crisis?".

[14] James Petras. (2011). US Working and Middle Class: Solidarity or Competition in the Face of Crisis?".

[15] James Petras. (2011). US Working and Middle Class: Solidarity or Competition in the Face of Crisis?".

[16] Sources: US Department of Commerce, Bureau of Economic Analysis. (2010). News Release, BEA 10-47, September 30; Bureau of Labor Statistics. (2010). Employment and Earnings, January, http://www.bls.gov/cps/tables.htm; US Total Private Non-Farm Sector Layoffs and Separations 2006 – 1999; U.S. Department of Labor, U.S. Bureau of Labor

standards it seeks to force on the developing countries. The rate of growth in the US was well below that which leading neoliberal ideologue Bhagwati (2004)[17] stipulated an economy needs to grow at in order to achieve any degree of real economic stimulation and success. While in the current neoliberal period the growth rate seems to determine whether a country is developing or not, saving played the role as the bedrock for investment and growth in earlier periods.

Sir W. Arthur Lewis (1954), the Nobel Laureate in economics argued the case for saving as the primary stimulant of economic growth. Lewis (1954) noted that

> The central problem in the theory of economic development is to understand the process by which a community which was previously saving and investing 4 or 5 percent of its national income or less, converts itself into an economy where voluntary saving is running at about 12 to 15 percent of national income or more. This is the central problem because the central fact of economic development is rapid capital accumulation (including knowledge and skills with capital).[18]

Under neoliberal capitalism however, saving is now blamed for stimulating the current economic and financial crises through what is described as a "global saving glut."[19] According to the "global saving glut" hypothesis an important feature of emerging economies in the early to mid 2000s was that desired saving vastly exceeds desired investment. This saving glut led to the flow of capital from these countries into the US, which in turn pushed down long-term interest rates that stimulated the housing boom that led to the current recession. In the US nonetheless, the saving rate fell

Statistics. (2008). Extended Mass Layoffs in 2006, Report 1004, April; U.S. Department of Labor, U.S. Bureau of Labor Statistics. (2006). Extended Mass Layoffs in 2005, Report 997, September; U.S. Department of Labor, U.S. Bureau of Labor Statistics. (2004). Extended Mass Layoffs in 2003, Report 982, December; U.S. Department of Labor, U.S. Bureau of Labor Statistics. (2003). Extended Mass Layoffs in 2002, Report 971, August 2003; U.S. Department of Labor, U.S. Bureau of Labor Statistics, Extended Mass Layoffs in 2002, Report 971, August. U.S. Department of Labor U.S. Bureau of Labor Statistics. (2010). Extended Mass Layoffs in 2008, Report 1024, June 2010. BLS. (2010). News Release USDL-10-1102, August 11. NB data for 2001–1999 represent total private layoffs and separation.

[17] Jagdish Bhagwati. (2004). *In Defense of Globalization*. New York. Oxford University Press.

[18] Sir W. Arthur Lewis. (1954). "Economic Development with Unlimited Supplies of Labor." *The Manchester School*, Vol. XXII, No. 2, May pp. 139–91.

[19] Ben Bernanke. (2005). The Global Saving Glut and the U.S. Current Account Deficit, Remarks at the Sandridge Lecture, Virginia Association of Economists, Richmond, Virginia, March 10.

to zero and eventually became negative, and its economy failed to achieve an economic growth level of 5 percent between 2000 and 2009.

The US economy grew by 4.1 percent in 2000, but it failed to achieve that level of growth again by the end of 2009. The closest it came to achieving that level of growth was 3.6 percent in 2004 and 3.1 percent in 2005. Growth in the US economy was only at 1.1 percent in 2001, 1.8 percent in 2002, 2.5 percent in 2003, and 2.7 percent in 2006. The economy experienced zero economic growth in 2008 and negative 2.6 percent in 2009.

Also, the US unemployment rate skyrocketed between 2000 and 2009, the period under review. The unemployment rate was 4.0 percent in 2000 the lowest in the period, and 9.3 percent in 2009, the highest. The average unemployment rate in the period 2000 to 2009 was 5.5 percent. Undoubtedly, with such meager levels of economic growth and high unemployment, the US economy has faltered badly between 2000 and 2009. The data on worker-layoffs between 2000 and 2009 also illustrate the plight of the US working and middle classes.

Layoffs and Separations 2007–2009

According to the International Labor Office (ILO) layoffs, redundancy and dismissals are not the same thing. It defines layoffs as the "failure, refusal or inability of an employer to continue the employment of an employee on account of shortage of raw materials, power, or the breakdown of machinery, etc."[20] In its view "layoff is normally of a temporary nature and is without prejudice to the worker." The term "redundancy" is used "for permanent workforce reductions at the enterprise level for economic reasons (e.g. bankruptcy, restructuring or technological change) affecting a sizeable number of workers."[21] Neither layoff nor redundancy must be confused with "dismissal" which indicates "the termination of employment when initiated by the employer."[22]

Extended mass layoffs, as defined in the Mass Layoff Statistics (MLS) program, refers to layoffs of at least 31 days' duration that involve the filing of initial claims for unemployment insurance by 50 or more individuals from a single establishment during a consecutive 5-week period.

---

[20] See ILO Thesaurus, http://www.vocabularyserver.com/ilo/index.php.
[21] See ILO Thesaurus, http://www.vocabularyserver.com/ilo/index.php.
[22] See ILO Thesaurus, http://www.vocabularyserver.com/ilo/index.php.

De Wolfe and Klemmer (2010) defined monthly total *separations* as "the number of employees separated from payroll during the reference month, and "annual total *separations*" as "the number of employees separated from payroll during" a given year. Furthermore, de Wolfe and Klemmer (2010) classified "separations" as "quits, layoffs and discharges, and other separations." Quits are identified as "cases in which people left a job voluntarily but did not retire or transfer," while layoffs and discharges involve "involuntary separations initiated by employers" and other separations refers to "retirements, transfers, deaths, and separations caused by disability."[23]

The political economy of neoliberal capitalism from the 1980s to present is associated with massive involuntary layoffs and job separations of workers by age, race, and gender in every economic sector. Neoliberal economics has placed the blame for the crises associated with the falling rate of profit in the 1970s, squarely on the shoulders of the working class. The neoliberal view is that the high cost of employment – wages and benefits payments – continues to increase unabated, eating into capitalist profits, causing the rate of profit to fall. The neoliberal remedy to this situation, that is, to reverse the falling rate of profit is to cutback on employment costs. The reduction in employment costs means in essence worker layoffs, reductions in worker benefits, lower wages, and an overall increase in the rate of exploitation of workers.

According to de Wolf and Klemmer (2010), the recession, which began in December 2007, continues to have a negative impact on the US economy. Indeed, they pointed out that "data from the Job Openings and Labor Turnover Survey (JOLTS) reflect the continued impact that the recession" has had "on the demand for labor and worker flows." The data showed that "Job openings – a measure of labor demand – and hires and separations – measures of worker flows – all declined during the 2007 – 09 period and reached series lows in 2009." Indeed, not only did the "job openings rate, seasonally adjusted, dropped from 3.1 percent in December 2007 to 1.9 percent in December 2009," but "the job openings rate reached a series low of 1.8 percent in April 2009," while "the annual hires rate declined from 46.1 percent to 37.2 percent, a series low, during the 2007 – to – 2009 period." Furthermore, compounding this dismal situation for the US working class, "the unemployment rate reached a peak of 10.1 percent in

[23] Mark de Wolf and Katherine Klemmer. (2010). "Job openings, hires, and separations fall during the recession." *Monthly Labor Review*, May, pp 36–44.

October 2009, having climbed from 5.0 percent in December 2007" as "nonfarm employment reached a low of 130 million in December."

Economic conditions did not improve in 2008 when "employers laid off about 1.5 million workers in 8,263 private nonfarm extended mass layoff events." Indeed, "both layoff events and separations rose sharply from 2007," as 2008 recorded the highest number of layoffs and the second high-est level since annual data became available in 1996. A substantial chunk of the increase in layoffs was registered in the fourth quarter of 2008.

The US Department of Labor Bureau of Labor Statistics reported in its publication entitled Extended Mass Layoffs in 2008 that, "in terms of worker separations, historic highs for the data series were reached in 7 of 18 industry sectors, 3 of 9 geographic divisions, and 14 States."[24] The report on Extended Mass Layoffs in 2008 stated that "more than 500,000 worker separations, the highest annual level on record" were attributed to layoffs due to "business demand factors (especially slack work or insufficient demand)." Another "60,950 workers lost their jobs in extended mass lay-offs because their employers moved work to other U.S. locations or to loca-tions outside of the United States." This figure was almost "one-third higher than the number of workers in the same position in 2007." In 2008, the closure of worksites permanently was the cause of "11 percent of all tended mass layoff events and affected 216,322 workers." However, it was antici-pated by 41 percent of employers reporting an extended mass layoff in 2008, the lowest proportion since 2001 that they would engage in some type of recall of workers.[25] Layoffs and separations totaled 11,824 and 2,108,202 respectively, in 2009.

Industry Distribution of 2008 Mass Layoffs and Separations

The data on the industry distribution of mass layoffs in 2008 showed that "manufacturing establishments accounted for 31 percent of extended mass layoff events and 32 percent of all separations in 2008." This was an increase "from 25 percent for both events and separations in 2007." The percentage of layoff events in the manufacturing sector in 2008 was the highest since 2003, while the percentage of separations in 2008 was

---

[24] U.S. Department of Labor U.S. Bureau of Labor Statistics. (2010). Extended Mass Layoffs in 2008, Report 1024, June.
[25] U.S. Department of Labor U.S. Bureau of Labor Statistics. (2010). Extended Mass Layoffs in 2008, Report 1024, June.

the highest since 2002. Forty-five percent of the separations in 2008 were accounted for by the transportation equipment (largely automobiles) and food processing (mostly fruit and vegetable canning and fresh and frozen seafood processing) firms within the manufacturing sector.

The report on Extended Mass Layoffs in 2008 stated that there was a 19 percent increase by 21 manufacturing subsectors, in the number of separations due to extended mass layoffs from 2007 to 2008. This increase was "led by transportation equipment (increasing by 96,038), food products (increasing by 20,404), wood products (increasing by 16,987), and fabricated metals (increasing by 15,282)."[26]

The construction industry accounted for the second highest number of mass layoffs and separations. Represented mainly in specialty trade contractors and in heavy and civil engineering, construction "accounted for 21 percent of private nonfarm mass layoff events and 14 percent of separations in 2008." As reported by the US Bureau of Labor Statistics "The number of laid-off construction workers reached a historic high at 205,327, with annual data available back to 1996." The BLS stated that, "69 percent of all construction layoffs were due to the completion of contracts and the ending of seasonal work." Also, it was expected that employers would recall roughly 56 percent of the construction layoff events. That percentage recall was "the second lowest percentage on record for the industry."

The administrative and services sector "accounted for 8 percent of layoff events and 9 percent of separations," which was due primarily to "business demand reasons in the administrative and support services subsector." The number of mass layoff separations in administrative and support services was 141,03 in 2008, reaching their highest levels since 2003.[27]

Comparatively, in the garments industry in 2008 "manufacturers and distributors of clothing reported extended mass layoffs of 69,328 workers, up 91 percent from 2007." The US Department of Labor report on Extended Mass Layoffs in 2008 stated that, "Layoffs due to financial issues accounted for the largest number of separations in this selected industry grouping (19,973), followed by layoffs due to seasonal reasons (16,744)." Furthermore, in the clothing grouping, the West of the US "registered the highest number of laid-off workers (29,297), followed by the South (16,362).[28]

---

[26] U.S. Department of Labor U.S. Bureau of Labor Statistics. (2010). Extended Mass Layoffs in 2008, Report 1024, June.

[27] U.S. Department of Labor U.S. Bureau of Labor Statistics. (2010). Extended Mass Layoffs in 2008, Report 1024, June.

[28] U.S. Department of Labor U.S. Bureau of Labor Statistics. (2010). Extended Mass Layoffs in 2008, Report 1024, June.

The food processing and distribution industry, excluding agriculture, "accounted for 10 percent (152,928) of private nonfarm separations due to extended mass layoffs in 2008." However, when compared with the 2007 level that separations figure represented a slight decrease. Nonetheless, "in 2008, 17 of the 19 major sectors posted over-the-year increases in separations when compared with 2007," led by manufacturing, and followed by administrative and waste services and the construction sector.

In addition, the US Department of Labor reported that, "among the 87 three-digit (National American Industry Classification Code) NAICS-coded industry groups in the private nonfarm economy identified in the Mass Layoff Statistics (MLS) program, 71 posted increases in the number of separated workers during 2008." The industry groups in the forefront of the increases in the number of separated workers were "transportation equipment manufacturing," which "recorded the largest increase (96,038), followed by administrative and support services (84,673) and general merchandise stores (25,359)." According to the US Department of Labor "eleven industries registered decreases, led by food and beverage stores with 52,788 fewer separated workers than the previous year."

Perhaps the decrease in the number of separated workers in the food and beverage stores is an indication that American workers take to eating and drinking as a means to forget about their plight. It is plausible that because American workers are eating and drinking more as a coping mechanism for the crisis that food and beverage stores had fewer separations. Small wonder that obesity, diabetes and alcoholism are increasing social and health problems in the US.

Also, "general merchandise stores moved into the top 10 in terms of worker separations in 2008," at the three-digit NAICS industry level, "with food and beverage stores dropping from the top 10." The US Department of Labor reported that, "among the six-digit NAICS industries, professional employer organizations and discount department stores moved into the top 10 in terms of separations, replacing child day care services and supermarkets and other grocery stores."[29]

The data on US economic growth and unemployment for 2000 to 2009, layoffs and separations between 2007 and 2009, and the industry distribution of 2008 mass layoffs and separations provide overwhelming evidence that the US was in severe crisis. According to the push-pull theory of migration, people should begin leaving the US, and immigrants should be

---

[29] U.S. Department of Labor U.S. Bureau of Labor Statistics. (2010). Extended Mass Layoffs in 2008, Report 1024, June.

deterred from wanting to go to the US. The data below showed that immigration to the US actually increased in the same time period that the country experienced its most severe economic and financial crises since the Great Depression.

Increased Migration During the Great Recession 2007–2009[30]

The US is a metropolis that sits at the center of its empire, and although it leads the way in cutbacks in benefits, wages, and worker-layoffs, it continues to attract migrant workers from the Caribbean and other migrant-sending locations around the globe. Persons obtaining legal permanent status in the US were 1,130,818 in 2009; 1,107,126 in 2008; and 1,052,415 in 2007, increasing steadily during the great recession years. In this period, family sponsored immigrants were 747,413 or 66.1 percent of total immigration in 2009; 716,244 or 64.7 percent in 2008; and 689,820 or 65.5 percent in 2007. Employment-based preferences immigrants were 144,034 or 12.7 percent in 2009; 166,511 or 15.0 percent in 2008; and 162,176 or 15.4 percent in 2007.[31] These latter percentages were the result of government restrictive action, not because people did not want to migrate to the US.

Thus, although the US economy experienced such low levels of growth, and high levels of layoffs and separations between 2007 and 2009, persons obtaining legal permanent status in US increased consistently in the same period. However, employment based immigrants fell by 2.7 percent from 15.4 percent in 2007 to 12.7 percent in 2009,[32] due to restrictive measures.

The increase in legal immigration was 2.1 percent between 2008 and 2009 and according to Monger (2010), Legal Permanent Resident (LPR) "adjustments of status increased 4.2 percent from 640,568 in 2008 to 667,776 in 2009." The "adjustments of status in 2009 were driven by a decrease in applications pending a decision rather than an increasing number of applications received during 2009" (Monger 2010). Indeed, "fifty-nine percent of new LPRs in 2009 were adjustments of status and 41 percent were new arrivals" (Monger 2010).

[30] U.S. Department of Homeland Security. (2010). Yearbook of Immigration Statistics 2009, Office of Immigration Statistics, August.
[31] Randall Monger. (2010). "U.S. Legal Permanent Residents: 2009," *Annual Flow Report*, US Department of Homeland Security, Office of Immigration Statistics, April.
[32] Randall Monger. (2010). "U.S. Legal Permanent Residents: 2009," *Annual Flow Report*, US Department of Homeland Security, Office of Immigration Statistics, April.

Monger (2010) pointed out that, "In 2009, a total of 1,130,818 persons became LPRs of the United States." Of this figure, the majority "(59 percent) already lived in the United States when they were granted lawful permanent residence," and approximately "two-thirds were granted permanent resident status based on a family relationship with a U.S. citizen or legal permanent resident of the United States." The leading countries of birth of new LPRs were "Mexico (15 percent), China (6 percent), and the Philippines (5 percent)."

New arrivals in the legal permanent resident category increased from 41 percent in 2007 to 42.1 percent in 2008, but declined to 40.9 percent in 2009. Persons adjusting their immigrant status to become legal permanent resident was higher than new arrivals, and increased consistently from 50 percent in 2007 to 59.1 percent in 2009.[33] This does not look like economic crisis is a deterrent to people wanting to migrate to the US.

In the category persons obtaining legal permanent resident status by type and major class of admission between 2000 and 2009, the data showed that employment based preferences increased in the period.[34] However, from 2005 the numbers in this category declined. The crisis seems not to have restricted the importation of priority workers whose numbers increased consistently between 2007 and 2009. The number of professionals with advanced degrees or of exceptional ability obtaining legal permanent resident also increased dramatically between 2007 and 2008 but declined in 2009.

Also, the data on legal permanent resident flow by region and country of birth for 2007 to 2009 showed that the bulk of immigrants to the US are from Asia (36.5 percent in 2009), dominated by China (5.7 percent in 2009).[35] The North American region comes second (33.2 percent in 2009) dominated by Mexico (14.6 percent in 2009). Other North America was 16 percent, followed by the Caribbean 12.9 percent, and Africa 11.2 percent, in 2009. By far Mexico sends the most immigrants to the US followed by China, the Philippines and India. The Dominican Republic, Cuba, Haiti

---

[33] Randall Monger. (2010). "U.S. Legal Permanent Residents: 2009," *Annual Flow Report*, US Department of Homeland Security, Office of Immigration Statistics, April.
[34] Randall Monger. (2010). "U.S. Legal Permanent Residents: 2009," *Annual Flow Report*, US Department of Homeland Security, Office of Immigration Statistics, April.
[35] Randall Monger. (2010). "U.S. Legal Permanent Residents: 2009," *Annual Flow Report*, US Department of Homeland Security, Office of Immigration Statistics, April.

and Jamaica are the leading Caribbean countries sending people to the US.[36]

Data for the group classified as legal permanent residents by gender between 2007 and 2008 showed that more women than men are migrating to the US. In 2007 55.2 percent of the legal permanent residents admitted were women compared with 44.8 percent men. In 2008 the figures were 54.2 percent women and 45.8 percent men, and in 2009 the numbers were 54.6 percent and 45.4 percent, respectively.[37]

Legal permanent resident flow by marital status data in 2007 showed that 58 percent of these persons were married compared with 36.8 percent single. This pattern was the same in 2008 (57.6 percent married and 37.1 percent single) and in 2009 (57.9 percent married and 36.9 percent single).[38]

Caribbean Migration to the US 2000–2009

Migration from the Caribbean Community (Caricom) countries to the US seems not to have been adversely affected by the economic and financial crises that have had a devastating effect on the US workforce since 2007.[39] According to the data on persons obtaining legal permanent status by country of birth between 2000 and 2009, despite the crises migrants from the Caricom countries to the US held steady between 2007 and 2009. In 2007 there were 68,778 persons from the Caricom countries that obtained legal permanent resident status in the US. Of this number there were 30,405 Haitians, 19,375 Jamaicans, 6,829 from Trinidad and Tobago, and 5,726 Guyanese.[40]

These four countries are the leading exporters of people from the Caricom region to the US. The number of Caricom migrants to the US increased to 75,502 in 2009 in spite of the economic and financial crises. This increase was represented by, 24,280 Haitians, 21,783 Jamaicans,

[36] Randall Monger. (2010). "U.S. Legal Permanent Residents: 2009," *Annual Flow Report*, US Department of Homeland Security, Office of Immigration Statistics, April.
[37] Randall Monger. (2010). "U.S. Legal Permanent Residents: 2009," *Annual Flow Report*, US Department of Homeland Security, Office of Immigration Statistics, April.
[38] Randall Monger. (2010). "U.S. Legal Permanent Residents: 2009," *Annual Flow Report*, US Department of Homeland Security, Office of Immigration Statistics, April.
[39] U.S. Department of Homeland Security. (2010). Yearbook of Immigration Statistics 2009, August.
[40] U.S. Department of Homeland Security. (2010). Yearbook of Immigration Statistics 2009, August.

6,670 Guyanese, and 6,256 from Trinidad and Tobago. Although the overall number increased between 2007 and 2009 those for Haiti, and Trinidad and Tobago decreased. Migrants from Jamaica, Guyana, Saint Lucia, the Bahamas, Barbados, and Suriname, among others, drove the increase.[41]

A similar pattern is evident from the data on persons naturalized by region and country of birth between 2000 and 2009.[42] There were 53,493 Caricom nationals who became naturalized US citizens in 2008, compared with 33,112 in 2007. In 2008 there were 21,324 Jamaicans, 8,290 Guyanese and 7,305 other Caricom nationals that became US citizens in 2008.

It must be considered however that although these numbers occur in 2008, there were in the making for sometime before 2008 due to the time lag in the US naturalization process. Thus, the naturalized citizens had no control over the year in which they became citizens. However, they had a choice not to become citizens and leave the US in the light of the economic and financial crises.

It should be noted that the slight slowdown in immigration to the US mentioned above is not due to people not wanting to migrate to the country during economic crises. Undoubtedly, it is due to US federal and state policies, which have becomes more restrictive. However, in 2008 the total figure was the second highest between 2000 and 2009. Indeed, the slow down in 2009 was higher than the figures for 2001 to 2005, and 2007. It cannot be the crisis that caused the slowdown.

Conclusion

It is not in every case that a high level of economic growth attracts people to migrate to a country, since low growth is also correlated with a high incidence of immigration as the economic growth and immigration data for the US between 2000 and 2009 showed. The view is held here that the high level of capital accumulation and not economic growth is a more plausible reason why people will migrate to a particular country. The high incidence of immigration into the US simultaneously that the US experienced economic and financial crises, seems to debunk the age-old view that the lack of economic growth is a deterrent to immigration.

---

[41] U.S. Department of Homeland Security. (2010). Yearbook of Immigration Statistics 2009, August.

[42] U.S. Department of Homeland Security. (2010). Yearbook of Immigration Statistics 2009, August.

Wherever capital accumulates on the scale as is has in the US and in the European metropoles, the standard of living is much higher than countries in which there is a low level of capital accumulation. Due to capital flight in the developing countries nonetheless, it is understandable that economic growth does not always translates into capital accumulation. However, the metropolis states such as the US and those in Europe have had many years of accumulating capital. The consequence of the centuries of capital accumulation in the metropolis is that even if they experience economic crises their socio-economic conditions will be relatively better than in countries with a low level of capital accumulation. Thus, the metropolis countries do not have to be growing in order to attract immigrants, their comparatively advanced socio-economic conditions due to capital accumulation, will.

PART TWO

NEOLIBERAL PERSPECTIVES ON DEVELOPMENT IMPACT
OF MIGRATION

CHAPTER FOUR

LIBERALIZATION AND FINANCIALIZATION OF MIGRATION

Introduction

The ebb and flow of socio-economic development policies that favor working people was a concrete feature of the twentieth century. The evidence of this characteristic attribute is provided by the prevalence of tangible development alternatives to the capitalist system during the first half of the century up until the 1980s, the forced and voluntary retreat from them in the 1990s, and the resurgence of searches such as critical development studies[1] for another way forward. The neoliberal counter-revolution however has had a stranglehold on domestic and international political economy since the 1980s, and finance capital has emerged at its apex.

The crises in global capitalism in the twentieth century that produced the first and second world wars spawned theoretical and policy options in which the capitalist state was called on to perform a definitive developmental role. The result was that not only had Britain, the leading capitalist power at the time, lost its global hegemonic position to the US, the central issue that surfaced for global capitalism was that of finding the correct theoretical and policy mix, which would stimulate economic growth in the capitalist states for them to maintain their competitive edge amongst themselves and against the development alternatives provided by the socialist states. The policy solutions proffered and put into practice to stimulate economic growth in the leading capitalist countries to counteract both the crises and socialism, as well as the socialist alternatives, depended heavily on state-directed policies.

Thus, when profits began to fall by the 1970s, which signaled the end of the so-called "golden age of capitalism" that began at the end of World War II in 1945, a new consensus emerged among the conservatives on the cause and solution of the crisis. Under the banner of Thatcherism and Reaganism what we call neoliberalism, the conservatives blamed the crisis

---

[1] See Henry Veltmeyer ed. (2011). *The Critical Development Studies Handbook: Tools for Change*, London and New York, Pluto Press; and Halifax and Winnipeg, Fernwood Publishing.

on the state-capitalist policies in the capitalist countries. These policies were founded on Keynesianism, which the neoliberal conservatives lumped together with socialism. Keynesianism and socialism were lumped together because of the centrality of the state in both approaches. But, the neoliberals did not stop at blaming the state for the crisis. They went a step further to finger specifically the social programs provided by the state as the main culprits cutting into capitalist profit driving it downwards.

The neoliberals therefore set for themselves the principal goal to dismantle the social structures and benefits that working people struggled for and won through collective bargaining, the primary mechanism by which these benefits are secured and maintained. The neoliberal campaign against state-led development and social welfare benefits, therefore has taken the form of a crusade against social safety nets, state-owned enterprises, public sector workers, and trade unions. Liberalization inclusive of privatization, union busting, and measures to roll back safety nets became the focal points of neoliberal policy alternatives.

The neoliberal liberalization policy prescriptions are leaving nothing untouched in its wake including the age-old phenomenon referred to as migration. Neoliberalism, nonetheless does not acknowledge the primacy of the state it its own ideology and policy initiatives. Undoubtedly, it is the capitalist state that protects and regulates the economy in favor of neoliberal capitalism. The capitalist state is placed in charge of dismantling its role in the economy, the social safety nets, union busting, and suppression of dissent by working people. The central contradiction is that the capitalist state undertakes these regulatory activities in the interest of the form or type of capital that is the most influential at the time. Thus, it is neoliberal capital dominated by financial capital, which claims that the state is the culprit for the crisis, but yet depends on the state to un-regulated itself by setting in place new regulations to enforce un-regulation in favor of neoliberal capital.

In other words, the state is dismantling the state to rid the economy of state control by instituting a different set of state controls. Thus, the state replaces one set of state controls associated with the type of capitalism associated with the "golden age of capitalism," with another set of state controls associated with neoliberal capitalism dominated by finance capital. To achieve this feat the state is vilified by neoliberal capital, while neoliberal capital depends on the state to implement policies that favor it. In essence, what we are faced with today is intra-class conflicts by different brands of capitalism, all of which depend on the state for their survival.

It is the capitalist state and its regulations currently described as "de-regulation" that is responsible for the establishment of the extant form of global capitalism, involving the great financialization,[2] the financialization of capital accumulation[3] and the imperialist centered model of capital accumulation.[4] It is the capitalist state in all hitherto forms of capitalism, which was responsible for providing the super-structural arrangements that govern the economy and society. Thus, the neoliberal view that the state should be driven out of the capitalist economy is false, and merely a ploy to reform the state to suit the interest of neoliberal capital. The capitalist economy needs the state to regulate it, and the regulations may favor one or the other type of capital.

The regulations implemented in the post-Great Depression period did not favor finance capital but the real economy, as manufacturing and other forms of capital in the real sectors flourished. However, in the current period of neoliberal capitalism, in which state regulation is mistakenly but commonly referred to as "de-regulation," it is finance capital, which is favored, and so capital is fleeing the real economy into the financial sector lured by super profits from speculation. The new regulations are the multiple laws and bilateral and multilateral agreements that forbid states from performing one or the other economic function.

These new regulations are said to be freeing the economy from regulations. In the new regulatory process called liberalization nonetheless, production is hampered, workers are laid-off, and their wages and benefits are reduced. It is in this liberalization regulations milieu, which purports to remove government regulations in the financial sector that speculative financial capital emerged at the helm of neoliberal capitalism.

The discussion on financial liberalization and migration begins with an analysis of labor mobility and capitalist globalization. Thereafter a descriptive analysis is provided of the principal neoliberal global agreement on international migration, the General Agreement on Trade in Services (GATS). This is followed by analyses of "the great financialization," and the financialization of migration. The principal argument supported by these

---

[2] Kari Polanyi Levitt. (2008). "The Great Financialization," John Kenneth Galbraith Prize Lecture, Progressive Economics Forum, University of British Columbia, Vancouver, Canada, June 8.

[3] John Bellamy Foster. (2010). "The Financialization of Accumulation," *Monthly Review*, Volume 62, Number 5 (October).

[4] James Petras. (2007). *Rulers and Ruled in the US Empire: Bankers, Zionists, Militants*, Atlanta, GA.: Clarity Press.

analyses is that neoliberal capitalism has only but one goal for labor migration – its exploitation to accumulate profit through the imperialist centered model of capital accumulation. With financial capital at its helm the principal value of migration to neoliberal capitalism is its financialization by regulating the financial framework for the entrapment by the financial sector of monies flowing in the migration sector. These monies will then become available to the financial elites to accumulate capital by speculation, which may also satisfy the conditions for the financialization of accumulation.

Labor Mobility and Capitalist Globalization

Trade liberalization and the restriction of migration from the developing to developed countries have emerged as major concerns under neoliberal globalization.[5] Indeed, neoliberal globalization has placed much emphasis on "the relationship between international trade and migration," which takes place "between the developing and developed world" especially with the pronounced increase in cross-border migration in recent decades.[6] The relocation of workers from developing to developed countries in search of employment and business opportunities thereby fulfilling labor shortages and contributing to economic growth in the developed countries, has forced policymakers to consider how to manage migration flows.[7]

According to the Center for European Policy Research (CEPR, 2000), however, international migration was conspicuously absent from the debate on the globalization of capitalism at the beginning of the twenty-first century. Thus, during the first decade of the century concerted efforts were made by the powerful neoliberal capitalist forces in Europe and the US to bridge the gap in the literature on migration and globalization. The international institutions in the control of global capitalist forces, academics, and policy makers began to produce reports and studies on

---

[5] Center for Economic Policy Research. (2000). "Trade and Migration," *European Economic Perspectives 24*, January, pp 6–8.

[6] Kamaal R. Zaidi. (2010). Harmonizing Trade Liberalization and Migration Policy Through Shared Responsibility: A Comparison of the Impact of Bilateral Trade Agreements and the Gats in Germany and Canada," *Syracuse Journal of International Law and Commerce*, 267, Spring.

[7] Kamaal R. Zaidi. (2010). Harmonizing Trade Liberalization and Migration Policy Through Shared Responsibility: A Comparison of the Impact of Bilateral Trade Agreements and the Gats in Germany and Canada," *Syracuse Journal of International Law and Commerce*, 267, Spring.

globalization and migration. CEPR (2000) argues that the evidence that stimulated the neoliberal push to study the relationship between migration and globalization stemmed from a basic observation.

It was detected that "trade flows and foreign direct investment [had] increased in the last 20 years" of the twentieth century "at a faster rate than world production," due to a decline in the costs of communication and transportation and "the reduction in policy barriers to commodity and capital flows," but that there had been little change in migration flows.[8] However, in earlier episodes of capitalist globalization during "the 19th and early 20th centuries and in the 1960s, international labor mobility played a key role in fostering economic integration" (CEPR, 2000). Why is it that neoliberal capital is adverse to the free movement of persons, while capitalism in earlier periods encouraged international migration as a foundation for capitalist economic integration?

It is not enough to argue as the CEPR (2000) does that the global capitalist system has shifted from the liberal stance it maintained on labor migration in the 19th century and in the 1960s when governments took an active role in encouraging migration. The current period of neoliberal globalization is characterized by an intra-class struggle between financial speculative capital and capital in the real economy, stimulated by the crisis in the 1970s. The earlier periods dominated by productive capital in which international migration was encouraged arguably led to overproduction and the crisis that catapulted finance capital into its current hegemonic position.

Finance capital is winning the struggle with productive capital and as a consequence its liberalization measures top the policy agendas of the international financial institutions in the control of the financial elites in the leading capitalist countries. Capitalism in the 19th century and in the 1960s favored migration because of its roots in production in the real economy in which labor is at the center. Financial capital, which is based on speculation and not production, is at the center of neoliberal globalization. But, finance capital has developed an interest in migration not as a mechanism to support productive capital, but as a means of accumulation of finance capital through remittances and the economic activities of Diasporas. Thus, migration is now a full-blown area of focus within the

---

[8] Riccardo Faini, Klaus F Zimmermann, Jaime de Melo, ed. (1999). *Migration: The Controversies and the Evidence*, published for Center for European Policy Research by Cambridge University Press, London.

international financial institutions such as the World Bank and the IMF, and in other United Nations agencies.

The contradiction nonetheless is that arguably, the disinterest of finance capital in migration in the sphere in production is the reason for the current aversion towards international labor migration, as the dominance of financial capital is associated with the decline in production and trade. For example, the annual percentage change in world GDP declined continuously from 3.7 percent in 2006 to 1.7 percent in 2008. Also, the annual percentage change in world exports declined from 8.5 percent in 2006 to 2.0 percent in 2008. Furthermore, the annual percentage change in world imports declined continuously from 8.0 percent in 2006 to 2.0 in 2008.[9] The fact that financial capital has temporarily won this struggle is the cause of the hostility towards international migration.

The observation however about the aversion of neoliberal capital towards international migration compared with productive capital in the 19th century and in the 1960s reinforces a prominent contradiction in neoliberal theory, namely that it preaches free trade but restricts free trade. Arguably, the restriction on the free movement of labor in the neoliberal period "reflects the fears that immigration may aggravate unemployment and worsen the domestic income distribution by widening the wage gap between the skilled and unskilled" (CEPR, 2000).

These arguments nonetheless are mere sidebars to the real issue, which is the fact that the finance capitalists do not need labor and production to become rich. It was only in the aftermath of the great crash of 2008 that social movements, policy makers and academics etc., began to learn about the workings of Wall Street. The financial elites created an array of financial instruments through which they raked in billions of dollars for themselves, without having to turn a straw in the sphere of production. Without producing anything the financial elites that run the banks, insurance companies, and hedge funds made billions.

The evidence in support of the fears about in-migration identified by the CEPR (2000) is not hard to find. The view is commonly held in the developed countries that excessive in-migration is "detrimental to the welfare of natives, and somehow that this provides a reason" to formulate and implement highly restrictive migration policies. The views to restrict migration nonetheless are more than economic in nature, and embrace concerns about social tensions, the erosion of national identities, and the

---

[9] World Trade Organization. (2009). World Trade 2008, Prospects for 2009: WTO Sees 9% Global Trade Decline in 2009 as Recession Strikes, Press Release 554, March 24 (08-0000).

exacerbation of domestic economic problems. In the EU for example, immigration policies have been highly divisive among domestic constituencies, although there has been considerable pressure to tighten immigration laws.

Also, restrictions on migration in the EU have caused conflict with sending countries in the developing world. This is especially so with the developing countries, which "rely on emigration to alleviate structural imbalances in their labor markets and earn valuable foreign exchange through workers' remittances" (CEPR, 2000). Furthermore, according to the CEPR (2000), although restrictive immigration policies abound in the EU they have been ineffective in curtailing the flow of the so-called undesirable populations into the EU. Thus, the idea was touted that the best policies under neoliberal globalization to address international migration would be to promote "equitable and sustained growth" in the countries of origin of migrants (CEPR, 2000).

Trade integration is advanced as an attractive strategy to assuage migration pressure. This strategy is founded on two sets of interrelated ideas gleaned from neoclassical economic theory. The first is that goods trade is said to represent an exchange in "the services of the factors embodied in those goods." Thus, the view is that as barriers to trade fall, and "commodity trade increases, the exchange of factor services will also increase and therefore the incentive for factors to move should diminish, in which case trade in goods and the international mobility of factors are 'substitutes'" (CEPR, 2000).

Second, it is believed that the convergence between countries with varying levels of income will be achieved faster with deeper trade integration. The EU is regarded as an example of this because of the speed with which "poorer regions have been rapidly catching up with relatively better off regions" in the EU. Also, the multinational and bilateral free trade agreements, which the US has with its poorer neighbors in NAFTA, CAFTA-DR, Chile, Peru, Colombia and Panama, are regarded as strategies along these same lines to promote income convergence as a factor that constrains international migration.

The view that poorer regions in the EU are rapidly catching up with richer ones is highly questionable. The current crisis in the Eurozone associated with the so-called PIGS (Portugal, Ireland, Greece and Spain), Europe's most heavily indebted countries, reflects the income gap in the EU, and threatens to plunge the entire globe into a deeper recession. The rich countries in the EU are reluctant to bail out the PIGS, and when they do impose stringent austerity measures on them.

There is great concern whether Greece will be able to repay the 300bn euros in government debt it currently owes. The deficit in Greece is at 12.7 percent more than four times higher than the European rules allow. The "Celtic Tiger" dumped 7bn euros to bail out its two biggest banks the Allied Irish Bank and the Bank of Ireland amidst deep public spending cuts and the establishment of a state-run agency to manage Ireland's bad debts. Spain continues to be submerged in recession due to the huge declines in the country's property market, as the government imposes a 50bn euro austerity package that freezes public sector hiring. The Portuguese people are facing a reversal in their fortunes as their country plunges into its worst financial and economic crisis without precedence in its recent history.

The neoliberal view nonetheless is that, "Trade liberalization of high-income countries with middle-income countries is more likely to foster convergence and discourage migration." A caveat however is that "liberalization in investment flows" could negatively alter the convergence outcome (CEPR, 2000). Also, it is held that the "integration of goods markets between economies with very different initial conditions could lead to the opposite outcome" to convergence. In this connection, the argument is that "the fall in trade costs could lead to more polarization of production and more migration," due in large measure to the possibility "that out-migration is impeded by a financial constraint that is relaxed by trade liberalization" (CEPR, 2000).

Furthermore, there are undesirable short-terms effects "when integration is between countries that are not at the extremes, as in the case of Mexico and the United States" (CEPR, 2000). NAFTA encouraged migration in agriculture in the short-term, disrupting "Mexico's maize production to the benefit of its US counterparts," which placed a "downward pressure on unskilled wages on both sides of the border." This is the result of over-protection and high labor-intensity in the maze sector in Mexico, and capital-intensive production in the US. However, it is expected that in the longer term "improved conditions in the Mexican economy" could "stem migratory pressures" (CEPR, 2000).

According to the CEPR (2000), therefore, there is no conclusive "theoretical and empirical evidence on the effectiveness of trade integration" and the reduction of migration. The CEPR (2000) expresses the view that, "trade liberalization will not always alleviate the incentives for migration from the poorer to the richer countries." However, the CEPR's (2000) view is trapped in the false assumption that poor people from the developing world are the ones who are migrating to the rich countries. But, the evidence is clear that the bulk of migration takes place within countries and at the cross-border level between countries.

In addition, the CERP (2000) holds the view that "trade liberalization and migration controls are not alternative policy strategies as suggested by a straightforward application of factor endowment trade theory," since they "work with differing effectiveness over different time horizons." Migration control is advocated in the short-term because of its effectiveness as the "main tool" in the avoidance of "massive, and largely undesired, immigration in receiving countries" CERP (2000). In the view of the CERP (2000), however, the objective to stem migratory pressures requires policy makers not to stop at short-run migration controls, but to search "for more forward-looking strategies to alleviate migration pressure in the medium term." Finally, even though there are "theoretical ambiguities and policy disputes," the CERP (2000) believes that "the evidence continues to point towards benefits from trade liberalization."

The General Agreement on Trade in Services (GATS) and Migration

The World Trade Organization (WTO) was established on January 1, 1995 to regulate trade between nations. It is the end product of the Uruguay Round of negotiations of the General Agreement on Tariffs and Trade (GATT), which started in September 1986 and ended on April 15, 1994. The GATS, which was negotiated in the Uruguay Round of global trade talks, also came into force in 1995. It is the first binding multilateral trade agreement to explicitly address the movement of persons.[10] The GATS was inspired by the same objectives as the GATT, its counterpart in merchandise trade. These objectives are the creation of "a credible and reliable system of international trade rules; ensuring fair and equitable treatment of all participants (principle of non-discrimination); stimulating economic activity through guaranteed policy bindings; and promoting trade and development through progressive liberalization."[11]

Services account for over 60 percent of global production and employment, but they represent no more than 20 percent of total trade (Balance of Payments BOP basis). The WTO has 140 member-countries and they are

---

[10] International Organization for Migration, "GATS Mode 4," http://www.iom.int/jahia/Jahia/about-migration/developing-migration-policy/migration-trade/GATS-mode-4.
[11] World Trade Organization, "SERVICES: GATS The General Agreement on Trade in Services (GATS): Objectives, Coverage and Disciplines," http://www.wto.org/english/tratop_e/serv_e/gatsqa_e.htm.

simultaneously all members of the GATS, and have assumed various commitments in individual service sectors. The GATS apply to all services with
the exception of "services supplied in the exercise of governmental authority," and measures affecting air traffic rights and services directly related to
the exercise of such rights.[12]

The basic obligations under the GATS are classified as general compulsions that "apply directly and automatically to all members and services
sectors," and particular "commitments concerning market access and
national treatment in specifically designated sectors," which are set out "in
individual country schedules whose scope may vary widely between
members."[13] The two major general compulsions are the Most Favored
Nations (MFN) treatment, and transparency. Through the MFN treatment
members "extend immediately and unconditionally" to services or services suppliers of all other members "treatment no less favorable than that
accorded to like services and services suppliers of any other country."

In essence, this obligation prohibits preferential arrangements among
groups of members in individual sectors or of reciprocity provisions,
which confine access benefits to trading partners granting similar treatment. The transparency obligation requires GATS members "to publish all
measures of general application and establish national enquiry points
mandated to respond to other member's information requests." There are
other generally applicable obligations that include "the establishment of
administrative review and appeals procedures and disciplines on the
operation of monopolies and exclusive suppliers."[14]

The specific commitments are market access that is negotiated in specific sectors, and which may be subject to various types of limitations,
such as "the number of services suppliers, service operations or employees
in the sector; the value of transactions; the legal form of the service supplier; or the participation of foreign capital." National treatment is a second specific commitment, which "implies that the member concerned
does not operate discriminatory measures benefiting domestic services
or service suppliers." In this connection it is considered that the key

---

[12] World Trade Organization, "SERVICES: GATS The General Agreement on Trade in
Services (GATS): Objectives, Coverage and Disciplines," http://www.wto.org/english/
tratop_e/serv_e/gatsqa_e.htm.
[13] World Trade Organization, "SERVICES: GATS The General Agreement on Trade in
Services (GATS): Objectives, Coverage and Disciplines," http://www.wto.org/english/
tratop_e/serv_e/gatsqa_e.htm.
[14] World Trade Organization, "SERVICES: GATS The General Agreement on Trade in
Services (GATS): Objectives, Coverage and Disciplines," http://www.wto.org/english/
tratop_e/serv_e/gatsqa_e.htm.

requirement is for members "not to modify, in law or in fact, the conditions of competition in favor of" their own service industry. Indeed, "the extension of national treatment in any particular sector may be made subject to conditions and qualifications."[15]

The GATS defines four ways known as "modes of supply," in which a service can be traded. These are Mode 1 – services supplied from one country to another, for example international telephone calls, officially known as "cross-border supply;" Mode 2 – consumers from one country making use of a service in another country, for example tourism, officially known as "consumption abroad;" Mode 3 – a company from one country setting up subsidiaries or branches to provide services in another country, for example a bank from one country setting up operations in another country, officially known as "commercial presence;" and Mode 4 – individuals travelling from their own country to supply services in another, for example an actress or construction worker, officially known as "movement of natural persons."[16]

Mode 4 is the only part of the GATS in which the issue of migration is officially addressed. According to Niessen (2003),[17] this is the reason why the community of scholars and agencies concerned with migration has neglected to discern the relationship between migration and the GATS. However, the Development Research Center on Migration, Globalization and Poverty (DRCMGP) (2005) has identified a number of limitations to Mode 4.

According to the DRCMGP (2005), few countries have made offers on Mode 4, and when they do the offers are limited to senior and skilled intra-corporate transferees, or to 'key' workers for intra-corporate movement. Very few requests are targeted at movement of low skilled workers, and some economic needs tests are specified but most do not provide criteria.

Also, there are in place quantitative limits on foreign employment, and other requirements such as associated training of local staff, the specification of restrictions on movement, either geographic or between firms, and the tendency for movement to be horizontal rather than sectoral. In addition, there are unspecified varying periods of stay and qualification

[15] Development Research Center on Migration, Globalization and Poverty. (2005). "GATS Mode 4: How Trade in Services Can Help Developing Countries," Briefing No. 4, November.

[16] Development Research Center on Migration, Globalization and Poverty. (2005). "GATS Mode 4: How Trade in Services Can Help Developing Countries," Briefing No. 4, November.

[17] Jan Niessen. (2003). Negotiating the liberalization of migration – Is GATS a vehicle or a model for global migration governance? *The European Policy Centre (EPC)* Issue Paper No. 6 Issued on 28/10/2003.

levels that constrain the movement of persons, and some make exemptions to the MFN requirement.[18]

The movement of persons is intertwined with the debate that has raged for many years between the developed and developing countries on whether to create an international agreement on minimum core labor standards, which the WTO or some other mechanism would enforce.[19] The EU and the US argue for example that rights such as the freedom to engage in collective bargaining, freedom of association, elimination of discrimination in the workplace and the elimination workplace abuse, including forced labor and certain types of child labor, are matters for consideration in the WTO. The developing countries are in agreement with these same standards but they believe that the issue of core labor standards is not a matter for the WTO. They see it as merely a ploy by the developed countries to protect their markets from goods produced in the developing countries, and a smokescreen for undermining the comparative advantage of low-waged developing states.

According to the DRCMGP (2005), Mode 4 does not contain any specific definition of the types of movement it applies to. Thus, it covers all international temporary movements to provide services, without distinguishing between movements from "developing to developed countries, developed to developing, or between developed or developing countries and including highly skilled, less skilled or unskilled."[20] Furthermore, the boundaries of temporary mobility are sometimes blurred, as the definition of a service "makes it difficult to know, for example, if a temporary agricultural worker is providing an agricultural service (covered) or seeking temporary employment in agriculture (not covered)." Also, a business producing its own goods or goods on behalf of another company is subject to similar interpretation, and the WTO's sectoral classification list is also ambiguous and open to interpretation.[21]

But, the DRCMGP (2005) argues that Mode 4 is still important because it was negotiated to counterbalance Mode 3 on "commercial presence" in

[18] Development Research Center on Migration, Globalization and Poverty. (2005). "GATS Mode 4: How Trade in Services Can Help Developing Countries," Briefing No. 4, November.

[19] Sandra Polaski (2003), Trade and Labor Standards: A Strategy for Developing Countries, Carnegie Endowment for International Peace, Washington, DC.

[20] Development Research Center on Migration, Globalization and Poverty. (2005). "GATS Mode 4: How Trade in Services Can Help Developing Countries," Briefing No. 4, November.

[21] Development Research Center on Migration, Globalization and Poverty. (2005). "GATS Mode 4: How Trade in Services Can Help Developing Countries," Briefing No. 4, November.

which companies are treated as persons, from which the developed countries benefit the most. The financial benefits from liberalizing the temporary movement of labor nonetheless in the view of the DRCMGP (2005) seem not to square with "the potential negative social effects of temporary migration including social exclusion of migrants in receiving countries and the break up of family units when working family members move independently of the rest of the family."

The perceived benefits of Mode 4 to the developing countries are that "it allows them to exploit a relative abundance of medium and less skilled workers," and provides their citizens with greater market access to developed countries allowing "them to yield economic benefits directly in terms of payments to workers and remittances as well as other less tangible benefits on return." Furthermore, the developing countries are said to benefit from productivity increases in workers who remain at home "through the transfer of ideas, technology, facilitating entry to markets, networks and so on." Although these benefits apply to all other types of migrants it is believed that "the economic benefits of Mode 4 are expected to accrue from the temporary nature of migration and the scale of migration that liberalization could potentially ensure." In addition, the view is held that "the temporary nature of Mode 4 movement is expected to help prevent the phenomenon of 'brain drain' (although for some small nations even temporary loss of skilled personnel could be damaging)" (DRCMGP, 2005)

The benefits of Mode 4 to the developed countries are construed in terms of plugging the gap created by their ageing populations, which is increasing the scarcity of less skilled labor. However, Mode 4 accounts for only a very small fraction, one percent, of total trade in services. This small percentage is regarded as a "reflection of the existing limits and restrictions imposed on the movement of people" (DRCMGP, 2005).

Before its implementation the debate on GATS stimulated a number of ideas on the treatment of migration under neoliberal globalization. However, in Niessen's (2003) view, migration must be incorporated into "economic, social and foreign policy." In this way the complexities of migration will be addressed at various levels of global society. It is believed that migration should become a subject of negotiations for the liberalization of "the cross-border movements of persons and to establish a rule-based migration regime" (Niessen, 2003).[22]

---

[22] Also see Timothy J. Hatton. (2007). "Should we have a WTO for international migration?" *Economic Policy*, Volume 22, Issue 50, pages 339–383, April 2007.

According to Niessen (2003), although the GATS had not attracted much attention from the migration community it was extremely relevant for the management and governance of international migration. The neglect to study the relationship between migration and the GATS in the view of Niessen (2003) was a result of the fact that the GATS is merely a treaty on trade in services, which has only partially addressed the issue of migration in its pronouncements on "the temporary movement of 'natural persons providing services'" (Niessen, 2003).

The GATS regards labor mobility in terms of "the movement of service providers," which takes place either in "mode 3 or Mode 4 of the agreement." Mode 4 addresses "the mobility of *natural persons*" identified as "individuals, as opposed to juridical persons such as companies and organizations, whose movement is provided for in mode 3 by way of commercial presence." The GATS specify nonetheless that its focus on the mobility of natural persons "does not apply to measures affecting individuals seeking access to the employment market of a member, or to measures regarding citizenship, residence, or permanent employment" (Niessen, 2003). This provision allows GATS members to regulate migration, regardless of their obligations under the agreement.

Three standpoints seemed to have emerged on the liberalization of migration in the context of the GATS. The developed countries, the MDCs and the LDCs, represent these three positions. Both the developed and developing countries are reluctant to take the plunge to fully liberalize labor migration. This unwillingness is said to places a severe constraint on the liberalization of migration including the free movement of service providers.

According to Niessen (2003), the current obligations to migration are more beneficial to the developed countries, favoring highly skilled persons and "especially service providers associated with a multinational company, which has an international commercial presence." Furthermore, "intra-company transferees are the group targeted by about 42 percent of all current horizontal commitments" in all sectors (Niessen 2003). In addition, "28 percent of commitments" on the movement of persons relate to "executives, managers, and specialists," while 13 percent is for "visitors for sales negotiations and ten percent" is for "other business visitors," and the remaining 7 percent is for "independent contractors and others" (Niessen 2003).[23]

---

[23] See also Steve Charnovitz. (2002). WTO Norms on International Migration. Paper Prepared for IOM Workshop on Existing International Migration Law Norms, April 30.

Liberalization, however, has been of "limited significance for developing countries," primarily, because, their "comparative advantage lies in the export of medium – and low-skilled, labor-intensive services" (Niessen, 2003). However, it is their highly skilled personnel that are gobbled up by the developed countries. The GATS has only about 17 percent of its commitments that "apply to low-skilled personnel, and these are often limited by an economic needs test that excludes applicants if it has not been shown that no qualified domestic workers are available" (Niessen, 2003).

According to Niessen (2003), the MDCs among the developing countries are in strong support of an increase in GATS commitments for the movement of service providers in areas in which they have an advantage such as in the "the sectors of professional services" including "computers and information processing, health services, tourism, construction, audiovisual and transport services." India has led the charge along these lines supported by countries in Latin America such as Colombia, Chile and those in Mercosur, the economic and political agreement now a custom union among Argentina, Brazil, Paraguay and Uruguay founded in 1991. In essence, the Indian proposal called for reform in GATS that would bring more benefits to the developing countries.

Countries as diverse as Argentina, Bolivia, Chile, China, Colombia, Dominican Republic, Egypt, Guatemala, India, Mexico, Pakistan, Peru, Philippines and Thailand had formulated a common position on the liberalization of Mode 4 under the GATS negotiations in 2003. They demanded substantial improvements to Mode 4 commitments to result in substantial liberalization of migration "through sector specific commitments." This demand was put forward in the light of the fact that there was greater convergence between the interests of the developed and developing countries concerning the movement of persons. These countries also wanted "a separate visa or sub-set of procedures for temporary movement" of persons, the "elimination of economic needs tests," and "better recognition of qualifications" of their services providers.

The LDCs, argued however that, "they depend on the export opportunities of Mode 4 and have little else to gain from the GATS as a whole." For this reason they demanded that together the LDCs should be treated as a special case. The GATS Special Council supported the LDCs position by adopting a paper on the special situation of the LDCs. The paper took "into account the economic and social situation" they faced, and their "lack of institutional and human capacities to analyze and respond to offers and requests." The Special Council agreed to "exercise restraint when seeking commitments from LDCs."

The liberalization of migration under the GATS Mode 4 has been quite limited in an overall sense. Member-countries of the World Trade Organization (WTO) have been particularly "slow to expand commitments to lower-skilled categories of service providers moving outside the framework of commercial presence" (Niessen, 2003). According to the International Organization for Migration (IOM), "liberalization of the movement of persons to provide services, pursuant to Mode 4 of the General Agreement on Trade in Services (GATS), has not kept up the pace." Also, the IOM argued that, "for many developing countries the liberalization of trade, such as under Mode 4, is seen as an important contribution to their economies and employment opportunities for their nationals" (IOM, 2006: 33).

Thus, the contradiction is that the GATS is really a barrier to the free movement of persons, whereas the GATS is supposed to liberalize the trade in services. Much of this barrier has to do with policies such as quantitative restrictions that constitute a direct ceiling on in-migration. Also, the enforcement of measures in the developed countries to ensure "minimum working conditions and consumer safety standards," generally tends "to establish the absence of a suitably qualified national for the job concerned." However, the discretionary, ambiguous, and non-transparent nature of these measures, "have attracted considerable criticism" (Niessen, 2003).

"The Great Financialization"

Montgomerie (2006)[24] argues that, "the concept of financialization is a more systematic approach to understanding the impact of the rise of finance on social organization and governance structures." But, a different view is advocated here, which is in association with Kari Polanyi Levitt's (2008),[25] characterization of "the great financialization," John Bellamy Foster's (2010),[26] definition of financialization, and James Petras (2007) classification of the imperialist centered model of capital accumulation characteristic of the current period of financialization.

---

[24] Montgomerie, Johnna. (2006). "The Financialization of the American Credit Card Industry," *Competition and Change*, Vol. 10, No. 3, September, 301–319.

[25] Kari Polanyi Levitt. (2008). "The Great Financialization," John Kenneth Galbraith Prize Lecture, Progressive Economics Forum, University of British Columbia, Vancouver, Canada, June 8.

[26] John Bellamy Foster. (2010). "The Financialization of Accumulation," *Monthly Review*, Volume 62, Number 5 (October).

The period characterized as "embedded liberalism" that was in operation before the great financialization "yielded three decades of high growth, [which] was underpinned by an institutional framework which regulated and restricted both the power and the mobility of capital" (Levitt, 2008). In that period "finance was subservient to production. Financial institutions channeled savings to investment and were strictly regulated" (Levitt, 2008). Levitt (2008) observed about the period that

> Central banks served as instruments of the government, with full employment as primary objective; price stability was secondary. Banks were not permitted to charge more than six percent interest on loans or to engage in mortgage or investment banking. There were exchange controls, and no private trading in foreign currencies. Social expenditures were financed by progressive income taxation (Levitt, 2008).

However, "Since the early 1980s we have witnessed a reversion to accumulation by dispossession, reminiscent of the old days of the mercantilist era that preceded industrial capitalism"(Levitt, 2008). Levitt (2008) states that, "the transformational process, which has unraveled the institutional framework that sustained the good times of the 1960s and 1970s, might be called The Great Financialization." In the view of Levitt (2008), the great financialization,

> [H]ad its origins in the dissolution of the Bretton Woods financial order, [which] gathered momentum in the 1980s, and exploded in the mid 1990s. Ever since dollar convertibility to gold was abandoned, the United States was able to sustain an ever-increasing external deficit by issuing ever-larger amounts of dollars. International liquidity increased and deregulation of financial institutions encouraged the progressive expansion of credit. Soon, cross border capital movements and trading in foreign currencies greatly exceeded the requirements of trade in goods and services (Levitt, 2008).

In this period of financialization governments increasingly financed public expenditures "by the sale of securities to domestic and foreign creditors, and public sector savings were negative." Furthermore, the state shifted the tax burden from the "corporations and the wealthy to middle and lower income groups and regressive sales taxes were introduced." Also, "High-income earners with greater discretional income generated pools of capital seeking returns in emerging markets and other financial investments" (Levitt, 2008).

According to Levitt (2008) the great financialization has transferred "the initiative of macroeconomic policy" from "national governments to financial markets." Furthermore, central banks, which were created as entities that were "independent" of finance ministries, are now "instruments for the protection of creditor interests of financial institutions, and governments." Central banks are "more sensitive to their credit rating than to opinion polls or election results."[27]

Financial markets now hold democracy hostage, as the "financialization of capital has been encouraged" in the past 25 years, "by disinflationary policies of central banks, which systemically favor creditors over debtors." These policies sustain the "profitability of mushrooming global financial transactions, resulting in the increasing vulnerability of the real economy—private and public—to debt finance." Financialization has shifted an increasing volume of capital "into the circuits by the lure of inordinate profits." The result is that, "manufacturing and other productive sectors have come under pressure to sustain profitability by mergers and acquisitions, downsizing, outsourcing and the search for new markets."

While the liberalization of capital is associated with "measures to break down barriers to trade and investment on an international scale," Levitt (2008) noted that, "the dynamics of financial liberalization are significantly different from trade liberalization." The "liberalization of capital proceeds by stealth as a progressive process of unilateral reduction of national regulatory constraint," but, "the liberalization of trade requires negotiated agreement between governments." Also, "Where negotiations take the form of free-trade agreements, they are legally binding international treaties of indefinite duration."

John Bellamy Foster (2010),[28] in his study on "the financialization of accumulation" defined financialization "as the long-run shift in the center of gravity of the capitalist economy from production to finance." According to Foster (2010), this shift is

> [R]eflected in every aspect of the economy, including: (1) increasing financial profits as a share of total profits; (2) rising debt relative to GDP; (3) the growth of FIRE (finance, insurance, and real estate) as a share of national income; (4) the proliferation of exotic and opaque financial instruments; and (5) the expanding role of financial bubbles.

According to Foster (2010), Paul Sweezy identified "the financialization of the capital accumulation process" as one of three main economic

---

[27] Kari Polanyi Levitt. (2008). "The Great Financialization," John Kenneth Galbraith Prize Lecture, Progressive Economics Forum, University of British Columbia, Vancouver, Canada, June 8.

[28] John Bellamy Foster. (2010). "The Financialization of Accumulation," *Monthly Review*, Volume 62, Number 5 (October).

tendencies at the beginning of the twentieth century, the other two being the growth of monopoly power and stagnation.[29] Foster (2010) noted that historically, the role of finance is usually separated from the "real economy" for analytical purposes, while "accumulation is conceived as real capital formation, which increases overall economic output, as opposed to the appreciation of financial assets, which increases wealth claims but not output."

According to Foster (2010) although finance is always central in the role of capital accumulation, "something fundamental has changed in the nature of capitalism in the closing decades of the twentieth century." Foster (2010) argues that, "Accumulation—real capital formation in the realm of goods and services—has become increasingly subordinate to finance," as speculation comes to dominate over production. Thus, neoliberal financialization in which an increasing volume of capital is shifted into the circuits of finance capital and speculation dominates over production, in Foster's (2010) view reflects Marx's observation concerning "an accumulation of debt" taking on the appearance of "an accumulation of capital," with the former obliterating the latter.

An important point to note here however is that the centrality of finance in capital accumulation becomes even dominant at a historical conjuncture subjugated by finance capital. Thus, although accumulation is defined in terms of real capital formation in the realm of goods and services, the dominance of finance capital is a vital component of that process.

Financialization is a central feature of the imperialist centered model of capitalist accumulation. According to Petras (2007) the functions of the imperialist centered model of capital accumulation needs to be examined to understand the dynamics of international migration in the current period of global capitalism. The current ICMCA created by the forces of neoliberal global capitalism including the IFIs, MNCs, and collaborators in domestic economies in dominated countries, "exports capital in the form of investments in stocks and bonds, and lends money to public and private enterprises, through the multinational corporations and banks" (Petras 2007).

In this way "it captures control over productive and financial sectors of the target economies, via buyouts of privatized and de-nationalized enterprises." The IMF and World Bank play a major role in this process to ensure that conditioned loans to borrower countries lower "protective barriers

---

[29] Paul M. Sweezy. (1997). "More (or Less) on Globalization," *Monthly Review* 49, Number 4 (September).

and the subsequent penetration and domination of local markets by subsidized agriculture exporters and large-scale manufacturers" (Petras,
2007).

The end result of this process is the replacement of "large numbers of
agricultural workers " by "machines and specialized production," as "millions of small peasant plots and medium size farms" are destroyed through
their inability to compete with subsidized first-world agriculture. Also,
due to labor displacement in retail trade and cuts in public spending "tens
of thousands of skilled public sector professionals and skilled workers are
losing their jobs," as the "bulk of profits and interest" are repatriated to the
home office in the imperial countries. In this process of the de-structuring
of labor, that is, the delinking of the "development of industry and infrastructure from the local population," a "permanent mass surplus labor
population" is created in the dominated country (Petras 2007).

Thus, financialization in the imperialist centered model of capital accumulation in the current period of global neoliberal capitalism is creating a
mass of surplus labor globally. This surplus labor becomes engaged in
domestic and international migration. Surplus labor is therefore not
merely existent in the traditional sector in the sense proposed by Lewis
(1954). The traditional sector in which the marginal productivity of labor
is below zero, and wages are below subsistence level a consequence of
economic backwardness. Surplus labor is created by the form or specific
model of capital accumulation. So that, it is not merely the pull of higher
wages and "greener pastures" that lies at the center of domestic and international migration but the form or model of capital accumulation, which
is creating surplus labor.

The Financialization of Migration

The financialization of migration is construed within the framework of
"the great financialization," "the financialization of accumulation," and
the imperialist centered model of accumulation. It involves the treatment
of remittances and Diasporas under neoliberal capitalism a period demar-
cated from hitherto forms of global capitalism by the "reversion to accumulation by dispossession," where "accumulation—real capital formation
in the realm of goods and services—has become increasingly subordinate
to finance," as speculation comes to dominate over production, and the
creation of a "permanent mass surplus labor population." The core
thrust of neoliberal capitalism in regards to the development impact of

migration is the central role it has assigned to remittances and Diasporas in the process of capitalist development in sending countries. Thus, the development impact of migration concerns the facilitation of remittances and Diasporas within the framework of the "great financialization," "the financialization of accumulation," and the imperialist centered model of accumulation.

Remittances are defined as a component of capital to be subjected to market liberalization. The financialization of migration taking place within the market liberalization framework is the process whereby domestic and international remittance capital is shifting into the circuits of financial capital or becoming a circuit of financial capital itself. This process is taking place through deregulation of the global remittance architecture to make it easier for migrants to send money back to their countries of origin, or within a country to their original communities. Thus, through deregulation international and domestic remittance capital is captured by finance capital and then put to use to generate profit for the financial elites operating both at the apex and middle layers of the global financial system, and at the domestic levels in sending countries.

Remittances depend on the ability of people to move, but migrant labor is not as mobile as capital under neoliberal capitalism. Thus, neoliberal capitalism is caught in a paradox in that it wants the migrants' money but not the migrants. In walking this tight rope, the elites in control of the global and domestic capitalist institutions have been mobilized to put their hands to the wheel to bring about the desired result of neoliberal capitalism with respect to migration – the financialization of remittances and promotion of managed migration.

A major assumption in neoliberal theory is that globalization is rapidly eroding national borders spurred-on by financial liberalization, which removes restrictions on the movement of capital. There has been considerable liberalization of trade in goods and some services in the international trading system, but the same cannot be said for the movement of labor on which there remains severe constraints. It appearance therefore, neoliberal theory is promoting the unrestricted movement of persons within and across national borders, to complement the movement of capital and to stimulate the processes of economic and human development. But, in reality however, only lip service is paid to the removal of restriction on the movement of labor.

The truth of the matter is that neoliberal theory is pushing for the financialization of migration that is the full integration of money transfers by migrants into the formal financial sector. The financialization of migration is rapidly becoming a centerpiece in neoliberal capitalism, disguised nonetheless as an essential ingredient in the economic and human development of both migrant-sending and migrant-receiving countries. Once remittance is fully incorporated into the financial system, the financial hawks could subject it and the millions earned from it in fees etc. to arbitrage, credit swaps, bets etc., to generate money for the super rich.

According to the IMF (2010) states have a right to limit capital flows by exercising such controls as are necessary to regulate international capital movements so long as they "do not restrict payments for current transactions or unduly delay transfers of funds in settlements of commitments." However, the IMF does have jurisdiction over "moderate remittances for family living expenses," which is included in the IMF's definition of "payments for current transactions," classified as part of the kinds of capital transfers that requires liberalization (IMF, 2010).

Remittances are therefore an integral part of global capital flows that neoliberal capitalism seeks to liberalize. The problem is however that "there are no widely accepted 'rules of the game' for international capital flows" in spite of the fact that these flows are the "principal conduit for the transmission of global shocks" (IMF, 2010). The IMF claims that it is "hamstrung in its efforts to forge such rules," which reflects the "perceived ambiguity in its Articles, divergent attitudes among members, and the legacy of a failed attempt to confront the issue in the late 1990s." Also, the fact is that the Executive Board of the IMF "has not had a broad ranging discussion of capital account liberalization and controls since 1997" (IMF, 2010).

The IMF sees its role as helping to develop "rules of the game for global capital flows and in fostering multilateral, nondiscriminatory, approaches that look to the interest of both the originators and recipients of capital." Furthermore, it seeks to "provide a more complete framework to address the complex issues related to international capital flows" (IMF, 2010). The IMF is therefore anxious to place its hands on remittances as it creates "rules of the game" on international capital flows. There could be only one true reason for this, which is to place remittances in the service of global neoliberal capitalism.

However, the debate is not settled on whether remittances are a source of capital for economic development. For example, Ernesto López-Córdova (2006)[30] in his study on "globalization, migration and

---

[30] Ernesto López-Córdova. (2006). Globalization, Migration and Development: The Role of Mexican Migrant Remittances, Institute for the Integration of Latin America and the Caribbean (INTAL) and Integration, Trade and Hemispheric Issues Division (ITD), Buenos Aires and Washington, Working Paper 20.

development," which examines "the role of Mexican migrant remittances," presented evidence in support of the argument that international migrant remittances generally lead to improved developmental outcomes. Chami, Fullenkamp and Jahjah (2005)[31] argue, nonetheless, "that remittances do not act like a source of capital for economic development." In their view this is because "despite their aggregate size, remittances are made up of millions of individual, private, nonmarket income transfers." They argue, "that the data confirms the countercyclical nature of remittances, which is consistent with" their "model's implication that remittances are compensatory transfers." But, the IMF's study entitled "The Fund's Role Regarding Cross-Border Capital Flows," "includes in its definition of 'payments for current transactions' certain items that are capital in nature from an economic perspective, including ... moderate remittances for family living expenses."[32]

Furthermore, Carlos Urrutia and Felipe Meza (2010)[33], did not find a significant role for migration remittances in their study on "financial liberalization, structural change, and real exchange rate appreciation." Their study accounted for "the appreciation of the real exchange rate in Mexico between 1988 and 2002." They used "a two sector dynamic general equilibrium model of a small open economy with two driving forces: (i) differential productivity growth across sectors and (ii) a decline in the cost of borrowing in foreign markets" (Urrutia and Meza, 2010).

However, there are lessons for the financialization of remittances that can be learned from the financialization of the American credit card industry.[34] According to Montgomerie (2006), "the advent of asset-backed securities, a financial innovation known as securitization, was the key to the enormous expansion of credit card profits and the continued proliferation and growth of the credit card market in the US."

In the view of Montgomerie (2006)

> This is because securitization moved credit card receivables off-balance sheet, allowing loan pools to be re-capitalized, lowering the cost of borrowing and increasing revenues from payments on securities issued. This financial innovation attracted non-banks, mostly large MNCs, into the credit card

---

[31] Ralph Chami, Connel Fullenkamp and Samir Jahjah. (2005). Are Immigrant Remittance Flows a Source of Capital for Development? *IMF Staff Papers*, Vol. 52, No. 1.

[32] International Monetary Fund. (2010). The Fund's Role Regarding Cross-Border Capital Flows, IMF Washington DC: November.

[33] Carlos Urrutia and Felipe Meza. (2010). Financial Liberalization, Structural Change, and Real Exchange Rate Appreciations, IMF Working Paper IMF Institute, WP/10/63.

[34] Montgomerie, Johnna. (2006). "The Financialization of the American Credit Card Industry," *Competition and Change*, Vol. 10, No. 3, September, 301–319.

market, facilitating greater integration between finance and the 'real' economy. The deepening integration facilitated mounting competition and lower
costs of borrowing and was the catalyst for the rapid expansion of the credit
card market and its unsurpassed profitability.

The most important lesson to be learned from this securitization is the
great crash in financial markets in 2008, from which the US and the EU
continue to be affected. The crash is a direct result of liberalization in financial markets that allowed non-bank financial intermediaries to operate as
banks and banks to engage in non-banking activities. The evidence is clear
that the capitalism system cannot function on its own as an economic
entity. It needs a political superstructure not only to mediate the property
relationships between the capitalists and working people but also to tame
the behavior of the voracious capitalists themselves. Without this supervi-
sion, the behavior of the rapacious capitalists will continue to generate
crisis after crisis that threatens to dismantle the capitalist system.

An inherent characteristic of the capitalist system therefore is not only
the tendency for periodic crisis, but also an intra-class struggle between
politics and economics. While the former seeks to save the capitalists from
themselves by regulating the economy, the latter pushes back against regulations. This conflict plays itself out in the realm of politics in the fight
over the control of the state particularly the legislative branch. The different sections of capital on the two sides of the issue struggle to control the
state to gain the upper hand.

Meanwhile, technological innovation has produced the possibilities for
new instruments to be developed to treat with remittances to rake in profits for the financial sector. In Africa for example monies are remitted
through a process called "mobile-cash," which is "a form of cashless consumption that uses a technology called near-field communication."
Mr. Lawrence Mafuru, the managing director of the National Bank of
Commerce in Dar Es Salaam, Tanzania, proclaimed that, "the introduction
of mobile phone money transfer services is a sure way of taking rural communities out of poverty." Furthermore, Mr. Lawrence noted that, "Vodacom,
Airtel, Tigo and Zantel deserve a pat on the back for their initiatives" concerning "mobile-cash." Their initiatives he said, "supplement efforts of the
banking sector in making financial services available to a majority of
Tanzanians in remote areas."[35]

---

[35] Samuel Kamndaya. (2011). "Mobile Cash Transfer Hailed," *The Citizen* (Dar es Salaam),
May 9.

Kevin J. O'Brien in his article entitled "Taking steeps towards mobile cash" published in The New York Times on Wednesday, July 2, 2008 explained how mobile cash works. O'Brien explained

> Rushed for time last month, Gerhard Romen jumped on a departing tram in Frankfurt and waved his Nokia cellphone across an electronic reader at the door. The transit operator, Rhein-Main-Verkehrsbund, instantly charged the €2.20, or $3.48, fare to Romen's bank account in Helsinki. The transaction was made possible by mobile payment – a form of cashless consumption that uses a technology called near-field communication, which sends encoded payment data over distances of less than 10 centimeters, or about 4 inches. Romen, the director of near-field communications at Nokia, the largest cellphone maker in the world, said mobile money had the potential to eventually replace many kinds of cash payments (O'Brien 2008).[36]

This is precisely the point about financialization of migration through bringing remittances into the powerful financial sector. Mobile-cash is revolutionizing money transfer and the biggest beneficiaries will be financial capital, the information communications technology companies such as Google, and the firms producing mobile telephones.

Conclusion

The conclusion to be drawn therefore is that despite neoliberal capitalist globalization propaganda to the contrary, the mobility of labor is encouraged merely to satisfy the interest of the particular type of capital in power. When productive capital is in power labor mobility is encouraged as a fillip to production for the various types of productive capitalists to accumulate capital. When financial capital is in power labor mobility is encouraged to facilitate the financialization of accumulation. In reality, nonetheless, whatever the type of capital in power labor mobility is restricted, it is just that there appears to be more restrictions under the supremacy of one type of capital than the other.

A second point is that the GATS the principal neoliberal institutional arrangement for dealing with labor mobility is not only severely constrained but is biased towards the rich countries. It allows the developed states to suck the skilled labor out of the developing countries. It financializes the remittances of migrant labor. It leaves these developing

---

[36] Kevin J. O'Brien. (2008). "Taking steeps towards mobile cash." *The New York Times*, Wednesday, July 2.

countries with a false illusion that they have greater access to markets in developed countries. Also, it leaves them with the bogus promise that they will benefit from the transfer of ideas and technology by the migrants to their home countries. Finally, it gives the developing countries the phony assurance that they will profit from the networks with which their migrants are associated.

The third point is that both domestic and international migration policies are being currently formulated at a historical conjuncture characterized by "the great financialization." This is a period in which all forms of capital, including capital derived from migration processes, are being transferred to the financial sector thereby fueling the financialization of accumulation.

The fourth and final point is that neoliberal theory is advocating for the full integration into the formal financial sector of all forms of money transfers by migrants. Thus, the financialization of migration through the capturing by the financial sector of the capital involved in migration processes is apparently at center stage of global neoliberal capitalism. The neoliberal theorists are selling this process, as the lofty ideal to promote economic and human development in both the developed and developing countries.

Thus, when viewed from a class analysis perspective what parades today as new directions and thinking in migration and development is nothing more than the chewing over of old bones. The difference is that the migration and development debate is being revisited at a historical conjuncture characterized by neoliberal capitalism under control of financial capital.

CHAPTER FIVE

THE DEVELOPMENT IMPACT OF REMITTANCES AND DIASPORAS

Introduction

A central feature of the neoliberal views on the development impact of migration is the positive role accorded to remittances and Diasporas in the economic and social development of the sending countries. The preceding chapter examined remittances and Diasporas in the context of the financialization of migration. This chapter focuses on the case made out for the development roles of remittances and Diasporas by leading neoliberal global institutions. The sheer volume of remittances globally as gleaned from data provided by the Migration and Remittance Unit of the World Bank (2010) speaks to the issue of the developmental role that such monies could play in sending countries.

The World Bank also has a complex web of initiatives to promote the role of Diasporas in the economic and social development of their home countries. Along these lines for example, the World Bank launched its Africa Diaspora Program (ADP), in September 2007. The ADP is in search of avenues to further facilitate and improve the human and financial capital contributions of African Diasporas to economic and social development in their natal countries. To make this outcome possible the World Bank concentrates on the amplification of policy, financial, and human capital development in Africa. This is done through a collection of actions and support in collaboration with agencies such as the African Union (AU), African Diaspora Professional Networks, Hometown Associations, partner countries and donors.

In addition to the World Bank's efforts in this connection, the International Organization for Migration (IOM), the Global Commission on International Migration (GCIM), and the Global Forum on Migration and Development (GFMD), also seek to enhance Diasporas in economic and social development. Moreover there is a plethora of other regional forums, programs, arrangements, and agreements that have advanced supporting arguments on the economic and social development role of Diasporas in their home countries.

The literature on this subject is also wide and varied. The direction of research in sociology, anthropology, political science and economics, on remittances and Diasporas studies has not had a focus on shifting the balance of power in sending countries. Instead, research has focused mainly on issues such as group identity and belonging, networks, and the collective dimensions of migrant behaviors. Diasporas are investigated through the study of transnationalism, meaning that the choices and trajectories of individuals surpass the nation state and single cultural and national characteristics and associations.

The IOM regards Diasporas as contributing to development and therefore focuses on measures to maximize their potential inputs. Additionally, some developing countries believe that membership in the IOM is significant in helping them to build up their capacity to handle the movement of migrants into and out of their countries, and to draw on IOM research to tackle various developmental issues they face. Antigua and Barbuda in the Caribbean for example, one of the most recent members of the IOM believes that its membership would lead to such results. Antigua and Barbuda High Commissioner Dr. Carl Roberts stated that the country "looks forward to further enhancing its developmental policy particularly in advance of the free movement of Caribbean nationals within the sub-regional grouping of the Organization of Eastern Caribbean States and the Caribbean Community."[1]

Membership in the IOM is also considered as better equipping countries to "fight the growing problem of human trafficking," according to Dr. Errol Cort, Antigua and Barbuda's Minister of Labor. The IOM's activities cover four broad areas of migration management – migration and development, facilitating migration, regulating migration, and addressing forced migration.[2]

The summary of Diaspora-related development programs provided by Johnson and Sedaca (2004)[3] and Newland and Tanaka (2010)[4] is instructive in this regard. The focus on Diasporas and development is on areas

---

[1] Address at the 100th Session of the Council of IOM December 5, 2011 Palace des Nations.

[2] *Caribbean360*. (2011). Belleville, St. Michael, Barbados December 30.

[3] Johnson, B., and S. Sedaca. (2004). "Diasporas, Emigrés and Development, Economic Linkages and Programmatic Responses," US Agency for International Development (USAID) and Trade Enhancement for the Services Sector (TESS) Project.

[4] Newland, K. and Tanaka, H. (2010). Mobilizing Diaspora Entrepreneurship for Development Migration Policy Institute and US Agency for International Development, Diasporas and Development Policy Project, October.

such as remittances, community development, Diaspora business linkages, Diaspora investment instruments and knowledge transfers, and entrepreneurship. The Diaspora mechanisms as classified by Lowell and Gerova (2004)[5] further breakdown the area of activities that the IOM concentrates on regarding the role of Diasporas in development. These mechanisms include, optimal brain strain, return migration, financial instruments, entrepreneurial investments, hometown associations, immigration and trade and professional Diaspora networks.

Newland (2004)[6] analyzed the impact of Diaspora inputs on poverty reduction. It is suggested that by making transnationalism an engine for development donors could strengthen the effect of development assistance. Also, De Haas (2006)[7] focuses on host country strategies in case studies of the Netherlands, the United Kingdom and France, as well as on international agencies and ongoing initiatives targeting Diasporas for development.

This chapter focuses on the cases made out by these institutions for the role of remittance and Diasporas in socio-economic development. It provides a critique of the neoliberal formulation on the development impact of remittances and Diasporas. Also, it examines the possible role of remittances and Diasporas in the transformation of state power to working people in the developing countries. Radical approaches to the study of the role of remittances and Diasporas under neoliberal capitalism must concentrate on the ways in which these could be used to bring about a shift in the power base in society that favors working people.

Although migrants come from both rich and poor countries the focus here is on the neoliberal views concerning the influence that remittances and Diasporas exert on economic and social development in the developing countries located in geographical regions such as Africa, Asia, Latin America and the Caribbean. The purpose therefore is to critically analyze the neoliberal propositions pertaining to the development impact of remittances and Diasporas. The preceding chapter on migration and

---

[5] Lowell L., and S. Gerova. (2004). "Diasporas and Economic Development: State of Knowledge," Report to the World Bank, Washington, D.C., Institute for the Study of International Migration, Georgetown.

[6] Newland, K. (2004). *Migration and Development*, Migration Policy Institute; (2004). *Beyond Remittances: The Role of Diasporas in Poverty Reduction in their Countries of Origin*, Migration Policy Institute, MPI.

[7] De Haas, H. (2006). Engaging Diasporas: How Governments and Development Agencies can Support Diaspora Involvement in the Development of Origin Countries, International Migration Institute.

financialization presents the argument in support of the idea that an essential feature of neoliberal capitalism is the financialization of remittances. It is reasoned that the primary interest that the global financial institutions in the control of the neoliberal capitalists have in remittances is about how the financial sector could capture the billions of dollars that migrants remit as well as the fees, etc. and to use those dollars for speculative purposes to augment their profit.

The proposal here is to explore a wider range of issues concerning the neoliberal views on remittances and Diasporas in economic and social development. The proposition is that remittances and Diasporas do not bring about true socio-economic development for working people, but reinforce rather than transform the capitalist power structure and its imperialist centered model of capital accumulation. Remittances and Diasporas will only have a genuine impact on economic and social development in the developing countries when they contribute towards shifting the power base in those states decidedly in favor of working people. The big challenge to working people and the social movements in which they are organized therefore is how remittances and Diasporas are used. Whether to maintain the status quo of the capitalist power structure, or to transform it such that an alternative development model is fashioned in which working people are the primary beneficiaries. This is ultimately a political issue since it concerns the question of power – that is who controls the powers of the state.

Diasporas and Entrepreneurship

Newland and Tanaka (2010),[8] provides the most recent summary of neoliberal research on diaspora entrepreneurship. The view is held that diaspora entrepreneurs are indeed "first movers" because they are uniquely placed to spot opportunities in their home countries to establish businesses, create jobs and promote economic growth. The problem with this view however as with the idea that entrepreneurs are concerned with job creation, is that the first priority of business people is to make profit and not to generating economic growth and jobs. Jobs creation and economic growth are matters for the state, which must implement the appropriate

---

[8] Newland, K. and Tanaka, H. (2010). Mobilizing Diaspora Entrepreneurship for Development, Migration Policy Institute and US Agency for International Development, Diasporas and Development Policy Project, October.

policies to stimulate jobs, economic growth and improve the conditions of work and working people. The fixation of the neoliberal views on diaspora entrepreneurs nonetheless has blindsided neoliberal scholars and policy makers to this gaping hole in their theories and policies.

Thus, they believe that the developing countries need to reverse their limited success in attracting diaspora direct investors and entrepreneurs as a major step to promote their economic development. This position is embraced because of the entrenched view that diaspora entrepreneurship contributes to the development of countries of origin through businesses and jobs, innovation, creating social capital across borders, and the channeling of political and financial capital. However, there is disparity in the contributions of diaspora entrepreneurship to economic development.

Entrepreneurs classified as "necessity entrepreneurs" are said to have a minimal effect on economic development because these are merely individuals who create their own small businesses in the absence of finding other work – thus merely supporting themselves and helping to reduce overt unemployment. However, those who are called "opportunity entrepreneurs" are said to have a much more positive effect on economic development because they spot and exploit market opportunities.

Government has a role to formulate and implement policies that target these extremes of the business spectrum, as well as small and medium-size companies. According to Newland and Tanaka (2010),

> Countries with higher levels of diaspora entrepreneurship tend to have promising prospects for economic growth, as well as proactive diaspora engagement policies, good governance, positive socio-cultural perceptions of entrepreneurship, a critical mass of human and social capital, and accessible to financial institutions and pools of capital (p. 1).

The job of government is to refashion these opportunity structures, such that they appeal more to diaspora entrepreneurs and are more supportive of them.

Thus, Newland and Tanaka (2010) have identified policy responses to the challenges faced by diaspora entrepreneurs to include the following six options. First, government policies should "encourage access to capital, ... "through loans, competitions, and risk-sharing mechanisms for investors." Second, government policies should aim to "provide high-quality education and vocational training to develop the skills in business, science, technology, engineering, and mathematics to individuals interested in pursuing opportunities in knowledge-based industries." Third, government policies must "consider lowering tariffs on imported raw

materials and equipment into the country of origin to help diaspora entrepreneurs begin transnational businesses." Fourth, mechanisms should be
established "that encourage regular consultations with diaspora professionals." Fifth, it should be made "very clear that diaspora entrepreneurs
are welcome in their countries of origin." Finally, policies should be
adopted "that make it easy for diaspora business owners or investors to
come and go between their country of origin and their country of
settlement."[9]

Newland and Tanaka (2010) identified five main levels of commitment
or categories of organizations and initiatives that help to support diaspora
entrepreneurship. Essentially, these levels of commitment/categories
"are networking organizations, mentoring organizations, training organizations, investment organizations, and venture capital/partnership
organizations."[10]

Remittance and Neoliberal Capitalist Development

Historically, the motives for remittances have been identified as those
influenced by altruism or those intended for investment purposes.[11] In the
first instance the aim of remittances is "to support recipients in their daily
expenditure and/or compensate them for catastrophic events." Lin (2011)
argues that the end-use of these types of remittances is primarily for consumption purposes, and that they are "negatively correlated with economic conditions (real GDP growth and employment) in the home
country."

In the case of remittances made for investment purposes, the aim is "to
take advantage of high returns or other opportunities for profits in the
home country." In this connection, "remittances are positively related to
economic conditions and investment opportunities in the home country
(as indicated by real GDP growth and real interest rate differential between
the home country and the remitting country)."[12] Lin (2011) observed that

---

[9] Newland, K. and Tanaka, H. (2010). Mobilizing Diaspora Entrepreneurship for
Development, Migration Policy Institute and US Agency for International Development,
Diasporas and Development Policy Project, October.
[10] Newland, K. and Tanaka, H. (2010). Mobilizing Diaspora Entrepreneurship for
Development, Migration Policy Institute and US Agency for International Development,
Diasporas and Development Policy Project, October.
[11] Hannah Huidan Lin. (2011). Determinants of Remittances: Evidence from Tonga, IMF
Working Paper, Asia and Pacific Department, WP/11/18, January.
[12] Hannah Huidan Lin. (2011). Determinants of Remittances: Evidence from Tonga, IMF
Working Paper, Asia and Pacific Department, WP/11/18, January. Lin (2011), provides a
worthwhile survey of the relevant literature in this connection.

remittances affect long-term growth, which takes place through many channels. To this effect she surveys literature on the exchange rate, in particular on the effects of "changes in the real effective exchange rate" on "the distributional impact of remittance inflows," concluding that the evidence is mixed.

A major component of neoliberal theory nonetheless is the marketization of remittances. Neoliberal theory seeks the introduction of policy measures that would formally bring into the capitalist financial markets, the underground financial systems established by migrants to remit money to their relatives back home. The focus is on how the banking and non-bank financial intermediaries could capture through fees and pricing policies, their share of the billions of dollars that are remitted annually by migrants.

Undoubtedly, remittances are an increasingly multi-billion dollars industry, as noted by Mohapatra, Ratha and Silwal (2010) of the Migration and Remittance Unit of the World Bank. They pointed out that, "Officially recorded remittance flows to developing countries are estimated to increase by 6 percent to $325 billion in 2010." This figure had fallen by 5.5 percent to $307 billion in 2009. Remittances declined modestly during the global financial crisis, compared with foreign direct investment (FDI), which decreased by 40 percent between 2008 and 2009, and private debt and portfolio equity flows that fell by 80 percent from their peak in 2007. The sharp decline in FDI and private debt and portfolio equity flows, relative to remittance flows are presented as evidence of the importance of remittance as a source of external financing and capital flows in developing countries.

The World Bank estimated that remittances amounted to 1.9 percent of GDP for all developing countries in 2009 but were nearly three times as important, 5.4 percent of GDP for the group of low-income countries.[13] In line with the Bank's outlook for the global economy, the recovery in remittances is set to continue as it is estimated that they are "expected to increase by 6.2 percent in 2011 and 8.1 percent in 2012, to reach $346 billion in 2011 and $374 billion in 2012, respectively." These estimations are somewhat lower however, because the World Bank has changed its definition

---

[13] Afghanistan, Bangladesh, Benin, Burkina Faso, Burundi, Cambodia, the Central African Republic, Chad, the Comoros, the Democratic Republic of Congo, Eritrea, Ethiopia, The Gambia, Ghana, Guinea, Guinea-Bissau, Haiti, Kenya, the Democratic People's Republic of Korea, the Kyrgyz Republic, the Lao People's Democratic Republic, Liberia, Madagascar, Malawi, Mali, Mauritania, Mozambique, Myanmar, Nepal, Niger, Rwanda, Sierra Leone, the Solomon Islands, Somalia, Tajikistan, Tanzania, Togo, Uganda, Zambia, Zimbabwe.

of "developing country," which now excludes Poland the recipient of $9.1 billion in remittances in 2010 (Mohapatra, Ratha and Silwal, 2010).

Mohapatra, Ratha and Silwal (2010), have identified six reasons for the resilience of remittances in the face of economic crises in host countries. These are

> (a) Remittances are sent by the cumulated flows of migrants over the years, not only by the new migrants of the last year or two. This makes remittances persistent over time. (b) Tightening of border controls and fear of unemployment back home may encourage the migrant to stay abroad longer (i.e. increase the duration of migration). Those staying continue to send remittances. (c) Since remittances are a small part of a migrant's income; the migrant can cushion a fall in income by cutting costs (especially housing) and continue to send remittances. (d) A returning migrant is likely to take back accumulated savings, which are counted as remittances. (e) Fiscal stimulus packages in response to the financial crisis may also provide a cushion to migrant employment and outward remittances. (f) At the macroeconomic level, countries with diversified migration destinations are likely to have more resilient remittances (Mohapatra, Ratha and Silwal, 2010).

It is noteworthy however that the above "reasons for the resilience of remittances in the face of economic crises in host countries" do not tell the whole story. The resilience of remittances is not merely a phenomenon driven by migrants themselves, conditions in their home countries, or policy shifts. The capitalist institutions and technological change also have a role in influencing migrants to remit monies.

In the first instance, they overlooked the role of the financial institutions in the resilience of remittances. The financial institutions have made it much easier for migrants to send monies abroad from their host countries. Gone are the days when migrants had to stand in long queues in commercial banks or post offices and fill out a slew of paper work to send money back home. In addition, migrants are influenced by commercial advertisements that the financial institutions bombard them with in connection with sending monies abroad.

Secondly, they paid insufficient attention the role of advances in information technologies in facilitating the maintenance of the high level of remittances. This may be described as the technological effect on remittances. For example, cell phone technology has stimulated the use of "mobile cash" around the globe. Since cell phones have been foisted on consumers as almost a necessity, people use them to engage in activities they would not have engaged in prior to the cell phone era. The remittance of money is one such activity.

The outlook for remittance flows, however, is said to be "subject to the risks of a fragile global economic recovery, volatile currency and commodity price movements, and rising anti-immigration sentiment in many destination countries" Mohapatra, Ratha and Silwal (2010). Three trends are identified for the medium-term, which could affect the outlook for remittances the first being high unemployment in the migrant-receiving countries, which has prompted restrictions on new immigration. But, as we have seen in chapter two above, this position is not wholly correct since high unemployment in the US has not deterred migrants from going to that country. Second, the application of mobile phone technology for domestic remittances has failed to spread to cross-border remittances. Finally, it is the view of Mohapatra, Ratha and Silwal (2010) that "developing countries are becoming more aware of the potential for leveraging remittances and diaspora wealth for raising development finance."

Money transfers do not always pass through the formal capitalist financial houses. Thus, the neoliberal view is that restrictions on money transfers should be relaxed, and pricing policy should be implemented to make it cheaper for migrants to remit money. The remittances architecture should become more, user-friendly. The belief is that if this were to happen it would stimulate the capitalist development process in the migrant-sending countries by making more money officially available in the financial system for investment in development projects. The migrant-receiving countries will also benefit because of the gains to be had by having more money passing through and held in their financial institutions.

The neoliberal idea is that if the state makes it easier and cheaper for migrants to remit money, then migrants would use the formal financial system to do so rather than to go underground. This would ultimately increase profits in the financial sector. Furthermore, the state should also look into the financial agencies already involved in money transfers to curtail any practices they may have that hinder remittance. Specifically, in this latter case, the concern is with the price of remittance, which requires state intervention through policy prescriptions to keep prices low.

For example the five most costly migration corridors in US dollars are Tanzania-Kenya, Tanzania-Rwanda, and Tanzania-Uganda where the average cost of remittance in each case is US$47.24. These are followed by Australia-Papua New Guinea and Ghana-Nigeria where the average cost is US$40.84 and $38.94,[14] respectively.

---

[14] The World Bank, International Financial Corporation, Remittance Prices Worldwide, http://remittanceprices.worldbank.org/.

According to Peria (2010)[15] there are three main factors that drive the price of remittances. First, there seems to be a "volume effect that works either through scale economies and/or higher competition in a larger market." This conclusion is arrived at because according to data in the World Bank's Remittance Price Worldwide Database the "number of migrants in a corridor is negatively and significantly associated with remittance prices across different samples and different providers."

Second, it is surmised that the price of remittances is driven by higher per capita incomes in sending and receiving countries. These corridors "exhibit, on average, higher prices, which could reflect higher prices of non-tradable goods."

Third, the significance of market structure and competition are evident since migration "Corridors with a larger number of providers and countries with more competitive banking sectors exhibit lower prices." However, in corridors where there is a higher share of banks among providers, prices are higher. Peria (2010) observed that "Overall, country characteristics associated both with the cost structure of remittance service providers and with their pricing power are significantly related to cross-corridor variation in remittance prices."

However, although the price of remittances is lowest where there is greater competition within the banking sector, anti-terrorism and money-laundering measures involve state intervention in the remittances subsector to tract their destinations. The view is that persons identified as "terrorists" by the neoliberal capitalists, could use the remittances rout to finance their activities globally. Also, persons involved in drugs and other criminal activities could use remittances to launder money. However, the mission of the neoliberal capitalists is clear – the generation of profit for the capitalist financial institutions engaged in money transfers, while stifling the development of alternative forms of money transfer outside of the formal capitalist financial institutions.

Diasporas Role in Neoliberal Economic and Social Development

Another vital plank in the neoliberal interpretation of the relationship between migration and development is the pivotal role it ascribes to Diasporas in the economic and social development of sending countries.

---

[15] Maria Soledad Martinez Peria. (2010). What Drives the Price of Remittances?: New Evidence Using the Remittance Price Worldwide Database, http://blogs.worldbank.org/.

The definition of Diasporas nonetheless is problematic, as the term has no single acceptable meaning. There is no "legal recognition of the term which consequently has given rise to many different meanings and interpretations."[16]

The International Organization for Migration for example defines Diasporas in the broadest possible terms. It defines Diasporas as "members of ethnic and national communities, who have left, but maintain links with, their homelands."[17] From the perspectives of home countries, nonetheless Diasporas are denoted in different ways. For example they may be identified as "nationals abroad, permanent immigrants, citizen of (X) origin living abroad, non-resident of (X) origin, persons of (X) origin, expatriates, transnational citizens," etc.

According to the IOM there are multiple realities, which differ from country to country that are covered by these terms. In the understanding of the IOM they signify "people settled in a host country on a permanent basis, labor migrants based abroad for a period of time, dual citizens, ethnic Diasporas, citizens of the host country or second-generation groups."

Furthermore, "the UK House of Commons defines Diasporas as "International migrants who, although dispersed from their homelands, remain in some way part of their community of origin." This definition, in the consideration of the IOM captures a number of salient points. These are that "individuals are dispersed, possibly across several countries, but they maintain an interest and an affiliation to their home country, either 'real' or 'imagined.'" Thus, in the analysis of the IOM "Defining 'Diasporas' raises tangible issues of time, place of birth and citizenship, as well as subtle questions of identity and belonging."[18]

The neoliberal view is that the Diaspora comprises "many of the best and brightest, as well as wealthiest, members of any country or community" living outside their natal areas. The neoliberal theorists are targeting the wealth of the Diaspora as a source for raising development finance for the developing countries. Diasporas are seen as increasingly "organizing to

[16] Dina Ionescu. (2006). Engaging Diasporas as Development Partners for Home and Destination Countries: Challenges for Policymakers Prepared for IOM the International Organization for Migration, Geneva.

[17] Dina Ionescu. (2006). Engaging Diasporas as Development Partners for Home and Destination Countries: Challenges for Policymakers Prepared for IOM the International Organization for Migration, Geneva.

[18] Dina Ionescu. (2006). Engaging Diasporas as Development Partners for Home and Destination Countries: Challenges for Policymakers Prepared for IOM the International Organization for Migration, Geneva.

help economic and even political development in their countries of
origin – through philanthropy, through business investment, and even
(particularly in post-conflict settings) by returning to take up positions in
government."[19]

The problem is that the issue of Diasporas in the processes of economic
and social development in sending countries is promoted in a top-down
fashion by many international agencies. Agencies like the IOM for example, are creating policy frameworks on Diasporas in development processes to be implemented by the developing countries. According to
Ionescu (2006) the IOM has reviewed "existing policies aimed at engaging
Diasporas for development purposes." It discussed "the policy context and
factors that facilitate their mobilization." Furthermore, the IOM has identified "key policy challenges in the light of ongoing national practices, general research evidence, and IOM's research and operational experience,"[20]
concerning the role of Diasporas in economic and social development.

It is not only the IOM but also the European Union that has a stake in
enhancing the role of Diasporas in economic and social development.
In September 2005, the European Commission issued a communiqué entitled "Migration and Development: Some Concrete Recommendations,"
that build on its December 2002 communication on the subject. The EC's
2005 communiqué was developed in consultation with a number of international organizations. Its explicit purpose was to make "a contribution to
setting up a framework for integrating migration issues into the EU external relations and development policies." The EC recognized Diasporas "as
potential actors for development of the countries of origin." Furthermore,
the EC "emphasized two main areas of work: identify and engage Diaspora
organizations in development strategies, and set up databases where
members of Diasporas can register voluntarily."[21]

In addition, the Global Commission on International Migration (GCIM)
also has a focus on Diasporas in economic development. The GCIM was
established to improve cooperation between the United Nations and other

---

[19] Jennifer M. Brinkerhoff, ed. (2008). *Diasporas and Development: Exploring the
Potential*, Lynne Rienner, 2008.
[20] Dina Ionescu. (2006). Engaging Diasporas as Development Partners for Home and
Destination Countries: Challenges for Policymakers Prepared for IOM the International
Organization for Migration, Geneva.
[21] European Commission. (2005). *Communication on "Migration and Development:
Some Concrete Recommendations,"* September, in Dina Ionescu. (2006). Engaging Diasporas
as Development Partners for Home and Destination Countries: Challenges for Policymakers
Prepared for IOM the International Organization for Migration, Geneva.

international agencies. The GCIM aims "to provide a comprehensive response to migration issues." In its report released in October 2005, the GCIM devoted a chapter to "Migration and Development." The chapter identified a role for Diasporas "in particular, the role of hometown associations and the growth of social networks,"[22] in the development process.

Furthermore, the UN general assembly's high-level dialogue on international migration and development in September 2006 addressed the contributions of Diasporas to economic and social development. The dialogue discussed the issue of Diasporas in the development process at four main roundtables

> (1) Effects of international migration on economic and social development; (2) measures to ensure the respect for and protection of the human rights of all migrants, and to prevent and combat the smuggling of migrants and the trafficking in persons; (3) multidimensional aspects of international migration and development, including remittances and (4) promoting the building of partnerships and capacity building and the sharing of best practices at all levels, including at the bilateral and regional levels, for the benefit of countries and migrants alike.[23]

That the International Organization for Migration, the Global Commission on International Migration, the European Commission, the UN general assembly's high-level dialogue on international migration and development all engage the issue of Diasporas in economic and social development demonstrate the importance of this subject in the era of neoliberal capitalism. These multiple groupings are speaking in one voice on the subject. The reason for this is that these agencies are under the influence of neoliberal theory.

This is all part of the false neoliberal idea that private enterprise operating in free markets is the most efficient means to economic and social development and that the only role for the state is to facilitate private capital. In this context, it is the private capital of Diasporas that must become a driving force in the economic and social development of the sending countries. An examination of the typologies of Diasporas engaged

---

[22] *The Global Commission on International Migration (GCIM), October 2005* in Dina Ionescu. (2006). Engaging Diasporas as Development Partners for Home and Destination Countries: Challenges for Policymakers Prepared for IOM the International Organization for Migration, Geneva.

[23] *High-level Dialogue on International Migration and Development, UN General Assembly, September 2006* in Dina Ionescu. (2006). Engaging Diasporas as Development Partners for Home and Destination Countries: Challenges for Policymakers Prepared for IOM the International Organization for Migration, Geneva.

in economic and social development as identified by the IOM reinforces this point.

Typologies of Diasporas Engaged in Development

The IOM has identified a number of typologies of Diasporas initiatives geared towards economic and social development. The first, are "business networks" that link entrepreneurs of a particular country living abroad with business opportunities in their countries of origin. The IOM provides several examples in this connection such as the Lebanese Business Network that connects-up Lebanese business people living overseas with opportunities to do business in Lebanon. The Armenia High Tech Council of America, and Silicon Armenia are two more examples of business networks that link Diasporas to business projects in their home countries. In the view of the IOM Diasporas networks such as Indus Entrepreneur have played a central role in the attraction of foreign investors in their home countries by building up the confidence of overseas investors such as Hewlett Packard.

Chambers of Commerce, represent a second type of Diasporas initiatives, which are geared towards the economic and social development of sending countries. Usually, these organizations comprise entrepreneurs of a particular country or geographic region that promote development by involving Diasporas in direct economic activities in their countries of origin. The Caribbean American Chamber of Commerce and Industry (CACCI) is one such agency. The CACCI is a membership organization that provides small and start-up businesses with assistance in, the areas of business planning, financing, procurement, certification, expansion, and export-import opportunities. Its goal is to promote small business linkages between the US and the Caribbean. In the case of several other countries, such as India, Bangladesh, Bulgaria, Sierra Leone, and Columbia Diasporas enable business exchanges with support from the chambers of commerce. In some cases such as in Sierra Leone and Columbia Diasporas are actually members of the chambers of commerce of their host country.

According to the IOM "professional networks" are a third type of Diasporas initiatives that represent the interests of both develop and developing countries. The Advance Australian Professionals in America, which is funded by Australian companies in the US, is identified as one such professional network. Some others are the Global Korean Network, the Worldwide Indian Network, the Reverse Brain Drain Project Thailand, the Hungarian Medical Association of America (HMAA), and the

Ethiopian North American Health Professionals Association (ENAHPA). The aim of the Global Korean Network is "to promote the formation and expansion of decentralized cultural, social, and economic networks among Korean communities overseas."

The Office of the Higher Education Commission in Thailand for example initiated the Thailand Reverse Brain Drain Project. Its purpose is to bring overseas Thai professionals to Thailand to provide assistance to Thai higher education institutions by participating in actual research projects, seminars, workshops, training, and curriculum and research development. The Worldwide Indian Network serves the international Indian community. It seeks to further the needs, aspirations and goals of the Indian Diaspora community by promoting social, cultural, political, and educational causes.

The Hungarian Medical Association of America "is a voluntary organization of physicians and scientists of Hungarian heritage formed to preserve, promote, and foster Hungarian medical traditions and ideals." The ENAHPA, which is a partner for the IOM project MIDA in Ethiopia, has the mission to address the healthcare needs of Ethiopians. The ENAHPA endeavors to achieve this task by heightened access and delivery of medical services, the promotion of preventative care, and the transfer of knowledge, skills and state-of-the-art technology.

"Scientific networks" comprising Diasporas involved in promoting economic development constitute a fourth type of Diasporas initiative to promote economic and social development. There are numerous "scientific networks," which according to the IOM are frequently founded on "university networks." Some "scientific networks" that the IOM has identified are for example the Chinese Association for Science and Technology (CAST-USA), the African Scientific Network, the Ethiopian Knowledge and Technology Transfer Society (EKTTS), and the Latin American Scientific Association (ALAS).

The IOM identified a fifth type of Diaspora agencies that promote economic and social development as those that "build skill capacity." For example, the IOM has classified AfricaRecruit, an agency of the New Economic Partnership for Africa's Development (NEPAD) as one such agency. Through AfricaRecruit ways are identified that the African Diaspora can add value to capacity building in Africa. It organizes and supports recruitment and career events, and operates an employment database/search engine.

In addition, the *"Forum pour le développement de l'Afrique"* has produced an African expert database, while "The African Capacity Building

Foundation (ACBF)," an independent, capacity-building institution has started to develop a Directory of African Development Management Professionals. The "African Foundation for Development (AFFORD)," a charity in the UK regards the African diaspora as "an important stakeholder in Africa's development and it strives to involve Africans in sustainable projects for the promotion of development and jobs and skills." In Belgium, the "African Axis" operates along similar lines as AFFORD. The "Jamaican Diaspora Canada Foundation," draws on Jamaican police officers in Canada to lend their expertise to the police in Jamaica.

Finally, ABANTU for Development is a non-governmental organization (NGO) in special consultative status with the Economic and Social Council (ECOSOC) of the United Nations. ABANTU for Development has a Regional Office for West Africa (ROWA) in Accra, Ghana to coordinate all ABANTU programs in West Africa and focuses on sustainable development. The mission of ABANTU is "to build the capacity of women to participate in decision-making at all levels, to influence policies from a gender perspective and to address inequalities and injustices in social relations." These are achieved through "advocacy, training, research, institutional development and networking."

Skilled migrants are regarded as a resource to be tapped for the development of the sending country. It is believed that countries and the international organizations must promote international labor migration by encouraging international labor mobility and the freer movement of workers, which will increase the volume of remittances and brain circulation.

"Community initiatives" and a sixth type of Diaspora activities promote social and economic development in sending countries. For example, there are "hometown initiatives" in Ecuador, Mexico, Paraguay and Uruguay that support local development, micro-enterprise and local community projects in those countries. The "*Programa de Iniciativa Ciudadana 3 x 1 Mexico*" for example "matches migrant funds with federal, state and municipal funds," while the non-profit organization "the Catalan Fund for Development Cooperation (FCCD)" works "in Latin America and supports immigrants wishing to promote local development projects" in their home countries.

Also, there are migration and development associations such as the "*Association Migration Solidarité et Echanges pour le Développement* (AMSED) in France, Migration and Development and Alternative for India Development in the UK." These migration and development associations have a focus on harnessing the solidarity that arises from migration dynamics.

In the category labeled "gender and development," the IOM has identified another area in which Diasporas are called on to promote economic and social development. The examples provided in this connection are *"Femmes et développement en Algérie* (FEDA) and FAMAFRIQUE," in France which explicitly aim at women in Diasporas. FAMAFRIQUE for example is a website created by Environmental Development Action in the Third World (ENDA) in Senegal as a part of the project "Women's Information Highways in French-speaking Africa." Dedicated to French-speaking women, FAMAFRIQUE engages in activities for the promotion of sustainable development, by playing the role of coordinating networks, redistributing information and resources to and from sub-regions of Francophone Africa and the rest of the world.

Also the IOM has identified a number of "umbrella organizations" that focus their attention on the issue of Diasporas in the development process. For example, *"Forum des organisations de solidarité internationale issues des migrations* (FORIM)," in France is a national platform that "brings together 700 networks, federations and associations dedicated to both integration issues in the home country and development activities for the host country." In the US the "National Federation of Indian American Associations (NFIA) brings together 250 organizations" in the country with the aim to unify the East Indian American communities by coordinating and promoting the activities of its member associations. Also, there is the "National Ethnic Minorities Consultative Committee," set up by the Dutch government through which it consults with different organizations representing minority groups.[24]

There are many different information networks operating in different sectors in different countries, as well as co-development initiatives, which the IOM classifies as "Diaspora networking." These "Diaspora networking" arrangements facilitate contact and collaboration between sending countries and expatriate communities abroad. Also, there are overseas Diaspora agencies that offer an extra transnational bridge for both sending and receiving countries by connecting emigrant communities and members of the host country. Examples of theses identified by the IOM are AfroNeth a Dutch-African Diaspora organization, the "German-Serbian Economic Forum," and the "Co-operation for the Development of Emerging Countries

---

[24] A.A. Mohamoud. (2007). The Contribution of African Diaspora to Policy Dialogue, African Diaspora Policy Centre, The Netherlands, October.

(COSPE)" a non-profit association operating in the field of international cooperation in Italy.

Diasporas may also deliberately apportion a part of the monies they remit to finance specific development projects. This type of "finances" is undertaken for example by agencies such as "Opportunity International," which channels remittances specifically for poverty reduction. This is done through partnerships with micro-finance institutions such as Metropolitan Insurance Company Limited a Ghana-based financial institution that operates Metcare, which channels remittances into healthcare projects.

As noted by the IOM, there are informal transfer mechanisms that substitute for official channels in situations where the latter are unavailable, or inaccessible, and in some cases avoided for personal reasons. For example in East and South-East Asia, and Muslim countries the *"Hawala"* is a widely used traditional money transfer mechanism. The *"Hawala"* provides users with anonymity, besides being low-cost, fast, and provides home language services. Similar traditional money transfer networks exist in China *"Jeiqian,"* the Philippines *"Padala,"* Thailand *"Phei kwan,"* and India and Bangladesh *"Hundi."*

The Global Commission on International Migration (GCIM) (2005) is of the view that the activities of Diaspora associations and individual migrants, strengthens their home economies and serve as conduits for new ideas. Also, Diasporas augment the understanding between countries of origin and destination (GCIM Report, 2005: 23). These are only some of the benefits associated with Diasporas financial and other investments in their home countries.

The GCIM believes that the global community of states and international organizations must encourage Diasporas to increase their saving and investment and participate in transnational knowledge networks to promote development in their home countries (GCIM Report, 2005: 29). The Mexican Home Town Associations (HTAs) in the US are identified as good examples in this connection.

According to the GCIM (2005)

> Mexican HTAs have a long history – the most prominent were established in the 1950s. There are currently over 600 Mexican HTAs in 30 cities in the USA. They support public works in their localities of origin, including funding the construction of public infrastructure (e.g. new roads and road repairs), donating equipment (e.g. ambulances and medical equipment) and promoting education (e.g. establishing scholarship programs, constructing schools and providing school supplies) (GCIM Report, 2005: 27).

Although the activities of HTAs are commendable, the fact should not be lost sight of that they are mere patchwork solutions to a wider problem of inequality caused by the class divisions in capitalist society. The HTAs are not engaged in a process of the revolutionary transformation of capitalist society. Neither do they challenge the status quo of capital accumulation and the power configurations of capitalism. As a consequence, they are a problem so much so as they contribute towards the maintenance of the power structure of class oppression by helping their compatriots to merely subsist within the framework of global capitalism. This same criticism is applicable to the pluralist approach, which present patchwork solutions to inequality that derive from class divisions.

Diaspora investment nonetheless, is a big part of the argument in favor of migration as an instrument for socio-economic development in the poor countries. According to GCIM (2005) "There are some 30 to 40 million overseas Chinese living in about 130 countries." The OECD estimated that approximately 45 percent of China's total FDI in 2004, was investments made by Chinese Diaspora (GCIM Report, 2005: 30). It is also pointed out that the flow of foreign direct investment increases as the movement of service providers rises. India provides an example in which increased FDI and service providers are positively correlated. Due to the increasing role of Diasporas in investments in their home countries, the GCIM recommends that the global institutions and states "should formulate policies and programs that maximize the developmental impact of return and circular migration" (GCIM Report, 2005: 30).

The Global Forum on Migration and Development (GFDM) has declared objectives in connection with increasing the role of Diasporas in the provision of investment capital in their home countries. One such objective is to establish partnerships and cooperation on migration and development. These will be undertaken between countries and between countries and other participants. These stakeholders include international organizations, Diaspora, migrants, and academia.

Thus, at its forum in Brussels in July 2007, the GFDM focused among other things on maximizing opportunities and minimizing risks concerning human capital development and labor mobility; increasing the net volume and development value of remittances and other Diaspora resources; and on enhancing policy and institutional coherence, and promoting partnerships. The GFDM held subsequent forums in Manila in 2008, Athens 2009, and Mexico in 2010, each making recommendations that contribute to its overall objectives. The Manila roundtables focused inter alia on measures concerning shared responsibilities in protecting the rights of migrants, and empowering migrants and Diaspora to contribute to development.

Meanwhile, the IOM argues that the benefits of new technologies could be promoted through Diasporas due to the major role they play in the transfer of knowledge and technology between countries of origin and destination. These benefits will also accrue because Diaspora networks could form the basis for business partnerships, trade, and flows of investment (IOM, 2005). The idea of the "digital Diasporas" has emerged because of the pivotal part played by some Diasporas in promoting the presence and use of information and communication technologies (ICTs) in the countries of origin.[25] Arguably, this role of Diasporas helps to bridge the "digital divide" (IOM, 2006; IOM, 2005).

The problem here is that bridging the "digital divide" increases the profits of the capitalist companies involved in ICTs by expanding their markets. It will not necessarily lead the developing countries to experience self-sufficiency in ICTs through domestic research and production. However, it is also believed that the international initiatives and networks set up by global Diasporas contribute to the growth of global partnerships that work towards the success of the Millennium Development Goals (IOM, 2005; UNFPA/IPEA, 2007).

Views on the positive role of Diasporas in development have been a central focus of a wide variety of regional associations on migration. Examples of these associations are the Lima Declaration of the South American Conference on Migration; the Puebla Process of the Regional Conference on Migration in the Americas; the Regional Consultation on Migration, Remittances and Development in Latin America and the Caribbean (2006); and the Regional Consultation on Migration, Remittances and Development in Africa (UNDP/Government of Ghana, 2007).

Also, the Migration Dialogue for Western Africa (MIDWA) and the Migration Dialogue for Southern Africa (MIDSA) seek to explore the potential of contributions by Diasporas to the development of their home countries. These groups also want to know the associations Diasporas may have with regional associations such as the Southern African

---

[25] See Joseph Gueron and Anne Marie Spevacek. (2008). Diaspora-Development Nexus: The Role of ICT. USAID Knowledge Services Center, August 18. See also International Organization for Migration (IOM). (2005). International migration, development and the information society. World Summit on Information Society (WSIS) Concept Paper Geneva 2003-Tunis 2005.

Development Community (SADC) and the Common Market for Eastern and Southern Africa (COMESA) (IOM, 2005). The New Partnership for Africa's Development (NEPAD) had also mapped out strategies to maximize the benefits of Diasporas for the development of Africa, in its Program of Action in 2001. The Africa Union (AU) supports the program of action by NEPAD on the Diasporas in Africa's development. The AU itself is working towards strengthening the African Diaspora's involvement in the development of their countries of origin.

In addition, the African, Caribbean and Pacific Group of States (ACP) have focused on the link between migration and development in the Cotonou Agreement with the European Union. Also, migration and co-development, including the necessity to facilitate the involvement of migrants in the economic development of their region of origin, is a focus of the Western Mediterranean Cooperation Process known as the "5+5 dialogue." The "5+5 dialogue" is an instrument with rotating presidency for informal political dialogue that brings together Algeria, France, Italy, Libya, Malta, Mauritania, Morocco, Portugal, Spain and Tunisia. The program of action of the Manila Process, which is no longer active, and other regional processes such as the Asia Europe Meeting (ASEM) and the Bali Conference have focused on the linkages between migration and development at their meetings and in their statements.

The World Bank (2004) argues that access to markets in migrant-receiving countries could be enhanced if the migrant-sending countries maintain ties to their Diaspora. Through these ties the sending countries could promote programs to stimulate return migration of skilled workers thereby enhancing the flow of finance and knowledge. The Bank cooperates with research groups in developing countries through its research and country analysis programs as a means to improve the relative attractiveness for highly educated individuals to remain in their home country. The Bank's task force on low-income countries under stress for example, recommended that the Bank expands its Diaspora initiative for Afghanistan to other countries. It also explored ways concerning the use of its financed technical assistance programs to encourage the return of nationals living abroad (World Bank, 2004).

Critique of the Development Impact of Remittances and Diasporas

The "typologies of diasporas initiatives" involving business, professional, scientific, skill capacity building, and diasporas networks, as well as chambers of commerce, community initiatives, gender and development, umbrella organizations and finance, are all capitalist institutional arrangements. Their main function is to embed more institutions from and about the developing countries into the neoliberal global capitalist system, to bring them in line with the imperialist centered model of capital accumulation spearheaded by financial capital. Neoliberal theorists are therefore in search of ways to utilize existing and future Diasporas in their globalization project.

Diasporas are to become willing allies in the spread and strengthening of the globalization of neoliberal capitalism. Diasporas are identified to perform the role of front men and women in their individual capacities, as well as through their institutions, to bring global capital to the developing countries. Neoliberal capitalism is probably using Diasporas as front men and women for the following reason. Foreign capital has cultivated a bad name for itself in the developing world, especially after such studies as *The Pillage of the Third World*.[26] For centuries foreign capital has intervened in the developing countries, but it has produced very little or no concrete results of development in those states.

In the age of the Diasporas, given the high volume of external migration, foreign capital seeks to penetrate the developing countries, with little or no scrutiny and suspicion by locals. This is possible because the locals will only see the Diasporas who are the front men and women. It will be harder for the locals to detect the workings of foreign capital behind these Diaspora organizations and individuals. Behind the Diasporas are capitalist entities that fund their projects, and provide them with knowledge of the political, economic and social systems of capitalism.

The role of the Diasporas is to help to bring this knowledge about capitalist economy, politics and society to their countries of origin. This kind of cloak-and-dagger activity in which Diasporas are knowingly or unknowingly involved, is necessary for one simple reason. It makes it easier for the neoliberal capitalist to do business in the developing countries. This is because the global capitalists will be dealing with familiar economic, political and social institutions in whichever country they go, rather than having to negotiate with unfamiliar local agencies.

Historically, during the colonial days this trend of Diasporas playing an increasing role in their home countries was very much evident in politics in the developing countries. For example, the educated elites who studied

---

[26] Pierre Jalée. (1968). *The Pillage of the Third World*. New York, Monthly Review Press.

abroad at colonial educational institutions returned home to form and lead political parties. The platform of these political parties included, universal adult suffrage, political independence, and economic development. Members of the educated elite who won power became the neocolonial rulers in the their natal countries. They proceed to rule in the interests of colonial capital and the colonial political economy order.

Diasporas are being identified for a similar role by neoliberal capital in the economic, political, and social realms. For example, having held senior positions in international agencies that serve the interest of global capital, Diasporas are returning to their countries of origins to become Prime Ministers and Presidents. This trend is evident in Africa and Latin America, where for example elected and appointed officials carry out the agendas of the World Bank and IMF. These Diaspora elements who are well versed in the theories of neoliberal capitalism become the political candidates favored by the imperialist centers such as the US and the European Union.

For example in Nigeria Ngozi Okonjo-Iweala a former Managing Director of World Bank was appointed directly from the World Bank to become the Minister of Finance, in July 2011. President Ellen Johnson Sirleaf of Liberia was a Senior Loan Officer at the World Bank. President Alassane Dramane Ouattara of Côte d'Ivorie was an economist for the International Monetary Fund, and President Alejandro Toledo of Peru, worked for the World Bank.

There is another side to the emphasis on Diasporas acquiring skills abroad and returning to their home countries to engage in economic and social development. It has to do with the migration of highly accomplished professionals trained in the developing countries. These individuals will be encouraged to migrate under the guise that they will make future contributions to their home countries as members of the Diaspora. The implication of this is that the developing countries will invest in the professional development of their workforce, merely to export skilled workers abroad with a promise that they will participate in Diaspora networks to bring about the economic and social development of their home countries.

Neoliberal theory has now rebranded the brain drain as "brain circulation" (Skeldon, 2008a) to put a positive spin on it. The idea of "brain circulation" implies that skilled labor is not constrained by national borders. It is not stationary but moves around the globe from country to country based on market conditions. The "brain circulation" idea is a fall back to the neoclassical position on the allocation of labor based on supply and demand forces in the markets for skilled labor. Skilled labor is circulated according to both its demand and supply in different parts of the global capitalist system.

There is the view, however, that the specific place of origin of skilled labor is significant in the debate on the brain drain. In Haiti, for example, it is estimated that about 90 percent of the doctors are located in the country's capital Port-au-Prince, while in Ghana, the Greater Accra area accounts for 46 percent of the doctors in both the private and public sectors. When the figures for Great Accra and Kumasi, Ghana's second city are added together they account for 69 percent of the doctors in the country (Nyonator and Dovlo, 2005: 229). The problem here is that the migration of skilled workers from areas where such labor is concentrated may have less of a negative effect on the local population than in areas where the need for these skills may be greatest. The effects on Accra of the migration of doctors from that area where there is such a high concentration will be less severe, compared with the migration of doctors form Cape Coast, where there are fewer doctors.

Remittances, Diasporas and Power: An Alternative View

What is the role of Diasporas and remittances in the transformation of state power to working people in the developing countries? Many pro-working people political parties in the developing countries are cash-strapped and in desperate need of funding to mount effective challenges for state power. This dilemma makes many of these organizations vulnerable to shady foreign agencies such as the International Republican Institute (IRI), and the National Endowment for Democracy (NED) both US organizations that fund political institutions in the developing countries. The IRI and NED give financial support primarily to institutions in the developing countries that support the neoliberal agenda.

The IRI for example has assumed for itself the mission to build democracy in foreign countries. The work of the IRI in Haiti however, has led to the overthrow of the democratically elected government of President Aristide. The IRI is regarded as an organization that "serves only as a screen for its energetic and unscrupulous promotion of an ultraconservative Republican foreign policy agenda."[27] It is supposed to be a research

---

[27] Leight, Jessica. (2004). The International Republican Institute: Promulgating Democracy of Another Variety. Washington. Council On Hemispheric Affairs, Memorandum to the Press 04.40, July 15.

institution but it is really a "cloak-and-dagger operation." There is evidence that the IRI was allied with the extreme antidemocratic forces in Haiti and contributed towards inciting the coup that overthrew President Aristide, while asserting that it was involved in "party building," and "educational seminars" in the country (Leight 2004).

Furthermore, the IRI received $1.2 million from the NED for its operations in Haiti. Together, the IRI and the NED funded two anti-Aristide conservative trade unions, the Federation of Trade Union Workers and the General Organization of Haitian Workers, to scuttle the radicalism of Haiti's left leaning trade union movement. These unions were regarded as a threat to the US and local business interests in Haiti. The NED also funded the Haitian Center for Human Rights (CHADEL), led by Jean-Jacques Honorat, a former prime minister in the Haitian military junta a brutally repressive government that beat and murdered thousands of political dissidents between 1991 and 1994.[28]

As a counter to these kinds of unsavory activities by foreign agencies in the developing countries, working people's movements in the developing countries could harness financial resources from Diasporas. There should be a concerted effort by Diasporas and migrants to deliberately fund pro-working people political parties in their countries of origin. This could help these political parties to avoid the pitfalls of taking money from shady foreign sources. Diasporas could also use the very mechanisms established by neoliberal capital to remit monies to political parties and civil organizations engaged in political struggle to shift the political balance in their home countries.

Conclusion

The above discussion is evidence of the comprehensive approach neoliberal capitalism has to the issue of migration and development. The key point here however is the manner in which neoliberal capitalism utilizes the international institutions in its control to bring its message of the development impact of migration globally. No part of the globe is excluded from its reach to profit from migration processes. The neoliberal line of reasoning outlined above on the role of Diasporas in the development process is devoid of class analysis. The Diasporas are really being encouraged to become involved in the deepening of neoliberal capitalism, without

---

[28] Dennis C. Canterbury. (2010). *European Bloc Imperialism*. Boston, Brill.

challenging the structural asymmetries associated with the capitalist system, and the power dynamics of its class structure nationally, regionally and globally.

The examples of the different "typologies of Diasporas initiatives" geared towards development merely buttress the capitalist status quo. In no way do they really broach the issue of genuine alternative development in which working people gain the upper hand. The problem is that the directions on the development impact of remittances and Diasporas are not coming from the developing countries but from the leading imperial states and the global agencies they dominate. These directions are designed to strengthen the global capitalist order.

CHAPTER SIX

THE MILLENNIUM DEVELOPMENT GOALS IMPACT OF MIGRATION

Introduction

The thirty-year historical conjuncture from the 1980s to the second decade of the twenty-first century is characterized by the ascendancy of neoliberal capitalism. Neoliberal capitalism is headed-up by a class of financial or speculative capitalists whose ideas are now the ruling ideas. The financial capitalists are currently the ruling material and intellectual force of neoliberal capitalism. They have control over both the means of material and mental production. This is evidenced by the fact that although they do not produce agricultural and manufactured commodities fundamental to human existence, they control the productive sectors by subjecting production to their ideals.

For example, the productive sectors are being reorganized on the basis of a slew of neoliberal free market fundamentalist ideas such as those on, market reforms, the extrication of the state from direct production, market deregulation, tax-breaks for the rich, the reduction in non-wage labor costs by cutting the social benefits of workers and retrenchment. The institutions of higher learning in both the developed and developing countries have reformed their curricula to produce a cadre of professionals well versed in neoliberal theoretical ideas. These individuals go on to occupy senior positions in political institutions and civil society. They are perched in both private and public agencies at the national, regional and global levels where they implement the neoliberal theoretical ideas.

Thus, in the current historical conjuncture politics, economy, and civil society are subjected to the ideas of the ruling classes – the neoliberal capitalists dominated by the financial capitals. Karl Marx[1] made the following observation about the ruling classes in their historical contexts.

> Insofar, therefore, as they rule as a class and determine the extent and compass of an epoch, it is self-evident that they do this in its whole range, hence among other things rule also as thinkers, as producers of ideas, and regulate

---

[1] Karl Marx and Friedrich Engels. (1998). *The German Ideology*. New York. Prometheus Books.

the production and distribution of the ideas of their age: thus their ideas are
the ruling ideas of the epoch.

This is the contextual framework for an analysis of the emergence of the
new ideas and challenges concerning the development of the former
European colonies in Africa, Asia and Latin America in the neoliberal era.

The experiment with capitalist development in these countries continues to fail as evidenced by the persistence of poverty in them. However,
the global institutions in the control of the different types of capital subsumed under neoliberal capitalism currently dominated by financial capital insist on formulating and implementing new policies to bring social
and economic development to the developing nations. These new policies
nonetheless are really designed to reshape the form of capitalism in the
developing countries to bring it in line with the dominant ideas of the
financial capitalists.

As former colonies the developing countries were ravaged by mercantile and industrial capitalisms. Their economies are structured within an
international division of labor such that they feed low-priced raw materials into the developed countries and consume the high-priced commodities manufactured from those raw materials. Now, in the era of neoliberal
globalization, the economies of the developing countries are being
restructured to allow financial capital to operate freely in them, as did
mercantile and industrial capital.

The essence of the neoliberal reforms therefore is to allow the capitalist
system albeit neoliberal capitalism to continue to extract the greatest
profit from the reformed system of production, exchange and speculation
by operating at the lowest possible cost. The reforms, therefore, are merely
in form, which means that the global institutions are bent on restructuring the way the capitalist system is organized to extract profit based on the
dominant ideas of financial capital rather than on transforming the capitalist system.

The unabated experimentation with capitalist development in the
developing countries currently takes the form of the Millennium Declaration signed by 189 countries in September 2000, which consists of
eight goals and 18 specific targets. The Millennium Development Goals
(MDGs) embraced by the global community are currently the guiding
principles for the socio-economic development of the developing countries. The MDGs seek to eradicate poverty, and to improve the welfare of
the people in the developing states.

Ban Ki-Moon, the General Secretary of the United Nations puts it this
way in his foreword to *The Millennium Development Goals Report 2011*,

"Since they were first adopted, the Millennium Development Goals (MDGs) have raised awareness and shaped a broad vision that remains the overarching framework for the development activities of the United Nations."[2] The MDGs have also become a strategic framework of reference for international development agencies.[3] But, it was only a few years after the global elites formulated the MDGs that they claimed that they had made a major omission – the exclusion of migration.

Why did the global elites considered it a serious problem that they omitted to discuss the implications of migration for the MDGs? They claim that at the time of the formulation of the MDGs migration was not on the global scene, meaning that the development impact of migration was not a primary consideration of neoliberal capitalism. Thus, five years later in 2005 when they broached the issue of migration and the MDGs at an international meeting, migration had emerged on the global scene as an issue worthy of their consideration. It is clear however that the view that migration was not on the global scene in 2000 is not consistent with the historical facts.

Migration was on the global scene long before 2005, as evidenced by the literature on migration and development. As we have observed in chapter two, the global significance of migration was attracted by a variety of theoretical traditions including classical, neoclassical and Keynesian economic theory in the 19th and 20th centuries. While, for example, the neoclassical model subjected migration to static equilibrium analysis in domestic and international labor markets, development economics has focused its attention on the relationship between migration and development.

The real reason why the neoliberal capitalists were forced to forge a link between migration and the MDGs is to ensure that the ideas of neoliberal capitalism permeates every facet of the material organization of society. This means that the debate on migration must also be subjected to the dominant ideas of the financial capitalists. The linking of migration and the MDGs is another neoliberal strategy that makes it easier for the global elites to implement neoliberal policies in the developing countries. The MDGs and migration theory both of which are founded on neoliberal principles, when combined will deliver a heavier dose of neoliberalism

---

[2] United Nations. (2011). Millennium Development Goals (MDGs) Report 2011, United Nations, New York.

[3] International Office for Migration. Migration and the Millennium Development Goals (MDGs) Facts and Myths. http://www.belgium.iom.int/InternationalConference/documents/issue%20papers%20final/Session%201%20-%20Migration%20and%20MDGs.pdf.

on the developing countries. Thus, by implementing the MDGs and migration policies the developing states will eventually surrender control of their economies and societies to the dictates of financial capitalism.

Global agencies such as the World Bank, the United Nations Development Program (UNDP), and the International Organization for Migration (IOM) among others emphasize the significance of the linkages between migration and the MDGs. However, in the Millennium Development Goals (MDGs) Report 2011, surprisingly, there is not a single reference to migration in the achievement or non-achievement of the MDGs. The Millennium Development Goals (MDGs) Report 2011 merely gives a big pat on the back of the agencies involved with the MDGs. It is loud in its praise for the work done by these agencies and the actual levels of progress made by the developing countries towards their achievements of the MDGs.

The summary achievements of the MDGs are stated in the MDGs Report 2011 as follows

> Poverty continues to decline in many countries and regions... Some of the poorest countries have made the greatest strides in education... Targeted interventions have succeeded in reducing child mortality... Increased funding and control efforts have cut deaths from malaria... Investments in preventing and treating HIV are yielding results... Effective strategies against tuberculosis are saving millions of lives... Every region has made progress in improving access to clean drinking water... The poorest children have made the slowest progress in terms of improved nutrition... Opportunities for full and productive employment remain particularly slim for women... Being poor, female or living in a conflict zone increases the probability that a child will be out of school... Advances in sanitation often bypass the poor and those living in rural areas... Improving the lives of a growing number of urban poor remains a monumental challenge... [and] Progress has been uneven in improving access to safe drinking water.[4]

The obvious problem with this approach is that it does not really cut to the chase of the material conditions of human existence in the developing world. It is merely a litany of empirical facts without any reference to the class dynamics and power configurations in the developing regions that produced those facts. Knowing that malaria deaths have been cut does not tell us why there are malaria deaths in the first place. It will never be discerned from those facts that the organization of production in the developing countries and the social relations that derive from them are the driving forces behind the problems identified for solution by the MDGs.

---

[4] United Nations. (2011). Millennium Development Goals (MDGs) Report 2011, United Nations, New York.

But, merely setting targets to reduce the volume of those problems such as we see in the above quote, is not a real solution, because the material conditions that generate them will continue to exist unabated.

Combining migration and the MDGs has more to do with the consolidation of neoliberal economic, political and social policies for the developing countries. While the MDGs are a unified group of specific policies aimed at precise treatment of the developing countries in specified areas, migration policies were not as integrated. By its incorporation into the MDGs, migration could now be fashioned into the neoliberal capitalist development scheme for the developing countries.

The MDGs must not be confused with the need for genuine alternative development in the developing countries. They are merely targets that seek to bring the former colonies subjected to imperialist exploitation up to similar standards in specified socio-economic areas like health, education, sanitation, etc., to make them become more like the advanced capitalist states. But, there has been a series of such policies in the past, such as "growth with equity," and the first and second development decades to name a few. These were spearheaded by the rich capitalist countries with the failed goal of bringing about the socio-economic development of the former European colonies. The development policies have been couched within the theoretical frameworks of free trade and mercantilism, a pre-industrial capitalist trade system organized by European city- and nation-states enforced by their naval and military power. The end-result of these policies, however, is that the gap between the rich and poor countries has widened.

It is doubtful that the MDGs will break that cycle of pauperization of the developing countries through international development policies intended to help them develop. The rich countries do not remain static as international development policies are implemented in the developing countries. The developed countries too get something out of the deal. And what they get is more of what they already have, wealth, as poverty is dispensed to the poor. The MDGs therefore are about strengthening the capitalist system that is the cause of the very economic, social and political problems that they seek to reverse in the developing countries.

As the end period of the MDGs 2015 approaches, however, it is a good time to assess the initiative, and the debate on its relationship with migration, while pondering the dilemma of the developing countries in a post-MDGs globe. Undeniably, the socio-economic conditions in the developing countries will remain basically the same in the post-MDGs globe as they were, before and during the period of the MDGs.

Genuine change for the better in the conditions of the poor in the developing countries will only take place with the appropriate forms of alternative development that the poor lead themselves. There should be no illusion that neoliberal policies on development and migration spearheaded by the IMF and World Bank will lead poor people out of their misery. Those policies are really designed to serve the interest of the neoliberal capitalist, who will remain their principal beneficiaries.

Description of the Millennium Development Goals

The Millennium Declaration contains 8 goals and 18 targets, which are complemented by 48 technical indicators. The technical indicators are to measure the progress that the developing countries make towards achieving the Millennium Development Goals. These indicators were adopted by consensus by a group of experts drawn from the United Nations, the International Monetary Fund, the Organization of Economic Cooperation and Development and the World Bank.

The first of the eight goals is to "eradicate extreme hunger and poverty." The first target is to "halve between 1990 and 2015 the proportion of people whose income is less than $1 a day." The three indicators identified by the World Bank to measure progress towards this target are the proportion of the population below $1 (1993 PPP) per day; the poverty gap ratio (incidence x depth of poverty); and the share of poorest quintile in national consumption.

The second target is to "halve, between 1990 and 2015, the proportion of people who suffer from hunger." The United Nations Children Fund-World Health Organization (UNICEF-WHO) and the Food and Agricultural Organization (FAO) provide the indicators for this target. Respectively, they are the "prevalence of underweight children under five years of age," and the "proportion of population below minimum level of dietary energy consumption."

The second goal is to "achieve universal primary education," with the target to "ensure that, by 2015, children everywhere, boys and girls alike, will be able to complete a full course of primary schooling." The United Nations Educational, Scientific and Cultural Organization (UNESCO), has formulated three indicators for this goal. These are the "Net enrolment ratio in primary education; Proportion of pupils starting grade 1 who reach grade 5; and Literacy rate of 15–24 year-olds."

Goal 3 of the MDGs is to "promote gender equality and empower women," with the specific target to "eliminate gender disparity in primary and secondary education, preferably by 2005, and in all levels of education no later than 2015." The UNESCO indicators in this connection are the "Ratio of girls to boys in primary, secondary and tertiary education," and the "Ratio of literate women to men, 15–24 years old." The International Labor Organization (ILO) and the Inter-Parliamentary Union (IPU) indicators, respectively, are the "share of women in wage employment in the non-agricultural sector," and the "proportion of seats held by women in national parliament."

The fourth goal is to "reduce child mortality," with the specific target to "reduce by two-thirds, between 1990 and 2015, the under-five mortality rate." The UNICEF-WHO, have identified three indicators for this goal "under-five mortality rate; infant mortality rate; and proportion of 1 year-old children immunized against measles." Goal 5 is to "improve maternal health," which has the specific target to "reduce by three-quarters, between 1990 and 2015, the maternal mortality ratio." The indicators identified by the UNICEF-WHO in this connection are the "maternal mortality ratio," and the "proportion of births attended by skilled health personnel."

Goal 6 is to "combat HIV/AIDS, malaria and other diseases," with the specific targets first to halt by 2015 and to begin "to reverse the spread of HIV/AIDS," and second to halt by 2015 and to begin "to reverse the incidence of malaria and other major diseases." The indicators of the first target of Goal 6 formulated by the Joint United Nations Program on HIV/AIDS (UNAIDS)-WHO-UNICEF are "HIV prevalence among pregnant women aged 15–24 years," and the "ratio of school attendance of orphans to school attendance of non-orphans aged 10–14 years."

The UN Population Division has identified "Condom use rate of the contraceptive prevalence rate" as an indicator, which has three sub-indicators "condom use at last high-risk sex (UNICEF-WHO);" the "Percentage of population aged 15–24 years with comprehensive correct knowledge of HIV/AIDS (UNICEF-WHO);" and the "Contraceptive prevalence rate (UN Population Division)." The indicators identified by the WHO for the second target are the "prevalence and death rates associated with malaria;" the "prevalence and death rates associated with tuberculosis; and the "proportion of tuberculosis cases detected and cured under" the directly observed treatment, short-course (DOTS) an internationally recommended TB control strategy. The UNICEF-WHO indicator is the "proportion of population in malaria-risk areas using effective malaria prevention and treatment measures."

Goal 7 is to "ensure environmental sustainability," which has three targets. The first target is to "integrate the principles of sustainable development into country policies and programs and reverse the loss of environmental resources." The indicators associated with this target are first the "proportion of land area covered by forest" to be monitored by the FAO. The second indicator is the "ratio of area protected to maintain biological diversity to surface area" to be monitored by the United Nations Environment Program (UNEP)-World Conservation Monitoring Center (WCMC). The third indicator is "energy use (kg oil equivalent) per $1 Gross Domestic Product (GDP) Purchasing Power Parity (PPP), which the International Energy Association (IEA) and World Bank overseers.

The fourth indicator embraces "carbon dioxide emissions per capita" monitored by the United Nations Framework Convention on Climate Change (UNFCCC), and the United Nations Statistics Division (UNSD). Also, it involves consumption of ozone-depleting Chlorofluorocarbons (CFCs) (Ozone Depletion Potential (ODP) tons), monitored by the UNEP-Ozone Secretariat; and the "proportion of population using solid fuels" which the WHO overseers.

The second target for Goal 7 is to "halve, by 2015, the proportion of people without sustainable access to safe drinking water and basic sanitation." There are two indicators for this target. The first is the "proportion of population with sustainable access to an improved water source, urban and rural," which the UNICEF and WHO overseers. The second is the "proportion of population with access to improved sanitation, urban and rural" also monitored by the UNICEF and the WHO.

The third target for Goal 7 is to "have achieved by 2020 a significant improvement in the lives of at least 100 million slum dwellers." The indicator for this target is the "proportion of households with access to secure tenure. This is monitored by the United Nations and Habitat for Humanity.

Finally, Goal 8 of the MDGs is to "develop a global partnership for development." This goal has seven targets the first being to develop a trading and financial system that is more "open rule-based, predictable, nondiscriminatory." This means that both nationally and internationally, there must be "a commitment to good governance, development, and poverty reduction." The second target addresses the special needs of the Least Developed Countries. These are with respect to issues such as their tariff- and quota-free access in developed markets, and exports. They also include "enhanced program of debt relief for heavily indebted poor countries" (HIPCs), and "cancellation of official bilateral debt." Furthermore, they include "more generous official development assistance for countries committed to poverty reduction."

The third target is to "address the special needs of landlocked developing countries and Small Island Developing States (SIDS). The intention here is to do this "through the Program of Action for the Sustainable Development of Small Island Developing States and 22nd General Assembly provisions." The fourth target is to "deal comprehensively with the debt problems of developing countries through national and international measures in order to make debt sustainable in the long term."

Several corresponding indicators under the general rubric of Official Development Assistance (ODA) were identified for these targets. The first indicator is "net ODA, total and to LDCs, as a percentage of OECD/ Development Assistance Committee (DAC) donors' gross national income (GNI)," to be monitored by the OECD. The OECD will also monitor the second indicator, which is the "Proportion of total bilateral, sector-allocable ODA of OECD/DAC donors to basic social services (basic education, primary health care, nutrition, safe water and sanitation)." The other indicators concerning ODAs, which are all monitored by the OECD, have to do with the "Proportion of bilateral ODA of OECD/DAC donors that is untied; ODA received in landlocked developing countries as a proportion of their GNIs; [and] ODA received in small-island developing States as proportion of their GNIs."

There is another set of indicators that fall under the rubric of "market access." The first is the "Proportion of total developed country imports (by value and excluding arms) from developing countries and from LDCs, admitted free of duty." The United Nations Conference on Trade and Development (UNCTAD), the WTO, and the World Bank are the monitors of this indicator. They will also monitor the "Average tariffs imposed by developed countries on agricultural products and textiles and clothing from developing countries." The OECD and WTO will monitor the "Proportion of ODA provided to help build trade capacity," and the former will overseer "Agricultural support estimate for OECD countries as percentage of their GDP."

A third set of indicators falls under the rubric of "debt sustainability," which the IMF and World Bank monitor. The first is the "Total number of countries that have reached their Heavily Indebted Poor Countries Initiative (HIPC) decision points and number that have reached their HIPC completion points (cumulative)." The second is "Debt relief committed under HIPC initiative," and third "Debt service as a percentage of exports of goods and services."

The fifth target under Goal 8 is stated as follows: "In cooperation with developing countries, develop and implement strategies for decent and productive work for youth." The International Labor Organization (ILO) will monitor the indicator in this connection, which is "Unemployment rate of young people aged 15–24 years, each sex and total."

The sixth target for Goal 8 is stated as "In cooperation with pharmaceutical companies, provide access to affordable essential drugs in developing countries," with its indicator being the "Proportion of population with access to affordable essential drugs on a sustainable basis," to be monitored by the WHO.

The seventh target for Goal 8 is stated as "In cooperation with the private sector, make available the benefits of new technologies, especially information and communications technologies." The two indicators in this connection are both monitored by the International Telecommunication Union" (ITU). The first is "Telephone lines and cellular subscribers per 100 population," while the second is "Personal computers in use per 100 population and Internet users per 100 population."

What is the relationship between these MDGs and migration in the perspective of neoliberal capitalism?

The Impact of Migration on the MDGs

In this section we examine the neoliberal ideas on the impact of migration on the MDGs outlined above. The neoliberal literature has identified migration as a central vehicle through which the Millennium Development Goals could be achieved. The neoliberal view is that "migration can have a direct or indirect impact on all of the MDGs as it is an essential element of the globalization process and represents a livelihood option for many people."[5]

The World Bank (2004) takes the position that migration could help bring to fruition the "core goal" of the MDGs, which is "poverty reduction." In this connection, the World Bank believes that a major concern of the international community should be to facilitate an increase in migration. To this effect the World Bank seeks to improve the development impact of migration by facilitating "research, policy-oriented analysis, communications and lending operations." It has identified several key issues concerning the development impact of migration. These are remittances, the temporary movement of workers and the General Agreement on Trade in Services (GATS), ties to the diaspora, coping with the emigration of highly skilled persons, and the protection of migrants (World Bank 2004). Also the World Bank has identified the activities it is likely to undertake to address these issues.

---

[5] International Organization for Migration. Migration and the Millennium Development Goals (MDGs) Facts and Myths. http://www.belgium.iom.int/InternationalConference/

With respect to the linkages between the MDG 1 and its targets and migration the IOM (2005),[6] is of the view that migration could be both the cause and effect of poverty. Also it believes that poverty could be stimulated or reduced by migration depending on the situation in which migrants find themselves. According to the IOM, tough economic and social conditions stimulate migration, which "plays a significant role in the livelihood strategies of the poor throughout the developing world." The IOM (2005) argues that poverty and vulnerability have two conflicting effects on migration. They provide both an incentive for migration, and also simultaneously reduce the movement of person due to the high transfer costs involved. According to the IOM (2005), "Empirical evidence demonstrates that an increase in international migration can be positively linked to a decline of people living in poverty."

Furthermore, the relationship between Goal 1 and migration is identified in terms of the problematic concerning the rates of production of skilled professionals and their migration. The view is that skilled professionals from the developing countries migrate at a faster rate than which they could be produced exacerbating the skill shortages in those states. This depletion of skills is a serious challenge that contributes to the prevalence of poverty in the developing countries. But, on the other hand, the IOM (2005) states that the migration of skilled personnel from the developing countries has a positive effect on poverty alleviation in the sending countries. This perceived positive effect is thereby identified as a contributing factor towards the achievement of MDG 1. For example, Diasporas are said to have contributed significantly to the economic development of the Asian countries. They are considered to have helped to "establish close economic and political links between countries of origin and of destination," such as in the software industry in India.

It is believed however that "the real contribution to development depends on the extent of remittances sent by the migrants, on the skills they acquire whilst overseas and on whether they eventually return to their home country" (IOM 2005). Remittances and Diaspora involvement in investment, skills and knowledge transfer are therefore the areas in which migration is said to have the greatest impact on development. According to the IOM (2005) "The most direct link between migration and poverty reduction is through remittances – the funds migrants send home."

---

documents/issue%20papers%20final/Session%201%20-%20Migration%20and%20MDGs.pdf.

[6] International Organization for Migration. (2005). The Millennium Development Goals and Migration, IOM Migration Research Series, No. 20, Geneva, Switzerland.

Through Diaspora involvement migrant communities abroad are said to engage financially with their countries of origin, as well as help to "foster innovation, trigger learning processes or facilitate the transfer of knowledge and technology to their countries of origin." Furthermore, migrant communities are said to help "in developing new markets and creating trade links between the sending and the receiving country."

Migration is said to have an impact on the third MDG and its targets in two principal ways. First, it is believed that "migration can contribute to the empowerment of women, thereby helping to promote gender equality." Second, on the other hand "particular migration situations can pose a challenge to gender equality."

According to the IOM (2005) these two contradictory impacts of migration on Goal 3 of the MDGs is specially the case since about half of the world's migrants today are women. Women are said to be migrating on their own independently as heads of households and not just following their husbands and families as "dependents," as was the case in the past. The belief is that this has led "to greater independence and autonomy of women by increasing the proportion of women in paid employment situations." The deduction is that with more migrant women in paid employment, their potential to contribute to the attainment of Goal 3 will be enhanced.

Also, in the view of the IOM (2005), the migration of women leads to "heightened self-esteem associated with employment, education and knowledge that can render female migrants more powerful in their host and home communities." This assessment is highly problematic because it implies that women in the developing countries have low self-esteem. It conveys a disturbing impression about the cultures of the peoples in the developing world. It infers that these women have low-self esteem due to the backwardness of their cultures. The reverse is that the women in the rich capitalist countries have high self-esteem because they are employed, educated and knowledgeable. Also, to improve their self-esteem, women from the developing states must migrate to the rich countries. The IOM's assessment on the self-esteem of women from the developing countries makes no sense and borders on the discredited perspective, which blames people's cultures rather than capitalist exploitation for their poverty.

The view held by the IOM nonetheless is that the empowerment of women through migration "will effect subsequent generations, providing children with different female role models and helping to influence ratios of girls to boys in primary, secondary and tertiary education." This is all about the habituation of women to the capitalist labor process for their most efficient exploitation as migrants in the developed countries. The IOM argues however that simultaneously, with these positive effects, women and men who migrate independently of their families "can contribute to the disruption of traditional family relations and social systems in the countries of origin in ways which are only beginning to be understood."

Considering some other negative consequences the IOM observed that, "migration still holds more dangers for women than men." This is due to the assessment that "Women are more vulnerable to deprivation, hardship, discrimination and physical, sexual and verbal abuse when travelling and more likely to fall prey to human trafficking and exploitation." Another factor compounding the difficulties for women is that "upon arrival in the country of destination, a female migrant in a situation of relative dependency may face greater difficulty with regard to integration than a male migrant."

Also, the IOM believes that there is a "higher degree of marginalization of women migrants in the host country," due to "psychosocial pressures and divergent sets of cultural expectations." Women are often faced with double discrimination in the labor market because they are "both female and foreign." Because of this they "may have even more limited access to employment, social security and health programs than male migrants." In addition, "legally, many migrant women are vulnerable if their legal residence is tied to their relationship with a citizen or a 'primary migrant' " (IOM 2005: 19).

According to the IOM (2005), Goal 6 of the MDGs is interlinked with migration in two important ways, and besides, three of the MDGs focus on global health as a means to alleviate poverty. The first interlink between migration and Goal 6 is that "migrants are particularly vulnerable to health risks," during their travels and on arrival in destination countries. Public health programs, which should take into consideration the situation of migrants, do not. The corollary is that there is an increasing vulnerability to "the spread of infectious diseases, such as HIV/AIDS." The second health impact of migration albeit on the negative side is identified as "the emigration of health workers from developing countries," which "has become a major impediment to the functioning of some national healthcare systems."

Migration is acknowledged by the IOM as having a significant impact on Goal 7 of the MDGs on environmental sustainability. The achievement of this goal is considered a major challenge in the light of the existence of internally displaced persons (IDPs), refugees, and migration to urban

centers. According to the IOM (2005) camps to accommodate refugees
and internally displaced persons have a negative impact on local ecosys-
tems through "the depletion and deterioration of the areas in which camps
are located." This is associated with "the high demand for wood in order to
build shelters and cook food," building infrastructures, and poor access to
safe water and sanitation, which ultimately leads to "the outbreak and
spread of epidemics and diseases." The IOM (2005) believes "Environmental
degradation can also be the cause, rather than the effect, of the migration
of a large number of people." The examples provided in support of this
view are "environmental catastrophes, land degradation and drought."

Slum dwellers are reportedly on the increase globally as rural-urban
migration remains a vital strategy for individuals to improve their livelihoods. According to the IOM, this fact displays an important link between
migration and Goal 7 whose target is to improve the lives of slum dwellers.
Urbanization is considered alongside slum dwellers in that more than
50 percent of the world's population live in urban centers. Migration is a
major source of urban growth and it creates great pressure on infrastructure, access to safe water, sanitation, employment and the provision of
social services in the urban areas.

Urban growth increases the "demand for water and sanitation services,
transport and energy consumption" and pushes "the city limits further
into the surrounding areas." This situation contributes to environmental
degradation as people eke out a living in overcrowded urban centers.
However, rural-urban migration does have positive aspects as slums are
understood to be "areas in transition which ease the integration process of
migrants."

Linkages have also been identified between migration and Goal 8 of the
MDGs on the establishment of a global partnership for development and
its targets. The assessment here is that the target to develop further open
rule based trading and financial systems impacts on migration in two
important areas. In the first instance, there is "the issue of transfer costs
for remittances." These costs were as high as "20 per cent of the transferred
money." The neoliberal goal is to establish urgently "effective legal channels for the transfer of these financial flows at reduced cost." This should
be done "within the development of a non-discriminatory and predictable
financing system."

The second linkage identified here concerns the liberalization of trade
in goods, capital and some services. However, as liberalization of trade in
goods and capital markets have moved apace, "the movement of persons
to provide services, pursuant to Mode 4 of the General Agreement on

Trade in Services (GATS), has not kept up the pace." This situation reflects a negative dimension of the linkage between migration and Goal 8 of the MDGs.

The neoliberal views on the linkages between migration and the MDGs are constrained by a number of factors discussed below.

Migration and the Limitations of the MDGs

What is the relationship between the Millennium Development Goals and migration in the light of the weaknesses of the MDGs? Much of the debate on the impact of migration on the MDGs takes place in the shadow of the limitations of the MDGs. The energy driving the debate is concentrated on establishing the central avenues through which migration contributes towards and takes away from the achievement of the Millennium Development Goals. The futility and or problems of the MDGs never come into question in this debate. Do the limitations of the MDGs have anything to do with the way in which the MDGs are impacted by migration?

The proposition here is that understanding the impact of migration on the MDGs are primarily to provide the global elites with the necessary information to formulate socio-economic policies to increase the efficiency with which neoliberal capitalism dominated by financial capital extracts the economic surplus from global migration processes under the current imperialist model of capital accumulation. From this vantage point, we propose to examine the neoliberal propositions on the impact of migration on the MDGs and targets and to consider the limitations of the MDGs, which render the proposals on the development impact of migration on the MDGs problematic.

The proponents of the neoliberal ideas on the linkages between the MDGs and migration do not consider how the limitations of the MDGs would alter the associations between the two they have identified above. What are some of the most prominent limitations of the MDGs that would have an impact on the linkages identified between migration and the MDGs?

Amir Attaran (2005)[7] observed that, "many of the most important MDGs, including those to reduce malaria, maternal mortality, or tuberculosis

---

[7] Amir Attaran. (2005). An Immeasurable Crisis? A Criticism of the Millennium Development Goals and Why They Cannot Be Measured, *PloS Medicine* Volume 2, Issue 10 e318 pp 0955–0961. Also, see Sanjay Reddy and Antoine Heuty. (2004). Achieving the MDGs: A CRITIQUE AND A STRATEGY August 12th, on the unreliability of the data used to assess the MDGs.

(TB), suffer from a worrying lack of scientifically valid data." Attaran (2005) noted that, "While progress on each of these goals is portrayed in time-limited and measurable terms, often the subject matter is so immeasurable, or the measurements are so inadequate, that one cannot know the baseline condition before the MDGs, or know if the desired trend of improvement is actually occurring."

What are the implications of this for the linkage between migration and Goal 6 of the MDGs on health? In the absence of scientifically determined data there is no real way for the neoliberal proponents of the MDGs and the development impact of migration to know the true relationship between migration and the MDGs, with respect to health. The recommended policies based on the pretentious scientific data generated in this connection are doomed to fail and waste taxpayers' money, while enriching the burgeoning global neoliberal elites parading as "experts" on migration and the MDGs.

Second, the MDGs are linked to World Bank and IMF liberalization prescriptions that have wreaked havoc in the developing countries. However, as the saying goes "the chicken finally came home to roost" when the very policies led to the great recession in 2008, evidenced by the most dramatic and deepest financial meltdown in the Euro-American capitalist empire in the post-great depression era. The meteoric rise in poverty in both the developed and developing worlds under the hegemony of neoliberal globalization, simultaneously with increasing income inequalities within countries, and between the developed and developing states, shatters any illusion about the impact of migration on the achievement of the MDGs. "Income and wealth inequality have also increased in most countries, as have inequalities based on gender, ethnicity and region" (UNRISD 2010).

Migration and the MDGs are both said to alleviate poverty, but the neoliberal globalization policies promoted by the World Bank and IMF have stimulated poverty and income inequality, and it is these very institutions that are urging migration and MDGs measures as integral components of their tool kits. The policy prescriptions of IMF and World Bank on migration and the MDGs to stimulate development in the poor states are going around in circles "like a dog trying to catch its tail."

Third, the MDGs are top-down formulated by the rich countries for the poor in the same manner as the prescriptions on the development impact of migration. According to Davis (2009), the MDGs originated in "a series of international agreements on the most pressing needs of the developing world" reached by a number of key international organizations in the 1990s. The organization that reached these agreements were the World Summit for Children in 1990, the International Conference on Population and Development at Cairo in 1994, the World Summit on Social Development at Copenhagen in 1995, and the 4th World Conference on Women in Beijing in 1995.

According to Davis (2009), "These were brought together as a set of objectives in the Development Assistance Committee (DAC) of the OECD's International Development Targets in 1996, before being reiterated by the UN, with some alteration, as the MDGs in 2000."[8] This means that the migrants are not the ones who are driving migration and development policy in their self-interest and in the interest of the sending countries. It is the global elites in the service of neoliberal globalization, who are doing so. Thus, it is the interest of neoliberal capitalism that is being served by this top-down approach to the MDGs and migration, and the relationship between them.

A fourth issue is that the targets and indicators of the MDGs and the proposed development outcomes of migration tend to ignore quality concerns, such as in education and gender equality for example, by privileging school enrollment and arguing that migration could enhance women's status. The quality of education that children receive, as well as that of women migrants is underplayed, in favor of increasing enrollment and women migrants' labor-market participation,[9] as emphasized in the neoliberal approach. Thus, neoliberalism could boast about the increase in the number of children who have enrolled in schools, under its hegemony, although the quality of the education is highly questionable. Neoliberal capitalism celebrates itself with the claim that women are better off under its dispensation in that more of them are migrating independently of their families and joining the labor force. This is said to be fostering gender equality, but the disruption it causes to family life and the poor and unequal conditions under which these women survive undoubtedly takes a heavy toll on them.

---

[8] Thomas W D Davis. (2009). "The MDGs and the Incomplete Relationship between Development and Foreign Aid," Paper presented to the "Meeting the Millennium Development Goals: Old Problems, New Challenges" Conference 30 November-1 December, Institute for Human Security Latrobe University.

[9] See Bibek Debroy. (2011). What will happen to the MDGs? *Indian Express.Com* April 6 for a critique of the MDGs and concerning the sidelining of the quality of education in favor of enrollment.

Fifth, perhaps the most telling blow against the MDGs is the view that they obfuscate the causes of poverty, fail to say why it persists, and do not bring the poor countries closer to eradicating their problems (Sogge 2010).[10] Migration, it seems, is just thrown into the mix to determine how it might stimulate or hinder the achievement of the MDGs, which already does very little about poverty eradication. The United Nations Research Institute for Social Development (UNRISD) (2010) argues from an in-house critical perspective that, "current approaches to poverty often ignore its root causes, and consequently do not follow through the causal sequence," but that they merely "focus on measuring things that people lack to the detriment of understanding why they lack them."[11]

The UNRISD (2010), advocates a different approach to fight poverty to those of the IMF and World Bank-led Poverty Reduction Strategy Papers (PRSPs), targeted poverty reduction and social protection programs, and the UN–led Millennium Development Goals (MDGs). The UNRISD (2010) claims that its "approach contrasts with contemporary efforts to reduce poverty through discrete social policies that are often weakly related to a country's system of production or macroeconomic policies." Instead, the UNRISD (2010) "calls for comprehensive social policies that are grounded in universal rights and that support structural change, social cohesion and democratic politics." In its view, its approach to fight poverty "makes the case for civic rights, activism and political arrangements that ensure that states are responsive to the needs of citizens and that the poor have influence in how policies are shaped."[12]

The view that the MDGs do not tell much about the causes of poverty and how to eradicate them, throws a big spanner in the works, concerning the debate on the impact of migration on the MDGs. How could one determine whether or not migration alleviates or stimulates poverty if the cause of poverty is unknown? This is the conundrum in which neoliberal theory on migration and development finds itself. This riddle causes us to question the very usefulness of the neoliberal struggle to identify the impact of migration on the MDGs, and to provide the policy framework to address them. It is clearly a waste of resources to expend money in the dark like that, rather than to put it to better use, to genuinely help poor people.

---

[10] David Sogge. (2010). Millennium Development Goals for the Rich? Transnational Institute (TNI), September.

[11] UNRISD. (2010). Combating Poverty and Inequality: Structural Change, Social Policy and Politics, Geneva, Switzerland, UNRISD/2010/4.

[12] UNRISD. (2010). Combating Poverty and Inequality: Structural Change, Social Policy and Politics, Geneva, Switzerland, UNRISD/2010/4.

Sixth, because of the stranglehold that the IMF has over socio-economic policy in the developing countries the governments in these states pay no real attention to the MDGs in the preparation of their budgets, but focus instead on IMF conditionalities.[13] Thus, the IMF and the national governments do not take the MDGs seriously. This reveals a serious in-house conflict between different branches of the same organization in the control of neoliberal elites. The UN leads the way on the MDGs, but the IMF is a branch of the UN. Indeed, Hulme (2009)[14] reported that, in an interview with an IMF official the person said, "we mention the MDGs in the introduction of reports but they don't change anything" and that, "the MDGs are European social policy and the IMF does not do European social policy."

Seventh, donors also do not take the MDGs seriously since according to Sogge (2010), "they have yet to put more money where their mouths are." Indeed, "Donor spending in the four aid priority sectors in MDG number eight – basic education, basic health, nutrition and water/sanitation" has hardly changed (Sogge 2010). A part of the problem is that donor contributions are voluntary and cannot be enforced politically or legally, and "aid recipients have to toe the donor line, or face unpleasant consequences."

On close examination of aid nonetheless, it is unquestionable that the poor countries are aiding the rich states. Sogge (2010) noted that, "For certain interests in rich countries, results of these policies have been hugely rewarding," if we follow the money. Sogge (2010) pointed out that, "Especially since the late 1990s, most global flows, after netting out foreign aid, foreign direct investment and remittances, have gone from poor to rich." This point is summarized in Table 1 on the yearly average net transfers of financial resources to low-income world regions between 2000 and 2008.

Finally, the Third World Network (2010)[15] has identified a number of well-argued limitations of the MDGs that are worth mentioning in the context of our critical analysis of the impact of migration on the MDGs. The first point is that "there is a fundamental mismatch between the

---

[13] David Sogge. (2010). Millennium Development Goals for the Rich? Transnational Institute (TNI), September.

[14] David Hulme. (2009). Governing Global Poverty? Global Ambivalence and the Millennium Development Goals," Brooks World Poverty Institute, and Institute for Development Policy and Management University of Manchester, May 6.

[15] Third World Network. (2010). Achieving the Millennium Development Goals (MDGs) Requires Fundamental Reforms in the International Financial Architecture, TWN Info Service on Finance and Development, June 15.

Table 1. Yearly Average Net Transfers of Financial Resources to Lower-income World Regions 2000–2008

Africa	(negative) -$50 billion
East and South Asia	(negative) -$239 billion
Western Asia	(negative) -$105 billion
Latin America & Caribbean	(negative) -$65 billion
Transition Economies (mainly former East Bloc	(negative) -$75 billion
Total	(negative) -$534 billion

Source: David Sogge. (2010). Millennium Development Goals for the Rich? Transnational Institute (TNI), September, compiled from data drawn from UN-DESA, 2010, World Economic Situation and Prospects 2010, New York: UN Department of Economic and Social Affairs, Table III.1, p. 73; IMF, World Economic Outlook Database, October 2009; and IMF, Balance of Payments Statistics.

ambitious framework of the MDG targets and the predominant economic model in many developing countries, including the least developed countries (LDCs)" (TWN, 2010). This is due to the fact that the "developing countries have not had the national policy space, market and technology access, and symmetry of rules required in the international economic architecture to be able to pursue a development-oriented national strategy" (TWN, 2010).

The developing countries are embroiled in the financial and trade liberalization agenda of the neoliberal economic model. This agenda has resulted in "a serious lack of public investments and spending that scale up productive capacities through strategic economic diversification and employment-creation, and through the development of public social services in health, education, and housing" (TWN, 2010). The Third World Network (2010) came to the conclusion that the disjuncture between the MDGs targets and the neoliberal economic model "highlights the underlying need to lay out a conceptual and analytical basis for new MDG-based national development strategies, not just indicators, for post-2015." In its view, however, the main challenge in this connection "is not the lack of explicitly economic goals in the MDG framework, but rather the challenge of formulating a policy strategy, in the context of an imbalanced global financial and trade system, that would back up the human-development ambitions of the MDG framework" (TWN, 2010).

Second, the TWN (2010) has identified three key areas in which the international financial architecture impedes the MDGs. First, it is stated that, "the pro-cyclical and deflationary macroeconomic framework that has dominated policymaking both globally and nationally" focuses primarily on macro-stability. This means that, "IMF loans to crisis-stricken countries across the world still, as in the past, carry fiscal and monetary conditions for fiscal austerity, monetary policy tightening, and a prioritization on debt repayment and maintaining open capital accounts." The focus on macro-economic stability "predominantly serves creditors, investors, and markets." Moreover, this is "often at the expense of development-oriented macroeconomic policies that allow for consistent and scaled-up public spending, access to credit, and long-term investments in public services and production sectors across agriculture, industry, and services."

The second limitation of the international financial architecture that hinders the MDGs "is that of debt sustainability in developing countries and the palpable absence of an international debt resolution mechanism able to guarantee a speedy and fair solution to sovereign debt crises." The debt burdens and "debt overhang" in the developing countries "has persisted over many decades as result of the liberalization- and deregulation-led economic model that promotes borrowing as a source for capital." The consequence of this is that, "foreign exchange earnings are funneled into external debt servicing obligations." Whereas, these earnings should go "to the current account for key imports payments necessary for building the domestic economy or to public investments vital to strengthen the health and education sectors."

The third obstacle "is that of capital account, or financial, liberalization which allows for the free cross-border mobility of capital, and the liberalization of financial services." Capital account liberalization is "one of the key drivers of recurring financial and currency crises." This is because "financial liberalization enables speculative trading, capital inflow surges, and 'panic exits' of capital, which are some of the root causes behind financial crises."

What would the neoliberal elites who seek to determine the impacts that migration has on the MDGs have to say about these particular limitations of the MDGs? Would they alter their views on the relationship between migration and the MDGs in the light of these limitations? The limitations of the MDGs are well documented, but still the neoliberal elites consider it an omission not to include migration in the discussion on the MDGs without even considering these drawbacks. Although the MDGs do not address the real causes of the global asymmetries that condemn the vast majority of humans to conditions of poverty and its attendant problems, the neoliberal view is that migration policy must be fashioned as an instrument for the achievement of these highly problematic goals.

Conclusion

The following points are made in conclusion to the neoliberal idea about
the impact of migration on the Millennium Development Goals. First, the
MDGs are currently at the apex of a long list of failed development policies and programs, such as the UN development decades, basic needs, etc.
However, although the resources are there to bring about the achievement
of the MDGs, it is quite apparent that the MDGs will suffer the same fate
as its predecessors that sought to bring piecemeal changes to the human
condition in the developing countries, within the embedded capitalist
system rather than to transform the system.

Second, the problem is that the MDGs are severely constrained but
there is no attempt in the neoliberal literature to understand how migration impacts on the MDGs in the light of these constraints. Third, it is
unlikely that the MDGs and the impact that migration has on them
will break the cycle of failed top-down development approaches foisted
on the former European colonies in Africa, Asia, Latin America, and the
Caribbean.

CHAPTER SEVEN

THE HUMAN DEVELOPMENT IMPACT OF MIGRATION

Introduction

The purpose of this chapter is to critically analyze the inter-relationships between migration and human development under neoliberal globalization spearheaded by financial capital. The principal argument is that in appearance the human development approach promotes migration to redress a wide variety of inequalities that constrains human development, but in reality it stimulates capital accumulation from migration processes. Capital accumulation takes place from both international and internal migration processes.

Migration has been designated by the global elites in the international financial institutions (IFIs) and the relevant global organizations, as a factor that could help to achieve human development by correcting the imbalances in the global distribution of human capabilities. In essence, the argument emanating from these institutions is that migration could be a conduit to reduce global inequalities or alternatively it could increase equality. The human development approach focuses primarily on the factors that reduce inequality and those that hinder equality.

However, the human development approach is disputed on the grounds that although it is a good idea, it does not attack the development problem at its core namely ensuring the transformation of the capitalist power structures that perpetuate global inequalities. Because of this weakness, there will only be cosmetic results from the functions that the human development approach has ascribed to migration, specifically the reduction of inequality or the promotion of equality. In the human development approach, migration is not intended to perform a transformative role under global capitalism. It is merely a variable in a larger scheme to increase capitalist freedoms that is the freedoms for capital to operate unhindered, and the freedom of working people to avail themselves to the capitalist for their exploitation.

The emphasis on freedom in the human development approach is in itself an oxymoron because of the incompatibility of real freedom and capitalism. Freedom under capitalism is merely freedom for the rich, and freedom for the laborer to be flexible to work for any capitalist. The human development approach does not seek to bring about substantial transformation of the global neoliberal capitalist economic order. It merely reinforces the status quo albeit heightening the access of more people to global and domestic economic, political and social resources in the capitalist system.

The designation of migration as a phenomenon to further the objectives of human development therefore is nothing more than the use of migration to maintain the exploitative capitalist power structures facilitating the imperialist-centered model of capital accumulation in the age of neoliberal globalization. How does the human development paradigm buttress the status quo of the global neoliberal economic order? The human development model plays down income accumulation in favor of improving the capabilities of humans. It does not challenge the exploitative methods of capital accumulation by neoliberal capitalism, but seeks to enhance the capabilities of humans to participate in the capitalist development process. Its basic position is that if human capabilities are increased then these individuals would have greater access to their basic needs and other goodies such as participation in politics, recreation, freedom, etc., within the capitalist system.

The analysis on the human development impact of migration commences with a brief discussion on the way human development is theorized in biology, psychology, and development studies. This is followed by a descriptive analysis of the neoliberal views on migration and human development, and the impact of migration on human development. Thereafter, the discussion shifts to the idea that migration serves neoliberal capital as a cost reduction mechanism. The foci here are on migration as a cost saving devise, the financial cost of moving, and cell phones and money transfer costs. The subsequent section engages in a discussion on migration and health. It concentrates specifically on health and low-skilled workers, and the migration of health professionals. Thereafter the analysis shifts to the question of migration and human rights. Finally, there is a critical analysis of the policy reforms identified by the human development approach to enhance the human development impact of migration.

On Theories of Human Development

The idea of human development is theorized in different ways in different academic disciplines. Biology for example, concentrates on human development in terms of the process by which humans become biologically mature beginning with fertilization and moving through different stages thereafter. These stages include birth, adolescence and puberty, adulthood and death. In this case, human development has a beginning, a middle and end, as humans are born, mature and then decline to their death. Thus on the biological human development trajectory every individual looks something like the Laffer curve on the relationship between government revenue raised by taxation and all possible rates of taxation. The Laffer curve begins at zero at the intersection of the X and Y-axes, rises to a maximum point and then falls back to zero on the X-axis.

Developmental psychology on the other hand, studies human development in terms of the systematic psychological changes that occur in humans over the course of their life span from infants and children through adolescence, adulthood, and aging.

The concern in this chapter however is with the human development approach from the perspective of critical development studies. The field of development studies had its beginnings as a sub-discipline of economics, political science and sociology. For several decades it nested within those specialties until its recent emergence and classification as a social science discipline in its own right. In development studies, the human development approach promotes linkages between growth in national income and increases in individual human choices. It emerged from a critique of mainstream socio-economic development theories in the 1980s, as a pretender for an alternative development model to those that have existed in the past. Critical development studies rethinks development theory and practice and the assumptions and beliefs that underlie them, seeing the world as empirically given (Veltmeyer 2010).

Human Development Approach in Development Studies

The human development approach in the field of development studies emerged in the United Nations Development Program (UNDP). It is closely associated with the Human Development Report published yearly by that institution since 1990. The HRD consists of a Human Development Index (HDI), which is a composite statistic that was developed to measure human development. It ranks countries on the bases of "very high," "high," "medium," and "low" human development. The HDI is therefore a comparative measure of life expectance, literacy, education and standards of living for countries worldwide. Academics and policy makers consider the HDI as a yardstick to tell if a country is developed or underdeveloped.

Scholars and policy makers such as Amartya Sen[1] and Mahbub ul Haq[2] among others pioneered the human development approach at the UNDP. Sen is credited with providing the conceptual foundation for an alternative human development approach. This alternative approach is "defined as a process of enlarging people's choices and enhancing human capabilities (the range of things people can be and do)." Also, it is about boosting human "freedoms, enabling them to: live a long and healthy life, have access to knowledge and a decent standard of living, and participate in the life of their community and decisions affecting their lives."[3] It is believed that there are many dimensions to human development relating to the different ways in which humans could enhance their choices, and that "the key or priority parameters of human development can evolve over time and vary both across and within countries."

The proponents of the human development approach have identified seven most central issues and themes in human development.[4] The first is "social progress," which refers to the ideal for individuals to have greater access to knowledge, and better nutrition and health services. The second central issue is in the realm of "economics." The view here is that economic growth is important not merely to accumulate income but to reduce inequality a central indicator of human development. The third set of issues and themes in human development has to do with the efficient use of resources and their availability from a pro-growth and productivity perspective, which "directly benefits the poor, women and other marginalized groups."

Fourth, is that there should be "equity" in "economic growth and other human development parameters." The fifth set of issues that are central to the human development involves measures such as "empowerment, democratic governance, gender equality, civil and political rights, and cultural liberty," to increase people's participation and freedom. It is the "marginalized groups defined by urban-rural, sex, age, religion, ethnicity, physical/

---

[1] The body of work that helped to shape the human development approach includes among others Amartya Sen. (1973). *On Economic Inequality,* New York, Norton, (1982). *Poverty and Famines: An Essay on Entitlements and Deprivation,* Oxford, Clarendon Press, and (1987). *On Ethics and Economics,* Oxford, Basil Blackwell.

[2] Mahbub ul Haq is credited with being the originator of the Human Development Index. He is recognized as the person who provided the intellectual impetus for the World Bank's commitment to poverty reduction in the early 1970s. His works include Mahbub ul Haq. (1976). *The Poverty Curtain: Choices for the Third World,* Columbia University Press; and (1996). *Reflections on Human Development,* Oxford University Press.

[3] Quote taken from http://hdr.undp.org/en/humandev/.

[4] These seven points were obtained from http://hdr.undp.org/en/humandev/.

mental parameters, etc.," for whom increased participation and freedom are seen to be particularly significant.

"Sustainability" in "ecological, economic and social terms" is the sixth central issue for human development as a guarantee for the survival of future generations on planet earth. The final issue/theme is "human security" to ensure that there is "security in daily life against such chronic threats as hunger and abrupt disruptions including joblessness, famine, conflict, etc."

The human development approach is presented as an alternative to "trickle down" theories that depend on capitalist markets to spread development. Also, human development is said to be a response to the high human cost of structural adjustment, and the pervasiveness of social ills consisting of crime, a deteriorating social fabric, HIV/AIDS, pollution, etc., even as some countries recorded consistent economic growth.

The human development approach based on the work of Amartya Sen has arguably shifted development theory "away from approaches that focus exclusively on income, growth and utility." Instead, it emphasizes "individual entitlements, capabilities, freedoms and rights."[5] Development is usually measured in terms of per capita income. Furthermore, food security and poverty were envisioned in terms of food availability and income deprivation, respectively. "Economic efficiency" became a major pursuit of countries bent on redressing the social ills associated with a lack of development.

The emphasis on economic efficiency in the development debate has led to the promotion of market forces over state interventionism. The market mechanism is regarded as the most efficient allocator of scarce economic resources. But Sen (2000) emphasizes however "fundamental freedoms, individual agency and human rights." He advocates that the market or state should be judged in the context of their "value of human ends."

The human development paradigm in the field of development studies focuses on changes in income, and economic growth. But more so it concentrates on the creation of an "environment in which people can develop their full potential and lead productive, creative lives in accordance with their needs and interests." It centers attention on enlarging people's choices to build their capabilities – "the range of things that people can do

---

5 *ODI Briefing Paper.* (2001). "Economic Theory, Freedom and Human Rights: The Work of Amartya Sen," November.

or be in life," and freedoms. Thus, the human development paradigm posits that, "The most basic capabilities for human development are to lead long and healthy lives, to be knowledgeable, to have access to the resources needed for a decent standard of living and to be able to participate in the life of the community.[6]

Without these, many choices are simply not available to marginalized peoples, and many opportunities in life remain inaccessible. The human development model recognizes people as the real wealth of nations. Its basic pillars are "equity, sustainability, production and empowerment." The accumulation of commodities and wealthy are not considered as the purpose and end of development. Although these are important aspects of human development, it is the enhancement of human wellbeing that is the principal concern of the human development paradigm.

A major limitation of the human development approach however is that it too depends on spreading the benefits of capitalism according to capitalist principles rather than according to the principles of an alternative socio-economic system. In other words, human development is capitalist development that increases the access of individuals to the "fruits" of capitalism.

However, since its inception the HDR, which is a measure of human development, has focused on different global themes. For example in 2010 the twentieth anniversary of the HDR the theme was *The Real Wealth of Nations: Pathways to Human Development.* In 2009 the HDR was entitled, *Overcoming Barriers: Human Mobility and Development.* The HDR that was published under this latter theme concentrates exclusively on the relationship between migration and human development.

Migration and Human Development

The dominant perception about migration is that people only move from poor countries in Africa, Asia, Latin America and the Caribbean, to the rich countries in Europe, North America and Australasia (UNDP 2009). In the analysis of the UNDP (2009), on the link between migration and development, however, most of the movement of people around the world does

---

[6] Richard A. Jolly, The Human Development Perspective, http://www.adb.org/Documents/Conference/Poverty_Reduction/chap1.pdf.

not take place between developing and developed countries or between countries. The overwhelming majority of people engaged in migration move inside their own country.

It was estimated that about "740 million people are internal migrants— almost four times as many as those who have moved internationally" (UNDP 2009: 1). Furthermore, the UNDP estimated that "only just over a third of people, fewer than 70 million, who moved across national borders go from a developing to a developed country." The data showed that "most of the world's 200 million international migrants moved from one developing country to another or between developed countries" (UNDP 2009: 2). The data also revealed that poor people are the least mobile and that 14 million or 7 percent of the world's migrants are refugees, the result of displacement by insecurity and conflict.

The point here is that capital accumulation from migration processes does not at all times requires the movement of people internationally. Internal migration is just as important to the imperialist-centered model of capital accumulation, as domestic and international capital flow into certain local districts or regions attracting migrant labor. This is very true for the mining enclaves in Africa, the Caribbean and Latin America, for example that usually attract migrant labor and squatting communities in the vicinity of the mines. The Wassa West District in Ghana in which seven large-scale gold mines are operating (Agbesinyale, 2003),[7] and the Omai Gold Mines in Guyana[8] are examples of areas to which migrant labor flows. The flow of migrant labor in the direction of foreign investment capital is primarily for the exploitation of that type of labor by foreign capital.

The UNDP now analyses migration in terms of its definition of human development. According to the 2009 Human Development Report "Human mobility can be hugely effective in raising a person's income, health and education prospects. But its value is more than that: being able to decide where to live is a key element of human freedom" (UNDP 2009: 1). The idea of freedom of movement ties in with Sen's (1999) work on *Development as*

---

[7] Patrick K. Agbesinyale. (2003). *Ghana's Gold Rush and Regional Development: The Case of Wassa West District*. Dortmund, SPRING Centre.

[8] See Dennis C. Canterbury ed., (1998). Guyana Gold Industry: Evolution, Structure, Impacts and Non-Wage Benefits, *Transition* Special Issue 27–28, Institute of Development Studies, University of Guyana.

Freedom. Sen (1999) advances two reasons why "freedom is central to the process of development." The first is *"evaluative reason,"* which considers whether progress enhances freedom, and second *"effectiveness reason"* that contemplates whether "development is thoroughly dependent on the free agency of people."

The 2009 HDR explores how better policies towards human mobility can enhance human development. It lays out the case for governments to reduce restrictions on the movement of people within and across their borders, so as to expand human choices and freedoms. It argues for practical measures that can improve the prospects of migrants on arrival in a destination country. The UNDP believes that this in turn will have large benefits both for destination communities and for places of origin (UNDP 2009: 1).

The 2009 HDR states that a majority of internal and international migrants "reap gains in the form of higher incomes, better access to education and health, and improved prospects for their children." Furthermore, the majority of migrants "are happy in their destination, despite the range of adjustments and obstacles typically involved in moving." Also, they "are often more likely than local residents to join unions or religious and other groups." However, the UNDP believes that "the gains from mobility are unequally distributed" (UNDP 2009: 2).

The UNDP (2009) takes the position that historical and contemporary evidence suggests that migration and development go hand-in-hand. It noted that, "the median emigration rate in a country with low human development is below 4 percent, compared to more than 8 percent from countries with high levels of human development" (UNDP 2009: 2). According to the UNDP (2009), the "share of international migrants in world's population remained remarkably stable at around 3 percent over the past 50 years." Importantly, as well, people move of their own volition to better-off places. This is evidenced by the fact that "more than three quarters of international migrants go to a country with a higher level of human development than their country of origin."

However, the UNDP (2009) posits that migrants "are significantly constrained, both by policies that impose barriers to entry and by the resources they have available to enable their move." These policies are stimulated by the fact that "low-skilled migrant workers" generate much of the controversy over migration. Fear about low-skilled migrants has to do with exaggerated concerns about "heightened risk of crime, added burdens on local services and the fear of losing social and cultural cohesion" (UNDP 2009). However, there is "broad consensus about the value of skilled migration to destination countries."

The Impact of Migration on Human Development

The intersection of migration and human development came into vogue with the Human Development Report 2009 entitled *Overcoming Barriers: Human Mobility and Development* published by the United Nations Development Program. The HDR 2009 presented a strong argument in favor of increased migration as a condition to boost human development. However, the HDR 2009 states, "international migration, even if well managed, does not amount to a national human development strategy. Migration is at best an avenue that complements broader local and national efforts to reduce poverty and improve human development" (HDR p 3).

Although the human development approach does not promote migration as a national human development strategy it regards it as an instrument of development. In other words, migration is a tool within the human development approach that stimulates national human development. This is the principal justification for dedicating an entire issue of the HDR report to the study of migration and its impact on human development. Also, by focusing on migration the human development approach is brought in line with neoliberal thinking on migration that is taking place in other global agencies.

However, while the surface manifestation of neoliberal thinking on migration is about bringing betterment to migrants, their home communities and countries, and the receiving states, the real issue is about how the powers that be could make more money from migration processes in the current period of globalization. The idea of globalization implies that people, and capital are free to move around the globe. The global movement of people and capital are processes from which financial capital generates the greatest profit. In the case of the liberalization of capital markets financial capital can move in and out of a country making billions overnight leaving crises in its trail. This was the situation that led to the Asian financial crisis in the late 1990s. The free movement of people also generates money for the neoliberal capitalists through remittances and cheap labor.

The HDR 2009 links migration and human development in several ways. In the first instance migration is regarded as a stimulant to economic output without adding any significant cost to locals in the receiving countries. Second, the HDR 2009 argues that migration impacts sending countries through "higher incomes and consumption, better education and improved health, as well as at a broader cultural and social level" (HDR p 3). The HDR 2009 envisages that the benefits of migration would include job creation for local workers generated by the spending of remittances, "behavior changes in response to ideas from abroad," and in particular the liberation of women from traditional roles.

A third related point mentioned by the HDR 2009 is that migration has a greater short-term impact at the community-level than at the national level. This is because people tend to migrate in large numbers from specific places. In the longer-term however "the flow of ideas from human movement can have far-reaching effects on social norms and class structures across a whole country" (HDR p 3).

The case laid out for migration by the HDR 2009 does not fail to meet expectations as justifications for neoliberal globalization. In the first instance, according to the HDR 2009 migration increases output while adding, "little or no cost to locals" meaning firms, households and the government. Cost reduction is perhaps the most critical concern of neoliberal capitalism because it leads to an increase in profit. Structural adjustment, rationalization of industry, and economic liberalization, terminology associated with neoliberal globalization, are all about cost reduction. Migration too is now considered as a factor in the neoliberal arsenal of cost reduction strategies. However, if output is increased while cost remains the same or increases only marginally relative to the increase in output, there is strong inference that migrants are exploited – working more for less pay.

Thus, albeit migration may increase human development, the human development approach is guilty of inadvertently promoting the exploitation of migrants. The HDR 2009 is just as guilty of advancing neoliberal globalization through migration, as the World Bank and IMF do through structural adjustment. The human development approach is promoted nonetheless as an alternative development paradigm to hitherto development models.

Second, the HDR 2009 argues that migrants are available for childcare freeing-up resident mothers to work outside the home. But, this fact is one way in which migrants subsidize resident families and contribute to family stability in receiving countries, while the families of migrants are disrupted and become unstable in the sending countries. Thus, migrants contribute to family stability in receiving countries, and to instability of their families in sending countries.

Third, the HDR 2009 has no qualms about the spread of capitalist culture, which it promotes over traditional cultures. Migrants are absorbed in the capitalist culture in the receiving countries. They have no choice but to fit into the ways of life in their newfound home. Although they may maintain some of their traditional cultures such as dress, ceremonies, customary foods, form ethnic associations, and establish ethnic markets, these are all done in the context of the capitalist culture in which they are immersed. In a real sense migrants maintain only vestiges of their traditional cultures preserved primarily by newcomers from the home country. But, these traces of the home culture begin to disappear among the offspring of the new migrants born in the receiving country. In this connection therefore migration spells doom for local cultures, as it advances in pace with the globalization of capitalist commodity production for market exchange.

Fourth, the HDR 2009 appears to be taking a pro-working class stance not merely because it alludes to the possible effects of migration on the class structures in society. It appears so because of its explicit pronouncement that "blaming the loss of skilled workers on the workers themselves largely misses the point." At the bottom of this argument is the idea that restraints on the mobility of skilled workers "are likely to be counter-productive – not to mention the fact that they deny the basic human right to leave one's own country." The brain drain is therefore presented as a human rights issue. The worker has the right to migrate if he or she choses to do so, and should not be blamed for exercising that right.

The real issue here however is not restraints on workers but constraints on capitalist profit. Restraining the movement of skilled workers will hurt big business that needs such skills regardless of their origins, to remain competitive. This point is well made by US Trade Representative Ron Kirk for example, who thinks that there is a need for a Third Great Migration of Americans but only this time "to far-flung cities around the world ... propelled by new opportunities opened up by advances in technology and the international removal of quotas, tariffs and outrageous export fees."[9]

The HDR 2009 is a staunch advocate of free trade of which migration is regarded as an integral component. In this connection, it sees the failure in the neoliberal model evidenced by the crash in financial markets in 2008, as an opportunity for migration. Referring to the 2008 crash in financial markets in the developed capitalist countries it states: "We believe that the current downturn should be seized as an opportunity to institute a new deal for migrants—one that will benefit workers at home and abroad while guarding against a protectionist backlash" (HDR 2009 9 3).

---

[9] George E. Curry. (2011). New Migration Needed For African-Americans, *The Seattle Medium* 6/8/2011.

Migration and Cost

There are two broad identifiable ways in which the human development approach treats with the issue of migration and cost. First, it regards migration as a possible cost saving device in that migrants reduce production cost in host countries. Second, the other set of costs it considers include the financial costs migrants face before they can actually move to other locations. We analyze in turn both of these ways in which the human development approach considers costs in its treatment of migration.

Migration as a Cost Saving Device

Undoubtedly, migration is a cost saving device to companies, households or individuals that hire migrant labor. The encouragement of migration by the human development approach is definitely to contribute to cost reductions for companies and individual households that hire migrant labor – legal or illegal. Companies will always prefer easy immediate access to labor rather than having to bear the costs of training workers for the long term. Cortes (2008)[10] for example has found that in the US "a 10 percent increase in the share of low-skilled immigrants in the labor force decreases the price of immigrant intensive services, such as housekeeping and gardening, by 2 percent" channeled through lower wages.

The counter arguments advanced by opponents to immigration for example are first that temporary immigrant labor are also subject to business cycles and therefore are sometimes made redundant. In their view the cost of the upkeep of migrants who are made redundant falls on taxpayers. Their argument is therefore that the costs to the economy of hiring migrant labor far outweigh the benefits.

Secondly, and along the same lines opponents to immigration argue that illegal immigrants are a drain on tax dollars, Medicaid, food assistance programs, etc. Camarota (2004)[11] found that "households headed by illegal aliens imposed more than $26.3 billion in costs on the federal government in 2002 and paid only $16 billion in taxes, creating a net fiscal deficit of almost $10.4 billion, or $2,700 per illegal household." He noted that the "largest costs are Medicaid ($2.5 billion); treatment for the

---

[10] Patricia Cortes. (2008). "The Effect of Low-Skilled Immigration on U.S. Prices: Evidence from CPI Data," *Journal of Political Economy*, Vol. 116, No. 3, pp 381–422.

[11] Steven A. Camarota. (2004). *The High Cost of Cheap Labor: Illegal Immigration and the Federal Budget.* Center for Immigration Studies Washington, DC, August, http://www.cis.org/articles/2004/fiscal.pdf.

uninsured ($2.2 billion) food assistance programs such as food stamps, WIC, and free school lunches ($1.9 billion); the federal prison and court systems ($1.6 billion); and federal aid to schools ($1.4 billion)" (Camarota 2004 p 5).

These types of arguments however, overlook the contribution of migrant labor to the reduction in production costs and the increase in profit of small, medium and large businesses. Also, by lowering production costs the prices remain low at which US consumers purchase commodities produced by migrant labor. In this way migrant labor does not only contribute to company profit, it also subsidizes the upkeep of consumers in receiving countries.

The costs that Camarota (2004) refers to are dwarfed by the trillions of dollars accumulated through the imperialist centered model of capital accumulation as a result of hiring cheap migrant labor. It is no secret that large, medium and small companies continue to hire illegal immigrants not merely because of labor shortages but as a means to lower production costs and increase profits. This is evident for example from the long list of US companies that are fined by the US Immigration and Customs Enforcement (ICE) agency for hiring illegal immigrants.[12]

Financial Costs of Moving

A central argument by the proponents of migration as a means to achieve human development is that "host country restrictions can raise both the costs and the risks of migration" (HDR p 53–54). The financial cost of moving includes "official fees for documents and clearances, payments to intermediaries, travel expenses and, in some cases, payments of bribes." Also, there are transaction costs associated with moving across borders involving agents who demand payment to match migrants with the right jobs, and provide them with the appropriate information about regulatory frameworks, language and other services, etc.

Agunias (2009) argues

> By providing information and extending critical services in many stages of migration and in places of origin, transit and destination, legitimate intermediaries build migrants' capabilities and expand their range of choice — the very essence of human development. However their value is, in many

---

[12] Susan Carroll. (2010). "Big names on list of companies ICE fined." blog.chron.com/ immigration/2010/09/big-names-on-list-of-companies-ice-fined/.

cases, overshadowed by the costs they impose on migrants, from charging exorbitant fees to outright abuse of basic human rights.[13]

The exploitation and ill treatment of migrants by agencies and individuals providing these "intermediation and facilitation services" are well documented. However, the involvement of brokers is not always beneficial to the migrants, who become dependent on them thereby increasing the risk of their exploitation.[14] Agunias (2010) reported for example that in the Philippines-United Arab Emirates migration corridor "low skilled workers with expected salary of around 1,600 dirhams (US$432) per month paid between 13,500 pesos (US$270) to 20,000 pesos (US$400) in placement fees." In the same migration corridor a "nurse or engineer pays between 20,000 pesos (US$400) and 40,000 pesos (US$800)" a much higher fee.[15] Furthermore, in some cases "excessive and unauthorized fees are often the first step in a cycle of dependency and coercion and are at the center of most recruitment irregularities." Also, highly visible in these relationships are "fraud and deceit, and outright human-rights abuse" (Agunias 2010).

These types of problems are so sever and prevalent in different migration corridors that recently US immigration officials announced that they "were teaming up with federal and state prosecutors, the government's commerce watchdog, lawyers and campaigners" to fight against "the 'epidemic' of bogus immigration lawyers" who defraud Caribbean immigrants to the US.[16]

The contradiction however is that the human development approach is celebrating migration middlemen of whom it is said help to build the human capacity of migrants, while simultaneously the very middlemen are engaged in some of the most vicious forms of exploitation of migrants that deny them of their human development.

---

[13] Dovelyn Agunias. (2009). Guiding the Invisible Hand: Making Migration Intermediaries Work for Development. United Nations Development Program Human Development Research Paper 2009/22.

[14] Ernst Spaan. (1994). "Taikongs and Calos: The Role of Middlemen and Brokers in Javanese International Migration," IMR Volume XXVIII, No 1.

[15] Dovelyn Rannveig Agunias. (2010). *Migration's Middlemen: Regulating Recruitment Agencies in the Philippines-United Arab Emirates Corridor.* Washington, DC: Migration Policy Institute.

[16] "US to protect Caribbean immigrants from bogus lawyers," Jamaica Observer, June 10 2011 http://www.jamaicaobserver.com/news/US-to-protect-Caribbean-immigrants-from -bogus -lawyers_8989104.

Migration, Cell-Phones, Money Transfer Costs and Human Development

There is a broad consensus among "international development agencies, donor organizations" and national governments "on the need to transform developing countries into information societies." The belief is that the adoption of ICT will lead to "economic growth, socio-economic development" and "poverty reduction" (Bon 2008).[17] This position on the role of ICT in development is shared by agencies such as the World Bank, UNESCO and the UNDP, among others. The fact that migrants routinely remit money to their home communities to help out their families and friends has led to further emphasis on the role of ICT in development and in particular the use cell-phones to transfer money.

The HDR (2009) observed that "For many people in remote rural areas of developing countries, the costs of receiving money remain high: recipients typically have to travel long distances to a regional or national capital to collect cash, or the cash has to be hand-delivered by an intermediary, who may take a sizeable margin." The solution proffered by the HDR (2009) to the high cost of receiving money is the use of cell-phones for remittances.

The idea behind the use of cell-phones in money transfers is that it will increase human development by lowering the cost of money transfers. According to HDR (2009) for example "in Kenya, a leading cell-phone company, Safaricom, teamed up with donors to pilot a system that subsequently led to the launch in 2007 of M-PESA (meaning 'Mobile-Cash'). Anyone with a cell-phone can deposit money in an account and send it to another cell-phone user, using M-PESA agents distributed across the country."

This solution however will certainly deplete the cash-strapped receiving countries of even more money, relative to the payments made to intermediaries. In the first instance, the cell-phone industry drains the African continent of billions of dollars annually. Anna Bon (2008) focused on this problem by investigating the impact of ICTs on Africa's development, analyzing in particular "the telecommunication markets for mobile telephony and the Internet, especially the infrastructural part of it." Bon (2008) pointed out that "infrastructure seems only a minor topic of the whole ICT

---

[17] Anna Bon. (2008). "Rethinking ICTs for Development." Conference on Rethinking Development Studies, Institute for Development Studies, University of Cape Coast, Ghana, November 3–6.

debate," but that "it is prerequisite and it illustrates several aspects of the digital divide."

In 2008 there were "more than 250 million mobile telephone subscriptions in the whole of Africa, out of a population of 933 million," while in 2000 there was less than 20 million (Bon 2008). The bottom line nonetheless is that the increase usage of cell-phones and the Internet "are exploited exclusively by international, not African, companies," as much of the way ICT infrastructure is organized "represents a disinvestment in terms of local capital" (Bon 2008).

Furthermore, "mobile-cash" is another example of the financialization of the remittance process in which the financial institutions headquartered in the developed countries stand to benefit the most in terms of earned profit and fees. It would seem that the M-PESA arrangement cuts out local middlemen, who could eventually develop into thriving small and medium businesses within the financial sector independent of the big banks. Also, cell-phones are imports they are not produced locally, which means that the M-PESA arrangement not only stimulates profit in the financial sector but also in the foreign-owned ICT sector in particular the cell-phone industry. The stimulation of profit in the cell-phone industry takes place not only through the increase in sales in cell-phones, but also in the fees paid to foreign companies for the use of the phones to make calls and undertake monetary transactions.

Thus, in the final analysis the use of ICT to facilitate remittance by migrants definitely will help to improve human development, but international capital is the real beneficiary from this process. International capital benefits in terms of the profit to be made in the financial sector from money deposited in banks through "mobile-cash," the payment of "mobile-cash" transfer fees, the squeezing-out of local independent intermediaries and their replacement with M-PESA vendors dependent on the banking sector, the increase in sales of cell-phones, and the increase in income from the fees collected for the use of cell-phones.

Migration and Health

This section is subdivided into three parts beginning with a presentation on the human development perspective on migration and health. This is followed by critiques of the human development perspective on migration and health, with a focus on health and low-skilled workers, and the migration of health professionals.

The Human Development Perspective

Gaining assess to improved health care is considered by the HDR 2009 as one of the principal motivation for migration. The links between health and migration nonetheless are regarded as a complex issue and not simply in terms of the latter stimulating the former. According to HDR 2009 "Migrants' health depends on their personal history before moving, the process of moving itself, and the circumstances of resettlement." However, although receiving countries have established mechanisms to screen migrants, "irregular migrants may have specific health needs that remain unaddressed."

By moving to the developed countries it is believed that migrants improve their "access to health facilities and professionals as well as to health-enhancing factors such as potable water, sanitation, refrigeration, better health information and, higher incomes." Furthermore, according to HDR 2009 there is evidence that "migrant families have fewer and healthier children than they would have had if they had not moved." Not only do migrants have fewer and healthier children but the HDR 2009 "found a 16-fold reduction in child mortality (from 112 to 7 deaths per 1,000 live births) for movers from low-HDI countries."

The problem in connection with migration and health however is that migration cuts both ways. This refers to the fact that migration depletes the poor countries of their health professionals. This problem is discussed in a sub-section below on the migration of health professionals.

Health and Low-Skilled Workers

The fact that migration improves the human development of migrants in that they have better access to health care does not mean that there are no downsides to the health of migrants in receiving countries. The health implications of migration are both good and bad thus it is the net health situation of migrants that must matter most. According to Benach, et al (2011)[18] "migrants workers often fill undesirable, low-skill positions characterized by flexibility, insecurity, precarious employment, and long working hours with low pay." Furthermore, several of them that are irregular are

---

[18] Benach J, Muntaner C, Delclos C, Menéndez M, Ronquillo C. (2011). "Migration and 'Low-Skilled' Workers in Destination Countries." PLoS Med 8(6): e1001043. doi:10.1371/journal.pmed.1001043.

"especially vulnerable to exploitation since they fear job loss, incarceration, and deportation" (Benach et al 2011).

Under these conditions migrant workers are therefore faced with urgent health issues including "occupational safety, injury prevention, work-related diseases, barriers to accessing health services, and the associated health risks for their families and communities, in addition to discrimination and exploitation."[19] In the view of Benach, et al (2011), this situation requires the collaboration of "governments, unions, and international organizations" to redress the situation. According to Benach, et al (2011), this partnership is necessary to "implement fair labor standards for both legal and illegal laborers." These labor standards must be "on par with citizen workers, standardize labor migration policies, and provide legal support for undocumented laborers to help eradicate human trafficking and other forms of extreme labor exploitation."[20]

The Migration of Health Professionals

The migration of health professionals from developing to developed countries is also another downside regarding the issue of health and migration. Indeed, "the international migration of health workers, especially of physicians and nurses but also increasingly of other health workers, has become a major global health concern."[21] Simultaneously that the rich countries are demanding more health professionals there is a shortage of health workers in the poor countries. This situation has an adverse effect on the developing countries that export health professionals.

Dovlo (2005) sees the issue here in terms of limiting the adverse effects of the migration of health personnel and promoting "fairer recruitment tactics by developed countries." According to Dovlo (2005) "Though some migration occurs between rich countries (and also between poor countries), most of the migration of health professionals is occurring from countries with physician densities of about 17 per 100,000 population to countries with densities of 300 per 100,000 population." Dovlo (2005)

---

[19] Benach J, Muntaner C, Delclos C, Menéndez M, Ronquillo C. (2011). "Migration and 'Low-Skilled' Workers in Destination Countries." PLoS Med 8(6): e1001043. doi:10.1371/journal.pmed.1001043.

[20] Benach J, Muntaner C, Delclos C, Menéndez M, Ronquillo C. (2011). "Migration and 'Low-Skilled' Workers in Destination Countries." PLoS Med 8(6): e1001043. doi:10.1371/journal.pmed.1001043.

[21] Dovlo D. (2005). "Taking More Than a Fair Share? The Migration of Health Professionals from Poor to Rich Countries." PLoS Med 2(5): e109. doi:10.1371/journal.pmed.0020109.

argues that, "This is a good example of the "inverse care law"—that countries that need the most health care resources are getting the least."[22] One of the main causes for the migration of health professionals is that "pay levels are up to 24 times higher in recipient countries than they are in source countries."

According to Dovlo (2005), there is considerable variation in the density of health workers. Dovlo (2005) pointed out that, "186 countries were designated as having low, medium, and high worker density clusters (below 2.5, between 2.5 and 5.0, and above 5.0 workers per 1,000 population, respectively)." In this connection, "the low- and high-density clusters" are "further subdivided according to high and low under-five mortality." It is noted that "Among low-density countries, 45 are in the low-density/high-mortality cluster; these are predominantly sub-Saharan countries experiencing rising death rates and weak health systems.[23]

Thus, according to Dovlo (2005), "Countries such as India, the Philippines, and Nigeria," which are "highly populated countries that train large numbers of health professionals and have a long-standing remittance culture, in which professionals working outside the country send money back home to relatives—have produced doctors and nurses for 'export.'" The fact of the matter nonetheless is that "demand for different kinds of health professionals can fluctuate." Thus, for example, "recent rises in demand for nurses in the United States led to reports of immigrant doctors in Florida who took up nursing to get into the job market." According to Dovlo (2005), "This doubly wastes the resources poor countries invest into training physicians; indeed, other anecdotes suggest that many immigrant physicians and nurses take on jobs completely unrelated to their training."[24]

The phenomenon of migrant health professionals taking on jobs completely or only partially related to their training is indeed a major problem. Migrant health professionals are not readily employed in the health care sector in the US for example. Health professional migrants have to take an

---

[22] Dovlo D. (2005). "Taking More Than a Fair Share? The Migration of Health Professionals from Poor to Rich Countries." PLoS Med 2(5): e109. doi:10.1371/journal.pmed.0020109.

[23] Dovlo D. (2005). "Taking More Than a Fair Share? The Migration of Health Professionals from Poor to Rich Countries." PLoS Med 2(5): e109. doi:10.1371/journal.pmed.0020109.

[24] Dovlo D. (2005). "Taking More Than a Fair Share? The Migration of Health Professionals from Poor to Rich Countries." PLoS Med 2(5): e109. doi:10.1371/journal.pmed.0020109.

exam before they can practice their profession, which it sometimes takes many years for them to pass. Many of these migrants give up trying to pass the exam and settle instead for some menial job, as their lives go on. Also, in many cases they take on menial jobs to raise the required amount of money to pay for the exam, which they otherwise could not afford.

In the light of this problem, Thomas and Hosein (2007)[25] presented an argument to help Caribbean Community (Caricom) health professionals maintain their dignity while simultaneously contributing to the improvement of the provision of health services in the Caricom region. They argue that due to the uneven economic attributes of the Caricom countries, the intra-regional movement of health professionals such as nurses can help to solve some of the regional shortages of those skills. In the view of Thomas and Hosein (2007) the intra-regional migration of health professionals would provide considerable benefits for the migrant nurses, without the drift of their skills beyond the region.[26]

Indeed, the idea about the promotion of intra-regional migration of health professionals in Caricom as a rebuff to their extra-regional migration has relevance to other regions around the globe. The same strategy could be implemented to retain health professional in Africa, Asia, Latin America, and the Caribbean. These regions should promote the benefits of intra-region migration of health professionals over their migration to extra-regional locations. For example, the fact that many migrant health professionals end up in menial jobs could be promoted as a downside relative to the benefits they would obtain by remaining in their profession in other regional settings.

Migration and Human Rights

The human development approach stresses the significance of human rights to the process of human development. However, Sen (2000) has identified three critiques that skeptics have about the "intellectual edifice of human rights."[27] These are what he calls the *legitimacy*, *coherence*, and

---

[25] Clive Thomas and Roger Hosein. (2007). "Caribbean Single Market Economy (CSME) and the Intra-Regional Migration of Nurses: Some Proposed Opportunities," *Global Social Policy*, Vol. 7 No. 3, pp. 316–338.

[26] Clive Thomas and Roger Hosein. (2007). "Caribbean Single Market Economy (CSME) and the Intra-Regional Migration of Nurses Some Proposed Opportunities," *Global Social Policy*, Vol. 7 No. 3, pp. 316–338.

[27] Amartya Sen. (2000). *Development as Freedom*. New York, Anchor Books.

cultural critiques. The *legitimacy* critique derives from the view that people are provided with well-defined rights in the absence of mechanisms to really give them justiciable rights, while the *coherence* problem "concerns the *form* that the ethics and politics of human rights takes," with the implication that human rights are hollow in the absence of the appropriate agencies that deliver them to people. The *cultural* critique is that human rights suggest that there exists a set of universal values, but the reality is that "there are no such universal values" recognized by all cultures. But, in contradistinction nonetheless Sen (2000) has founded his case for basic freedoms and the associated rights on "their *intrinsic* importance; their *consequential* role in providing political incentives for economic security; and their *constructive* role in the genesis of values and priorities."

So long as the case for human rights is accepted however, the human development perspective posits that the intersection of human rights and migration becomes more visible. Thus, the HDR (2009) declares that, "Even if there is no appetite to sign up to formal conventions, there is no sound reason for any government to deny such basic migrant rights as the right to:

> Equal remuneration for equal work, decent working conditions and protection of health and safety; Organize and bargain collectively; Not be subject to arbitrary detention, and be subject to due process in the event of deportation; Not be subject to cruel, inhumane or degrading treatment; and Return to countries of origin. These should exist alongside basic human rights of liberty, security of person, freedom of belief and protection against forced labor and trafficking (HDR 2009 p 101).

These basic migrant rights nonetheless do not have universal support among scholars and policymakers. According to the HRD 2009, "One argument against ensuring basic rights has been that this would necessarily reduce the numbers of people allowed to enter." The HDR 2009 takes the position however that generally the enforcement of basic migrant rights does not reduce the numbers of migrants allowed to enter a country, and that such "an argument is in any case not justifiable on moral grounds" (p 101).

The foregoing discussion on the intersection of human rights and migration is reflective of the human rights dilemma experienced by migrants under neoliberal capitalism. The human development approach promotes both human rights and migration as means to human development. It is founded on the idea that basic human rights are essential to human development. It therefore encourages the protection of the human rights of migrants, as a human development function. But, the contradiction is that the migration process is characterized by gross violations of the basic rights of migrants.

The violation of basic migrant rights and not the protection of those rights is a concrete condition of migration under neoliberal capitalism. Thus, by promoting migration the human development approach has the unintended effect of perpetuating the violation of basic migrant rights. Profit maximization in the bottom line of neoliberal capitalism with respect to migration – it is not the protection of the basic rights of migrants. Thus, the violation of the basic rights of migrants will persist under neoliberal capitalism. Meanwhile, the human development approach will continue to call on governments to respect the basic rights and freedoms of migrants and demand policy reform. These actions will only bring about piecemeal rather than fundamental transformations in the power structure that reproduces the concrete conditions of migration under neoliberal capitalism including the suppression of the basic rights of migrants.

Policy Reforms for Human Development Impact of Migration

The HDR (2009) has made a number of proposals on the policy reforms needed to enhance the human development impact of migration. According to HDR (2009)

> The principal reforms proposed center around six areas, each of which has important and complementary contributions to make to human development: opening up existing entry channels so that more workers can emigrate; ensuring basic rights for migrants; lowering the transaction costs of migration; finding solutions that benefit both destination communities and the migrants they receive; making it easier for people to move within their own countries; and mainstreaming migration into national development strategies (HRD 2009 p v).

These policy reforms are well intended but the problem is that although their goal is to increase human development, they will undoubtedly have unintended opposite effects. It is evident from the activities of the global institutions in the control of neoliberal capitalism that the current thrust in the area of migration is to stimulate capital accumulation. Neoliberal capitalism is bringing all global institutions to serve its interest and the policy reforms proffered by the human development approach are no different. Whatever human development takes place as a result of these policy reforms, will only do so as an aside to the principal goal of neoliberal capitalism, which is to generate the greatest profit from migration processes.

Human development is construed in terms of correcting the asymmetrical "distribution of human capabilities," which is "a major driver for movement of people." However, the human development approach does not adequately address the source of the problem of unequal distribution of human capabilities that causes people to migrate. It inadequately addresses the class bases of the capitalist power structure, which is the major constraint to "opening up existing entry channels so that more workers can emigrate," and "ensuring basic rights for migrants." Indeed, the human development approach is couched within the capitalist framework, and is not a plausible alternative to it.

Conclusion

The human development impact of migration is constrained by the class dynamics of the neoliberal capitalist power structure that facilitates the imperialist centered model of capital accumulation. The extraction of profit from the migration process cancels out whatever the benefits that accrue to migrants in terms of the reduction in the cost of remitting money back home, access to health care and improved human rights.

The concentration and centralization of capital that result from the imperialist centered model of capital accumulation entrenches a political and economic power structure that is at the bottom of the push and pull factors of migration. It regulates migratory flows and from time to time investigates migration issues to determine how migration processes could be updated and utilized in the most efficient manner to stimulate profit. Simultaneously, however, neoliberal capitalism pays only lip service for the most part to the democratic, welfare, and humanitarian ideals of capitalism, concerning migrants.

The human development approach fits into the scheme of things, which focuses on spreading to migrants the various benefits of capitalism including, health care, basic human freedoms, and modern technologies. But, the human development approach does not really challenge the status quo in terms of upturning the capitalist political and economic structures, which ensure that migration serves the interest of capital accumulation.

PART THREE

FAULT LINES IN NEOLIBERAL VIEWS ON MIGRATION

CHAPTER EIGHT

MIGRATION FAULT-LINES UNDER NEOLIBERAL GLOBALIZATION

In both Europe and the United States, the death toll that result from today's restrictive immigration policies is astonishingly high: over the past decade, thousands of people have died trying to make their own private dash for freedom.[1]

Introduction

The US is the biggest advocate of neoliberal free trade and the liberal democratic tradition around the globe except when it comes to protecting its domestic and foreign economic interests, borders, and satellite states. In those situations, the most degenerate forms of authoritarianism, apartheid, suppression of liberty and free movement of persons, and state-protectionist economic policies are tolerated and promoted at home and abroad by successive US administrations. Examples abound in Latin America, Africa, the Middle East, and Asia where the US fervently supports countries that engage in flagrant violations of human rights, and the suppression of the free movement of persons.

The separation walls in Israel and the US, the restrictive migration policies in the EU and US, along with anti-immigration neoliberal theory and anti-immigration movement reflect this degeneracy in human decency, and show the low levels to which the human spirit could sink to deny poor people work, food, shelter, health and social services so necessary for their existence in modern times.

But, immigrants are fighting back through pro-immigration mass movements. However, the ambivalence on immigration issues by the sections and sectors of capital that employ immigrant labor does not help the cause of immigrants. It merely serves to promote harmony between these capitalists and those that oppose immigration.

The callous behavior of the US towards immigrants has attracted the attention of the UN's Committee on the Elimination of Racial

---

[1] Jonathon Wayne Moses. (2006). *International Migration: Globalization's Last Frontier.* London, Zed Books.

Discrimination (CERD), of the Office of the United Nations High Commissioner for Human Rights. The CERD in its Shadow Report in response to the 2007 Periodic Report of the US Human Rights Network stated that "Immigrants and migrants in the United States are frequently denied their right to be free from discrimination" and that they "are often discriminatorily denied their fundamental civil and political rights, as well as their economic, social and cultural rights."[2] A migrant is a person outside their country of birth for a year or more.[3]

The CERD concluded that through its direct and indirect action, the US "has failed in its obligations under the Convention to guarantee the rights of immigrants to be free from discrimination on the basis of race, ethnicity, national origin and ancestry." The CERD states further that the US has also failed "to recognize and address the multiplicities of discrimination immigrants face and the intersection of gender, race, national origin and citizenship discrimination."[4]

This chapter analyses these major fault lines in the neoliberal approach to migration – the construction of separation walls to deny the entry to migrants coupled with restrictive migration policies, and anti-immigration movements. The neoliberal approach to migration is characterized as the development impact of migration. Commencing with a discussion on the contradictions in the neoliberal approach to migration, the focus is thereafter shifted to descriptive and critical analyses of separation walls in Israel and the US. Thereafter, it analyses some selective migration policy issues in the EU and US. The latter sections examine the issues of anti-immigration in theory and practice, the pro-immigration mass movements, and the sections and sectors of capital that employ immigration labor.

Contradictions in the Neoliberal Approach to Migration

The neoliberal dominated international financial institutions, policymakers, and academics argue in favor of increased migration, within the

---

[2] Committee on the Elimination of Racial Discrimination (CERD) Immigrant/Migrant Rights Working Group. (2007). Rights of Immigrants and Migrants to the United States: A Critical Look at the US and Its Compliance under the Convention: A Response to the 2007 Periodic Report of the United States of America.

[3] Philip Martin. (2006). The Economics of Migration: Managing the Flow of International Labor, *Harvard International Review*, July 17.

[4] Committee on the Elimination of Racial Discrimination (CERD) Immigrant/Migrant Rights Working Group. (2007). Rights of Immigrants and Migrants to the United States: A Critical Look at the US and Its Compliance under the Convention: A Response to the 2007 Periodic Report of the United States of America.

market liberalization framework to feed the imperialist centered model of capital accumulation. The desire by ruling elites to increase migration nonetheless is a factor that is ever present in the history of capitalism. As Ness (2007) observed, the increase in trade in labor at the international level is a recurring theme in capitalism, which was evident during the Victorian age, when the global trade in labor was only second to that of the trade in finance.[5] In the current period of neoliberal capitalism however the problem is that the neoliberal theorists and practitioners are not true to their own doctrine because they do not genuinely favor the unrestricted movement of persons, globally.

Neoliberal capitalism is characterized by two contradictory tendencies towards immigration – these are the simultaneous increase and restriction of migration. The examples that magnify this contradiction are the actions by Israel, the United States, and the European Union to restrict immigration targeted at specific poor countries in Africa, Latin America and the Caribbean, and elsewhere. Simultaneously advocating for an increase in managed migration however, are a complex of international institutions, academics, research programs, reports, policy prescriptions, and policy makers. They are also dedicated to facilitate the unhindered flows of capital globally in the service of neoliberal capitalism. Another dimension of the contradiction is that neoliberal capitalism promotes managed migration such that only the choice migrants with money and high-level skills are preferred for admittance into the rich countries.

This contradiction reflects a disjuncture between politics and economics under neoliberal globalization. There seems to be a time lag between the economic base and the political system on the immigration question. While neoliberal economic expediency to lower production cost and stimulate profit requires the hire of cheap migrant labor, the political system erected to facilitate the smooth operation of the neoliberal economic base is erecting barriers to entry by migrants.

Arguments in favor of migrant labor differentiate between migrants, workers in the sending countries, and workers in the receiving countries as inherently different groups of people.[6] This difference is artificial however since the only role of workers in a capitalist economy whether they are migrants, remain in the sending-countries or are new arrivals in the

---

[5] Immanuel Ness. (2007). "Forging a Migration Policy for Capital: Labor Shortages and Guest Workers," *New Political Science*, Volume 29, Number 4, December, pp 429–452.

[6] Philip Martin. (2006). "The Economics of Migration: Managing the Flow of International Labor," *Harvard International Review*, July 17.

receiving country, is to sell their labor-power to the capitalist that pays the highest wages.

Workers are distributed in the globe in such a manner as Martin (2006) observed that in 2006 "about 40 percent" of them were "employed in agriculture, 20 percent in industry, and 40 percent in services." At that time "about 60 percent of the world's almost 100 million migrant workers" were "in developed or industrial countries, and their distribution" was "markedly different from that of native-born workers." Indeed, "about 10 percent of the migrants in industrial countries" were then "employed in agriculture, 40 percent in industry, and 50 percent in services, while only 3 percent of native-born workers" were "in agriculture, 25 percent in industry, and 72 percent in services."[7]

Given that distribution of the global labor force, why is it that neoliberal capitalism is promoting the development impact of migration while simultaneously some countries and regions are erecting separation walls and other measures to deny entry to migrants? What is driving the urges to simultaneously increase managed migration and to restrict migration? Undoubtedly, this process is driven by the profit motive by both the companies that hire migrant labor and those that do not. The companies that hire migrant labor do so to lower production cost and increase profit, while the companies that do not hire migrant labor, want to restrict it so that they can be more competitive vis-à-vis the companies that hire migrant labor.

Neoliberal structural adjustment policies forced the developing countries to engage in what is termed the "rationalization" of state enterprises to reduce their operation costs. Migration policy is now a form of "rationalization" but of an entire country rather than of a particular state-owned enterprise. Redundancy measures were implemented in the public enterprises in the 1970s and 1980s that saw millions of workers in the public sector laid off from their jobs, with the view to cut cost and increase profit.

In the same manner that the public enterprises were supposed to become "lean and clean" through "rationalization" policies, it is intended that the country as a whole, namely society and economy, must become "lean and clean" through migration policies. This means that there should be no migrant hangers-on in the economy that taxpayers subsidize through social programs. The dialectics of the "rationalization" to rid the

---

[7] Philip Martin. (2006). "The Economics of Migration: Managing the Flow of International Labor," *Harvard International Review*, July 17.

EU and US of immigrants has spawned anti-immigration movements that embrace xenophobia and Islamaphobia in the EU and the US, and its opposite in terms of the pro-immigration mass movements.

This form of "rationalization" of the economy and society does not consider the contributions of underpaid migrants to the reduction in costs to the companies that hire them, and the fact that their employers are able to sell the products of migrants at lower prices because of the low wages paid to them. It does not consider the fact that it is the migrant workers who are subsidizing low food prices in the rich countries, which is also a direct subsidy to the consumers in these states.

Also, there is the issue of capitalist competition in the sense that some companies are more disposed to hire certain categories of migrant labor especially illegal migrants, which give them a cost advantage over those firms that are not in a position to do the same thing. The latter companies are the most vehement in their opposition to migrant labor. Thus, there are sections and sectors of capital, which employ migrant labor and those that abhor it.

The major fault line in the neoliberal case for migration presented in the 2009 Human Development Report, and in the debate on the new directions and thinking on the development impact of migration under neoliberal capitalism, is the contradictory actions by the ruling elites in Israel, the United States and the EU to restrict immigration. Israel and the US have taken the degenerate steps to build separation walls to keep out Palestinian and African and Mexican migrant workers, respectively, while the EU invested millions of Euros in Libya for that country to police the Mediterranean Sea to keep out African migrant labor from the EU. The EU-Libya migration agreement is the subject of a separate chapter.

The Israeli Separation Walls with Egypt and Palestine

There are two sets of overlapping arguments that the Israeli ruling elites present to erect separation walls with Palestine and Egypt to restrict Palestinian and African immigrants from entering into Israel. The first is that the walls are intended to protect Israeli civilians from infiltrators and terrorist acts by Palestinians, including suicide-bombing attacks. The Israeli authorities argue that terrorism in Israel has decreased since the construction of the separation walls. This claim is used as evidence that the separation barrier with Palestine is effective in preventing terrorism.

Second, it is argued that African immigrants will dilute the Israeli culture through intermarriage. The anti-immigrant view is that the Africans will bring about a rise in violent crimes in Israel. There have been demonstrations in "south Tel Aviv calling for the expulsion of the Africans." Indeed, "a group of rabbis in the area issued a religious edict several months ago against renting" apartments to Africans. Despite this edict, local landlords are making a fortune off of these immigrants who are in search of housing.

The rabbis warned against intermarriage and claimed that the newcomers have brought a rise in violent crime. The, residents in Tel Aviv "recited a litany of complaints against the migrants, accusing them of alcoholism, drug use and carrying diseases, as well as involvement in muggings, break-ins, harassment of women and even rape and murder."[8] But, according to Greenberg (2011), "police statistics show that the crime rate among the Africans is significantly lower than among the general population."

The African Development Center reported that government statements against the flow of Africans into Israel fuel hostility towards these migrants, which sometimes lead to assaults on the streets, as migrants are beaten and verbally assaulted in the Tel Aviv area. South Tel Aviv is an economically depressed area and officials there believe that the impoverished African migrants should not burden it further.

African immigration is regarded by Israeli officials as one of the most pressing issues facing the country, which places a stain on its security and welfare systems. Israel believes that immigration is the number one problem on the Israeli-Egyptian border, while security and smuggling occupy second and third places, respectively. The problem of the rise in human trafficking through Egypt into Israel is another key issue identified as justification for the separation walls. The argument is that the separation wall with Egypt will not only address these pressing problems, it will also protect Israel's Jewish and democratic character. Officials are of the view nonetheless that it is difficult to evict immigrants once they become embedded in Israeli society.

The Israeli-Egyptian separation wall is therefore an official response by the Israeli state to the perceived problems African migrants pose to Israel. However, the Israeli wall with Egypt is problematic on the grounds that it is allegedly in violation of the 1979 peace treaty between the two countries that limits military and security deployments on either side of the border.

---

[8] Joel Greenberg. (2011). "Flow of African Migrants Poses Dilemma for Israel," *The Washington Post*, Friday, April 15.

Despite the peace treaty the Israeli authorities decided in November 2010 to construct a detention camp near its border with Egypt to temporarily accommodate undocumented African immigrants attempting to enter Israel illegally.

Africans and Palestinians migrate into Israel to improve their economic and social conditions. The imperialist centered model of capital accumulation has enriched Israel making it an attractive site for African and Palestinian migrants. The data on the differences in per capita income between Israel, Palestine and the African countries speak for themselves. But, although the Israeli authorities would like to keep out the Africans, sections of the Israeli capitalist class are profiting by employing these immigrants and paying them low wages. The employment of immigrant labor in Israel is expected to accelerate as businessmen seek to lower production costs in the light of the economic crisis in the country.

The rising cost-of-living in Israel has brought social unrest that saw 250,000 demonstrators on the streets of Tel Aviv and other cities in early August 2011. The Israelis were demonstrating against high rent for housing, and for economic relief for the middle and working classes in the country. The demonstrators demanded economic reform that would redistribute income in Israel in favor of the Israeli middle and working classes.

The ascendancy of neoliberal capitalism, and the wars and increase in poverty with which it is associated, among other factors, has stimulated African migration to Israel. Thousands of African and other migrants fleeing conflict, drought and famine at home or searching for a better life migrate to Israel through its desert border with Egypt. It is believed that the deal made by Libya and Italy in 2009 cut off the African migrants from a popular sea route to Europe and helped to redirect the flow towards Israel, which is seen as offering better work opportunities and more Western standards (Knell 2010). It is reported that Sudanese, Ethiopians and Eritreans travel directly to the Israeli border after arriving in Egypt.

It is unclear if the war in Libya has reestablished that country as a transit rout for migrants to the European Union. Also, it is still to be seen if the Transitional National Council in Libya that has replaced the Gaddafi regime in October 2011 will enforce the 2009 agreement between Libya and Italy.

The Egypt-Israel border therefore represents a major transit route for African migrants, both political refugees and job seekers, coming mainly from Sudan, Ethiopia and Eritrea (Morrow and Al-Omrani 2010). These migrants including those from the war-torn Darfur region of Sudan find themselves in Israel by sneaking across the border from Egypt's Sinai desert, seeking asylum, jobs and a better life.[9] According to Greenberg (2011), migrants arriving from Eritrea, Sudan and more recently from Ivory Coast are granted special status by the Israeli government and are protected form deportation because of threats in their home countries.

The Israeli immigration authorities reported in early November 2010 that about 700 illegal immigrants a month are recorded as passing into Israel, an increase of about 300 percent since the start of 2010. Israel says the arrival of almost 15,000 refugees and asylum-seekers has put a strain on its security and welfare systems (Knell 2010). The Israeli authorities reported that 10,858 migrants entered the country over the January-November period, way above the figure of 4,341 migrants for 2009 (BBC 2010). According to Greenberg (2011), based on the most recent official statistics there are approximately 34,000 African migrants in Israel, mostly concentrated in Tel Aviv. These migrants "live in cramped apartments or shelters in poor neighborhoods where there is resentment against the newcomers' presence."

The surge in African migrants who make the harrowing journey to Israel began in 2007. These migrants are subjected to imprisonment, torture, rape and the extortion of high ransom payments by Bedouin smugglers in Sinai. When they finally cross the border the Israeli army hold them in "a detention center in southern Israel for several weeks" before they are placed on "buses to Tel Aviv, where they are left to fend for themselves."[10] They are not given work permits and are debarred from participating in government provided health care and social services. Furthermore the state authorities turn a blind eye to "employers who collect the migrants from street corners for menial day jobs, such as cleaning work, dishwashing in restaurants or construction."[11]

One of the leading considerations of the political elites is that of "preserving the Jewish majority in Israel." The problem nonetheless is that neoliberal capitalism like its predecessors is after profit. Thus, the Israeli capitalist who would make a fortune off of the African migrants in Israel

---

[9] Joel Greenberg. (2011). "Flow of African Migrants Poses Dilemma for Israel," *The Washington Post*, Friday, April 15.
[10] Joel Greenberg. (2011). "Flow of African Migrants Poses Dilemma for Israel," *The Washington Post*, Friday, April 15.
[11] Joel Greenberg. (2011). "Flow of African Migrants Poses Dilemma for Israel," *The Washington Post*, Friday, April 15.

will privilege capital accumulation over any idea about "preserving the Jewish majority in Israel." The imperialist centered model of capital accumulation could not be subjected to ideals such as the preservation of a race, an ethnic group or religious beliefs. Capital accumulation would not be subjected by views concerning the dilution of culture or increased crime allegedly caused by migration.

In response to the perceived problems of African migration into Israel, the Israeli government has decided to construct a new barrier on part of the some 266 km long Egyptian-Israeli border at a cost of an estimated \$270 – \$370 million. Indeed, 50 to 60 percent of Israel is cordoned off by fences along its borders with Lebanon, Jordan, most of the West Bank, and all of Gaza. The wall along Israel's southern border is separate from a 670 km barrier that already cuts off Israel from large parts of the West Bank.

The electric wall on the Egyptian-Israeli border is equipped with advanced high-tech surveillance cameras and electronic sensors. The barrier is seen to represents "a strategic decision to secure Israel's Jewish and democratic character." Israel claims that it would continue to accept refugees from conflict zones but that it "cannot let tens of thousands of illegal workers infiltrate into Israel through the southern border and inundate" the "country with illegal aliens" (McCarthy 2010).

It is reported that Israel had not informed the Egyptian authorities of its plan to build the wall. But, the Egyptians are of the view that the wall is entirely an Israeli matter so long as it is built on Israeli soil. Morrow and Al-Omrani (2010) noted however that Egypt supported Israel in the erection of the wall. The Egyptian government appeared indifferent to news of Israel's planned border fence, despite the 1979 peace treaty (Morrow and Al-Omrani 2010).

Meanwhile, Egypt has also been building "an underground steel barrier along its 14-kilometre border with the Gaza Strip with the ostensible aim of disrupting smuggling operations." This forces Gaza's roughly 1.5 million inhabitants to rely on cross-border tunnels for their most basic needs (Morrow and Al-Omrani 2010).

The Egyptian police have increased their current efforts at border patrol with Israel following a rise in human trafficking through Egypt. Since May 2009, the Egyptian police have killed at least 17 migrants attempting to cross into Israel from Egypt. Egyptian border authorities killed a Sudanese national attempting to cross into Israel in late October 2010. A recent report by Human Rights Watch noted that since 2007 Egyptian border authorities have killed at least 85 African migrants, recorded 24 fatalities in 2010 and 19 in 2009 (Morrow and Al-Omrani 2010).

Despite the Israeli/Palestinian conflict Palestinians in the Occupied Palestinian Territory (OPT) migrate into Israel in search of a better life. The economic conditions in the OPT are poor relative to those in Israel. The OPT suffers from high levels of poverty and unemployment and a low per capita income (Farsakh 2006; Farsakh 2005; and UNCTAD 2010). The Palestinian economy depends almost totally on Israel to which it sells approximately 90 percent of its exports. This is the case although the Palestinian Authority has free trade relations with, the EU, the European Free Trade Association (EFTA), the US, Canada, and Turkey and the Arab League agreed to preferential treatment of Palestinian products in 2004. Also, the OPT's imports from Israel represent an increasing share of total imports, reaching 80 percent in 2008 (Tillekens 2010).

The Israeli gross national income per capita in current international dollars was $27,110 in 2009, compared with $1,978 in the OPT. Net flows of foreign direct investment in Israel were $8,048 million in 2000, $4,818 million in 2005, $10,876 million in 2008 and $3,894 million in 2009. Israel is indeed a major capitalist state in the Middle East, where capital accumulation is taking place at a rapid pace. Theorizing about capital accumulation and corporate concentration in Israel, Nitzan and Bichler (2002 and 1999) argue that the large core firms at the center of Israel's economy are the principal actors in the process of accumulation and concentration, which are two sides of the same process. The heavy concentration and accumulation of capital in Israel and the lack thereof in the OPT is understandably a driving force behind Palestinian migration to Israel.

The state of Israel nonetheless decided to build a 640 km (400-mile) Israeli-West Bank separation barrier to keep the Palestinians out of Israel. The separation wall is on territory Israel occupied in 1967, rather than along the internationally recognized boundary between Israel and the West Bank. The International Court of Justice at the United Nations has ruled that the Israeli's West Bank barrier is illegal and construction of it should have been stopped immediately. The ICJ stated that the barrier is "tantamount to annexation" and stood in the way of the Palestinian's right to self-determination. The US, UK, and France argued however, that the ICJ should stay out of the issue, warning that any opinion it gives could interfere with the Middle East peace process (BBC 2004). The European Union, nonetheless, takes the position that the wall is illegal. The legality of the Israeli wall in the West Bank was also successfully challenged at the International Court of Justice.

Current US-Mexico Border Issues

There are several issues that can be gleaned from US official documents, which could be identified as the driving force behind the construction of the US-Mexico border fence. Furthermore, there are cultural, religious, ethnic, and economic objections by sections of the native-born US population to the arrival of new immigrants from Mexico and elsewhere in the US. The basic opposition some Americans have has to do with the effects of immigration on the public budget. This concerns the public services immigrants receive relative to their alleged non-payment of taxes, and on the private economy in terms of lowering wages and its consequences.

The US officials have identified Mexico as "a major producer and supplier to the U.S. market of heroin, methamphetamine, and marijuana and the major transit country for as much as 90 percent of the cocaine sold in the United States."[12] Reportedly, the most significant drug distribution network is in the control of a "small number of Mexican drug trafficking organizations (DTOs)," along the US Southwest border. The US Department of Justice's National Drug Intelligence Center (NDIC) characterizes these DTOs "as representing the 'greatest organized crime threat' to the United States today."[13]

The Mexican DTOs are said to have displaced "other Latin American traffickers, primarily Colombians," in recent years. Furthermore, it is evident that "the violence and brutality of the Mexican DTOs have escalated." This is due to "an increasing number of groups" that "battled each other for control of lucrative drug trafficking routes into the United States." Recent estimates by the Mexican government released in January 2011, have identified 34,500 people as having died in "violence related to organized crime between January 2007 and December 2010."

A related issue to drug trafficking is that of "money laundering and bulk cash smuggling." According to the Department of Homeland Security's United States-Mexico Bi-National Criminal Proceeds Study, published in June 2010, it is estimated that "between $19 billion and $29 billion in illicit proceeds flow from the United States to organized criminal groups in Mexico each year." Seelke (2011) noted that much of the money made from the illegal drug trade in the US is laundered in Mexico through bulk cash

---

[12] Clare Ribando Seelke. (2011). Mexico-U.S. Relations: Issues for Congress, Congressional Research Service, 7-5700 RL32724, February 15.

[13] Clare Ribando Seelke. (2011). Mexico-U.S. Relations: Issues for Congress, Congressional Research Service, 7-5700 RL32724, February 15.

smuggling, "the Black Market Peso Exchange, or placement in financial institutions, cash-intensive front businesses, prepaid stored value cards, or money services businesses" (Seelke 2011).

Seelke (2011) pointed out that the proceeds from these illegal transactions are then "used by DTOs and other criminal groups to acquire weapons in the United States and to corrupt law enforcement and other public officials." Operation Firewall launched by the US immigration and Customs Enforcement (ICE) and the US Customs and Border Protection (CBP) in 2005, have since made "679 arrests and 3,946 seizures totaling more than $302 million."

"Weapons trafficking" is another major issue that the US authorities have identified that shapes US-Mexico relations. The Mexican DTOs are said to "use 'military-style' firearms, including assault weapons," which have been traced back to the US, some even to the US military inventories. Through "straw purchases" the Mexican DTOs secure some of the most sophisticated weapons. Now, individuals who can legally buy weapons from licensed gun dealers or at gun shows in U.S., do so and then sell them to gun smugglers in the border-states who then take them across the border and resell them to the Mexican DTOs (Seelke 2011). These illegal weapons are then used "in conflicts between rival DTOs as well as between the DTOs and the Mexican government, military, and police" (Seelke 2011).

The US Bureau of Alcohol, Tobacco, Firearms and Explosives (ATF) leads the Project Gunrunner mission, which has "led to the arrest of 1,397 defendants – 850 of which had been convicted – and the seizure of over 6,688 firearms." Furthermore, "From calendar years 2007 – 2009, ATF traced more than 69,800 firearms for Mexican authorities, the majority of which appear to have a nexus to the United States."

"Human smuggling" and "trafficking in persons" (TIP) are other border issues that the US has with Mexico. In 2005, the US Customs and Border Protection (CBP) and the Mexican government implemented "Operation Against Smuggling Initiative on Safety and Security (OASISS), a bi-lateral program aimed at enhancing both countries' abilities to prosecute alien smugglers and human traffickers along the Southwest border." Between 2005 and 2009, "OASISS generated 1,579 cases."

Mexico is identified as "a significant source, transit, and destination country for people trafficked for forced labor or sexual exploitation." It was estimated by the Mexican government that "20,000 children are trafficked within the country each year for sexual exploitation." Also, TIP victims from Central America are transshipped through Mexico into the US.

Compounding the problems of drug trafficking, money laundering and bulk cash smuggling, weapons trafficking, human smuggling, and trafficking in persons, in US-Mexico relations, is the issue of migration. According to Seelke (2011) drawing on data from the Department of Homeland Security Office of Immigration Statistics (OIS), "Mexico is the leading country of origin of the legal permanent residents (LPR) population and unauthorized migrant population in the United States."

The US Immigration and Nationality Act (INA) has established a "ceiling on immigration from any one country at 7 percent" but "many Mexicans are exempt from the statutory numerical limits as immediate relatives of U.S. citizens." It is estimated that 58 percent of Mexicans who became LPRs in the US in 2009 "did so as immediate relatives of U.S. citizens," while "only 5 percent of the Mexicans who became LPRs in 2009 were employment-based immigrants." It was estimated that "3.4 million or 26.9 percent of LPRs living in the United States in 2008 had emigrated from Mexico," and that "Mexicans made up 62 percent of the unauthorized aliens living in the United States in 2009," representing "6.7 million Mexican nationals among the estimated 10.8 million unauthorized resident population in 2009."[14]

The US – Mexico Border Fence: "The Great Wall of Mexico"

The initial attempt to secure the southern US border with the construction of the San Diego Fence in 1990, has since the attack on the US in September 2011 been "morphed from a method to stem the tide of illegal immigration from Mexico into a legislated method to prevent the entrance of terrorists."[15] However, just as its close ally Israel is doing in the Middle East, the building of the US border fence to keep out so-called terrorists and illegal immigrant workers from Mexico is degrading to the human spirit. The per capita income in the US is over $30,000, while that of Mexico's is $4,000. This class divide between Mexico and the US evidenced by the per capita incomes in the two countries, is a principal cause of Mexican immigration in the US. Besides, the Mexicans take the jobs that US citizens do not want, such as working as farm laborers.

---

[14] Clare Ribando Seelke. (2011). Mexico-U.S. Relations: Issues for Congress, Congressional Research Service, 7-5700 RL32724, February 15.

[15] MAJ John T. Sherwood. (2008). Building the Wall: The Efficacy of a US-Mexico Border Fence, a thesis presented to the Faculty of the U.S. Army Command and General Staff College in partial fulfillment of the requirements for the degree Master of Military Art and Science, Homeland Security, December.

The Secure Border Initiative was launched by the US Department for Homeland Security in November 2005, as a "multiyear, multibillion-dollar program aimed at securing U.S. borders and reducing illegal immigration" (USGAO, 2009). The US Customs and Border Protection (CBP) has responsibility for the Secure Border Initiative (SBI) program. The SBI program office manages the SBI program and is responsible for developing a comprehensive border protection system in the US.

There are two components to the border protection system – SBI net that involves first the employment of "radars, sensors, and cameras to detect, identify, and classify the threat level associated with an illegal entry into the United States between the ports of entry." The second component is "SBI tactical infrastructure (TI), fencing, roads, and lighting intended to enhance U.S. Border Patrol agents' ability to respond to the area of the illegal entry and bring the situation to a law enforcement resolution (i.e., arrest)" (USGAO 2009).

The anti-immigration forces in the US a land of immigrants have created so much fear of immigrants that a majority of Americans are in favor of the 2,000-mile security fence. The number of illegal immigrants in the US is variously estimated between 8 and 20 million people. It is estimated that "each year between 400,000 and 1 million undocumented migrants try to slip across the rivers and deserts on the 2,000-mile (3,200-km) US-Mexico border" (GlobalSecurity.org). US officials believe that "the sea of illegal aliens provides a cover and an environment in which terrorists can hide, and the tide of in-coming illegal aliens provides terrorists with a reliable means of entry." The US Border Patrol apprehended over 1.2 million illegal immigrants in 2005. They catch about 1 in every 4–1 in every 5 illegal border crossers. Arrests along the southern border make up about 97–98 percent of the total arrests, most of whom on the US' southern border are Mexicans (GlobalSecurity.org).

The cost of the 2,000-mile state-of-the-art border fence is estimated at between four and eight billion dollars. Estimates also reveal that

> Costs for a wall that would run the entire length of the border might be as low as $851 million for a standard 10-foot prison chain link fence topped by razor wire. For another $362 million, the fence could be electrified. A larger 12-foot tall, two-foot-thick concrete wall painted on both sides would run about $2 billion. Initially it was estimated that the San Diego fence would cost $14 million – about $1 million a mile. The first 11 miles of the fence eventually cost $42 million – $3.8 million per mile, and the last 3.5 miles may cost even more since they cover more difficult terrain. An additional $35 million to complete the final 3.5 miles was approved in 2005 by the Department of Homeland Security – $10 million per mile (GlobalSecurity.org).

The millions of dollars spent on construction walls to keep Mexicans out of the US could be used instead to further the economic development of Mexico and the US. This would create jobs and help to ease the hard times that working people are experiencing in the current crisis in global capitalism.

Migration Policy Issues in the EU and US

Aspects of EU and US Immigration Restrictions and Entry Policies

The EU and US immigration policies reveal different dimensions of the fault lines in the neoliberal approach to migration. Both the EU and US are in the control of neoliberal capitalism dominated by finance capital – the US spearheading neoliberal globalization and the EU in the vanguard of "European bloc imperialism" through its economic partnership agreements. The variations in the operations of neoliberal capitalism in the EU and US are characterized as "European bloc imperialism" and "US-led globalization." The two approaches differ on immigration policies, although they are both restrictive and therefore are constitutive parts of the fault lines of neoliberal capitalism with regards to the movement of persons.

According to Niessen and Schibel (2003), "unlike the United States most European states do not consider immigration as a matter of national interest."[16] The regulatory immigration system in the US "aims to enhance the benefits and minimize the drawbacks of immigration" and there is "strong support from a wide variety of stakeholders" for "the country's bipartisan immigration policy." In the case of Europe, "the emphasis is on immigration restriction and prevention, reflecting the position of most stakeholders that the costs of immigration outweigh its benefits."[17]

The United States has pursued an open door policy to immigration for the first hundred years of its existence as a means to supply its agricultural and non-agricultural workforce. The immigration landscape was characterized by a situation "qualified as 'immigration management by the absence of it.'" A proper immigration policy that sets limits to immigrant numbers and implemented selection criteria was instituted at the beginning of the twentieth century. The implementing and enforcement

---

[16] Jan Niessen, Yongmi Schibel. (2003). EU and US Approaches to the Management of Immigration: Comparative perspectives. Migration Policy Group Brussels, May.

[17] Jan Niessen, Yongmi Schibel. (2003). EU and US Approaches to the Management of Immigration: Comparative perspectives. Migration Policy Group Brussels, May.

mechanisms introduced were the Department of Labor and the Department of Justice, respectively. Thereafter, immigration became a recurring issue on the US policy agenda.

According to Niessen and Schibel (2003) "family reunion, employment schemes, or humanitarian programs" are the principal means through which immigrants normally enter the US to live and work permanently. These immigrants can become US citizens after five years. According to official data roughly 800 thousand legal immigrants were admitted into the US each year in the 1990s. The considerable increase in immigrants in the US during the last 30 years reflects a change in the countries of origin from Europe to Latin America and Asia.[18]

In the EU however, "5.1 percent of the population were non-nationals, of which 3.5% or 13 million were non-EU nationals and 1.6% or 6 million were EU nationals," in 2000. Furthermore, "positive net migration was at around 700,000 net migrants," in 2000, "a net migration rate of 0.2 percent." Of these "almost three quarters were third country nationals," made of predominantly by Turkish nationals, with 2.7 million people, 1.9 million from the former Yugoslavia, 2.3 million from North Africa, just over 1 million from the rest of Africa, and 2.2 million from Asia.[19]

Niessen and Schibel (2003) noted that neither the EU nor the US pursue a laisser-faire policy in migration, which is considered to be unfeasible. Thus, "Immigration policies in the EU and in the US" are "a mix of accommodating and facilitating the movements of people. One of the consequences is that limits or ceilings are set in terms of numbers of immigrants and that admission criteria are defined."

Niessen and Schibel (2003) pointed out that "national origin" is at the heart of "exclusion/inclusion criterion" applied in several countries. However, the "racial overtones" of that system forced the US to abolish it in the 1960s, "which was an indirect effect of the civil rights movement." The granting of "opportunities and entitlements" regardless of "race, ethnicity, national origin" makes it "difficult to defend a position that this only applies to those who are already in and not to those who want to come in." Europe also has "many variations of this theme" particularly with respect

---

[18] Jan Niessen and Yongmi Schibel. (2003). EU and US Approaches to the Management of Immigration: Comparative perspectives. Migration Policy Group Brussels, May.

[19] Jan Niessen and Yongmi Schibel. (2003). EU and US Approaches to the Management of Immigration: Comparative perspectives. Migration Policy Group Brussels, May.

to "its history of reversed colonial migration and with the different status of immigrants coming from different types of associated states."[20]

Much of the policy debates in the EU and US is said to surround the issue of finding a balance between "economic, social and humanitarian considerations" for migration. They both identify many advantages of employment-based immigration, which is the economic pillar of immigration policy. However, the determination of economic needs based immigration policy force the EU and the US to make choices to meet their respective domestic conditions. According to Niessen and Schibel (2003) for many years "this was the main component of US policies and only in the second part of the 20th century other components were added." In both in the EU and the US "the assessments of employers and trade unions groups tend to differ markedly" on economic needs. In these conflict situations government tends to broker a compromise.

Also, the use of language as a selection criterion for entry, in cases is an important barrier to immigration. In the US for example, language has been used as a criterion in the determination of entry. In Europe language was a critical issue in the debate on integration. This was coupled with the fact that some countries linked "the issuance of permanent residence permits or the granting of social benefits" with the capacity of immigrants "to express themselves in the national language."

However, according to Niessen and Schibel (2003) the primary difference between the EU and US immigration policy stems from the fact that the US is a "well-established federation," while the EU is a "federation in the making." Whereas in the US "admission decisions are taken at national level in a federal system of complete freedom of movement," in the EU "national governments of Member States decide on admission in a Union system of severely restricted freedom of movement and settlement of immigrants." Thus, while the freedom is maintained in the US system, "it is highly unlikely that the federal government will share its full admission powers with governments of states." In the EU, however, it is unlikely that there will be complete freedom of movement, as long as its member-states jealously guard their sovereignty on immigration matters.[21]

---

[20] Jan Niessen and Yongmi Schibel. (2003). EU and US Approaches to the Management of Immigration: Comparative perspectives. Migration Policy Group Brussels, May.

[21] Jan Niessen and Yongmi Schibel. (2003). EU and US Approaches to the Management of Immigration: Comparative perspectives. Migration Policy Group Brussels, May.

Meanwhile, there are a number of other issues such as Islam, security, and terrorism that form barriers to immigration in the EU and US.[22] In Europe for example, there is the rhetoric that due to their fundamental difference, there is an inability by Muslims "to integrate yet alone assimilate to the mainstream" society. The false view of the inability of Muslims to integrate in European society is identified as the cause of social disintegration in the EU. This incorrect assessment that brands all Muslims as fundamentalists is accompanied with another view. In this case a link is established between immigration and security, and "a singular worldview" is perpetuated in debates on immigration of "us the mainstream versus them the immigrants/terrorists."[23] Thus, as economic, social and humanitarian considerations influence the erection of both entry and restriction policies, Islamophobia, security, and terrorism seem to operate at one extreme – the restriction of entry of certain people.

Under the US Immigration and Nationality Act (INA), an alien could only enter the US to perform skilled or unskilled labor if the following two conditions are determined. In the first instance, there must not be "sufficient U.S. workers who are able, willing, qualified, and available" to do the job. Second, "the employment of the alien will not adversely affect the wages and working conditions of similarly employed workers in the United States." The US Department of Labor has responsibility for the foreign labor certification program, which ensures "that foreign workers do not displace or adversely affect working conditions of U.S. workers."[24]

Immigration policy in the US nonetheless has been influenced by the ebb and flow of migration into the country, and the associated cultural, religious, ethnic, and economic objections by the native-born population to the arrival of new immigrants. These identical objections to immigration are present in the current period, although the national debate on the subject is focused on its economic effects namely on the public budget and the private economy.[25] The principal issue concerning the budgetary

---

[22] Didier Ruedin and Gianni D'Amato. (2011). Improving EU and US Immigration Systems' Capacity for Responding to Global Challenges: Learning from Experiences Social Cohesion Challenges in Europe, Research Report, Background paper, EU-US Immigration Systems 2011/04 European University Institute, Robert Schuman Centre for Advanced Studies, Italy.

[23] Didier Ruedin and Gianni D'Amato. (2011). Improving EU and US Immigration Systems' Capacity for Responding to Global Challenges: Learning from Experiences Social Cohesion Challenges in Europe, Research Report, Background paper, EU-US Immigration Systems 2011/04 European University Institute, Robert Schuman Centre for Advanced Studies, Italy.

[24] Ruth Ellen Wasem. (2010). Immigration of Foreign Workers: Labor Market Tests and Protections, Congressional Research Service (CRS), 7-5700, RL33977, August 27.

[25] Linda Levine. (2010). Immigration: The Effects on Low-Skilled and High-Skilled Native-Born Workers, Congressional Research Service (CRS) 7-5700, 95-408, April 13.

effects "is whether immigrants receive more in public services than they pay in taxes." Furthermore, the problematic concerning the relationship between immigrants and the private economy is that in their capacity as workers, immigrants affect the private economy. Thus, according to Levine (2010) the problematic is that

> [I]f the admission of foreign-born workers lowers wages, which, in turn, results in more goods being produced at lower prices, then U.S. consumers would benefit; however, if immigration results in lower wages, U.S. workers would be harmed. The debate over immigration policy has been devoted more to the well being of U.S. workers than to consumer welfare.[26]

These issues have taken center stage in the US in the wake of the economic recession, which began in December 2007.[27] There is a tendency for international migration to ebb during economic crises, as evidenced by the Great Depression, during which the lowest level ever of in-migration was recorded in the US. Although there is some evidence that economic growth has returned, unemployment remains high in the US, indicating that the crisis persists, but, although "preliminary statistical trends hint at a slowing of migration pressures, it remains unclear how the current economic recession will affect immigration."[28]

Wasem (2010) observed that some US employers continue to depend on "the 'best and brightest' workers, regardless of their country of birth, to remain competitive in a worldwide market and to keep their firms in the United States." However, while arguments against increasing employment-based immigration may gain momentum during an economic recession, "proponents argue that the ability to hire foreign workers is an essential ingredient for economic growth."

The opponents to increased in-migration of foreign workers assert that migrants "have a deleterious effect on salaries, compensation, and working conditions of U.S. workers." Also, they question the wisdom of the US issuing foreign worker visas, above all temporary visas, during an economic recession and propose that the government places a moratorium on the issuance of such visas.[29]

---

[26] Linda Levine. (2010). Immigration: The Effects on Low-Skilled and High-Skilled Native-Born Workers, Congressional Research Service (CRS) 7-5700, 95-408, April 13.

[27] Ruth Ellen Wasem. (2010). Immigration of Foreign Workers: Labor Market Tests and Protections, Congressional Research Service (CRS), 7-5700, RL33977, August 27.

[28] Ruth Ellen Wasem. (2010). Immigration of Foreign Workers: Labor Market Tests and Protections, Congressional Research Service (CRS), 7-5700, RL33977, August 27.

[29] Ruth Ellen Wasem. (2010). Immigration of Foreign Workers: Labor Market Tests and Protections, Congressional Research Service (CRS), 7-5700, RL33977, August 27.

According to Wasem (2010) there has been a marked increase in the number of foreign workers who legally entered the US over the past decade. The data showed that between FY1994 and FY2005 the number of employment-based legal *permanent* residents (LPRs) grew from under 100,000 to over 250,000, declining in 2009 to 126,874. Also, there was an increase in the number of visas issued to employment-based *temporary* non-immigrants between FY1994 and FY2007 from just under 600,000 to approximately 1.3 million, although the number dropped slightly to 1.1 million in FY2009.[30]

It is in these contexts of US immigration policy and debate on the significance of decreased or increased employment-based immigration, whether the economy is in recession or growing, and the current US-Mexico border issues stated above that the US-Mexico border fence must be understood and analyzed.

Anti-Immigration in Theory and Practice

Some Economic and Sociological Arguments

Another set of fault lines associated with the neoliberal approach to migration could be gleaned from an analysis of relevant economic and sociological arguments against migration. Historically, a key economic argument against migration has been that migrant labor suppresses the wage rate in the receiving countries. Accordingly, it was theorized that as the supply of labor increases with in-migration relative to demand the price of labor decreases. Labor migration is said to reduce the wage rate in three ways.

First, migrant workers are willing to work for lower wages and so employers will set the wage floor lower than it would have otherwise been in the absence of migrant labor. Second, a related point in neoclassical economic analysis is that the increase in supply of any commodity, relative to its demand lowers the price of that commodity subject to elasticity, and that the same applies in labor markets. Thus, migrant labor lowers wages, as well as the wage floor. Third, because migrant labor lowers wages, and the wage floor overall, it suppresses the total aggregate labor income and hence reduces potential consumer spending.

---

[30] Ruth Ellen Wasem. (2010). Immigration of Foreign Workers: Labor Market Tests and Protections, Congressional Research Service (CRS), 7-5700, RL33977, August 27.

Furthermore, it is theorized that migration exacerbates labor market imperfections otherwise referred to as labor market failures, adding losses to the population in receiving countries. Market imperfections are said to "affect virtually every transaction in some way, generating costs that interfere with trades that rational individuals make, or would make, in the absence of the imperfection."[31] Thus, the labor market is said to be inefficient, since there exists other efficient outcomes that would bring more gains to participants in it, which the imperfections hinder.[32]

It is believed that market imperfections involve information irregularities, non-competitive markets, externalities, and pubic goods. A market is imperfect when information is uneven or irregular allowing one party to a transaction to possess more or better information than the other. Market imperfection exist in a variety of non-competitive market conditions identified in the neoclassical literature as monopolistic competition, oligopoly, duopoly, oligopsony, monopoly, natural monopoly, and monopsony.

Also, a market is classified as imperfect when there are externalities, which could be negative in which case they are called transaction spillovers or costs, or they may be positive in which case they are called external benefits. These externalities are not transmitted through prices and are incurred by a party who did not agree to the action causing the cost or benefit. A public good is defined as a commodity, which must contain the following two important qualities – first, its use by one individual does not reduce the availability of the good for others to use, and second, no individual could be excluded from consuming the good.

Also, it is theorize that migration takes a toll on the welfare state because migrants benefit from various entitlement programs and public services, increasing the cost to the state in the provision of those programs and services.[33] According to Razin and Sadka (1996), "Being unable to perfectly exclude migrants from various entitlement programs and public services, the modern welfare state finds it more and more costly to run its various programs."[34] However, Borjas and Hilton (1996), observed that in the US for example, "The immigrant-native difference in the probability of

---

[31] Ramon P. DeGennaro. (2005). Market Imperfections, Federal Reserve Bank of Atlanta Working Paper Series, Working Paper 2005–12, July.

[32] Assaf Razin and Efraim Sadka. (1996). "Suppressing Resistance to Low-skill Migration." *International Tax and Public Finance*, Vol. 3, No. 3, pp 413–424.

[33] Assaf Razin and Efraim Sadka. (1996). "Suppressing Resistance to Low-skill Migration." *International Tax and Public Finance*, Vol. 3, No. 3, pp 413–424.

[34] Assaf Razin and Efraim Sadka. (1995). Resisting Migration: The Problems of Wage Rigidity and the Social Burden, NBER Working Paper No. 4903, Issued in June.

receiving cash benefits is small, but the gap widens once programs are included in the analysis: 21 percent of immigrant households receive some type of assistance, as compared with only 14 percent of native-households."[35]

Some sociological arguments against migration are that migrant workers promote crime, and dilute the local culture. In the UK for example, Mike Fuller the Chief Constable of Kent said "that 'migration surges' had contributed to an increase of more than a third in violent crime over five years to 7,800 incidents in 2007." The Chief Constable of Kent said "The influx of migrants from eastern European countries is placing a huge strain on resources and has brought greater complexity to the pattern of crime."[36]

Fabio Mariani (2010), however, has disputed the view that crime is usually high among migrant populations. According to Mariani (2010), the "concern about the propensity of immigrants to become involved in criminal activities is almost as old as migration itself." There are reports from the 1930s and 1940s[37] that document examples "of how, in the 19th century United States, immigration was regarded as a potential inflow of criminals" (Mariani, 2010). Mariani (2010) pointed out that currently the commonly held view in the OECD is that "immigrants commit more crimes than natives, thus determining an overall increase in crime." Mariani (2010) noted however that "empirical evidence says that crime rates are not necessarily higher among immigrants than among natives; however, in most cases, second-generations immigrants are more involved in criminal activities than natives."[38]

Meanwhile, the data showed that among Europeans migrants convicted in Britain in 2010 Polish migrants toped the list with 6,777 convictions. Romanians at 4,343, Lithuanians at 4,176, the Irish at 2,423, Latvians at

---

[35] George J. Borjas and Lynette Hilton. (1996). "Immigration and the Welfare State: Immigrant Participation in Means-Tested Entitlement Programs," *The Quarterly Journal of Economics*, Vol. 111, No. 2, May.

[36] Harriet Sergeant. (2008). "Commentary: The facts behind crime and migration." Mail Online, April. http://www.dailymail.co.uk/news/article-560181/Commentary-The-facts-crime-migration.html.

[37] Abbott, E. (1931). "The Problem of Crime and the Foreign Born," in *National Commission on Law Observance and Enforcement: Report on Crime and the Foreign Born*, Washington, D.C., United States Government Printing Office; and Van Vechten, C.C. (1941). "The Criminality of the Foreign Born," *Journal of Criminal Law and Criminology* 32, 139–147.

[38] Fabio Mariani. (2010). Migration and Crime: Preliminary Draft. IRES, Université Catholique de Louvain Paris School of Economics IZA, Bonn March 15. http://www.iza.org/conference_files/LeIlli2010/mariani_f2907.pdf.

1,938, and Portugal 1,842, followed on the Polish.[39] Tom Whitehead (2011) the home affairs editor of *The Daily Telegraph* reported that, "More than 54,000 European Union citizens have been convicted of crimes" in the United Kingdom in 2010, and that "Poles and Romanians are the worst offenders according to the figures, adding to concerns over the impact of the two most recent EU expansions."[40] According to Whitehead (2011), "Figures from the Association of Chief Police Officers showed that last year 27,056 such notifications were made and 27,379 in 2009. That is the equivalent of 520 a week or 75 a day." The data showed that the worse European immigrant offenders in Britain "with the exception of Ireland ... came from countries that joined the EU in either 2004 or 2007."[41]

The idea that migrants are criminals is not only prevalent in the developed countries such as the US and the OECD states. In India, the New Delhi Home Minister Chidambaram accused migrants of being the cause of an increase in crime in that city after an 18-year old girl was gang-raped in a moving car. ("P Chidambaram links crime to migrants, retreats after opposition backlash," *Economic Times Bureau*, Dec 14, 2010). Although Chidambaram was severely criticized by his opponents for his anti-immigration statement, the sentiment that immigrants are criminals is still present among the ruling elites in India.

In the Caribbean there are reports of an increase in hostility towards Guyanese immigrants in Barbados. Some native Barbadians are of the view that the island is getting over-populated by Guyanese, and that these immigrants are allegedly involved in crime, particularly drugs and prostitution. Also, it is said that race plays a role in than many of the immigrants are of East Indian extraction, who are seen be threatening to over-run the country, numerically. Mr. Joseph Atherley, the Minister of State for Immigration in Barbados, a country with a black majority is reported to have said, "I think that a lot of (anti-Guyanese) utterances is being driven in the minds of people that Barbados is being overrun by non-nationals, particularly Guyanese and more specifically East Indian Guyanese."[42]

---

[39] Tom Whitehead. (2011). EU Migrants Commit 500 Crimes a Week in UK, Sunday 17 April.

[40] Tom Whitehead. (2011). EU Migrants Commit 500 Crimes a Week in UK, Sunday 17 April.

[41] Tom Whitehead. (2011). EU Migrants Commit 500 Crimes a Week in UK, Sunday 17 April.

[42] Quoted in Bertram Niles. (2006). Are Guyanese welcome in Barbados? *BBC Caribbean. com* September 7.

Examining the case of migration between China and Tibet, John Pomfret (1999)[43] in his article "A Less Tibetan: Many Residents Fear Chinese Migration will Dilute Culture" published in the *Washington Post Foreign Service*, highlights the issue of the dilution of culture due to migration. Indeed, the World Bank approved a $160 million loan for the resettlement of 58,000 people including Han Chinese on land traditionally claimed by Tibet, designed to give farmers from an overpopulated region access to more land and water to "speed the assimilation of Tibetans, a deeply religious people whose language, world view and customs differ sharply from the Chinese." The resettlement is opposed on the grounds that it threatens to swamp the culture of Tibet. Similar arguments are made in Israel, the US and Australia among other places, about immigrant population diluting or threatening to over-run the local culture. This non-economic factor is also advanced as a reason in support of separation walls in Israel and the US.

The Ascendancy of Anti-Immigration Movements

Why have the anti-immigrant sectors gotten the upper hand over capital that wants/exploits immigrant labor? Currently, the anti-immigration sectors in the US have gained the upper hand over the pro-immigrant capitalist sectors. But the argument here is that this is only a temporary development because historically anti-immigration hysteria tends to be a cyclical phenomenon. It took the form of anti-catholic, anti-Irish and anti-Italian sentiments in the US during the 1920s. This led to the passage of the Immigration Act of 1924 that basically outlawed Asian immigration and instituted national origin quotas that favored Northern European immigrants.[44] The Act of 1924 remained the standard bearer of US immigration policy until 1965 when it was replaced by the Immigration and Nationality Act in that year, which finally abolished the national origin quota system.

The current wave of anti-immigration sentiment focuses on Latin Americans, and especially after the September 11, 2001 attacks on the World Trade Center and the Pentagon, and the declaration by the US of its "war on terrorism," on Muslims and people from the Middle East. According to the Southern Poverty Law Center (SPLC), the anti-Hispanic

---

[43] John Pomfret. (1999). "A Less Tibetan: Many residents fear Chinese Migration will Dilute Culture. Washington Post Foreign Service, Sunday, October page A31.
[44] Heidi Beirich, The Anti-Immigrant Movement, Southern Poverty Law Center, http://www.splcenter.org/get-informed/intelligence-files/ideology/anti-immigrant/the-anti-immigrant-movement.

sentiments could be traced back to the 1960s and even before, although it gained momentum in the 1970s with the formation of certain hate groups that are presently at the foundation of the anti-immigration movement.[45] Also, "the association between the" September 11, 2001 "attacks and immigrants in the minds of voters has created a complex shift in public sentiment about immigrants."[46]

The concern of the anti-immigration movement in this connection is to "protect" the US from "outsiders" to guarantee the country's security against "terrorist acts." Arabs and people who look like Arabs feel the brunt of this anti-immigrant sentiment. Also, there is even greater paranoia among some Americans who believe that the country should close its borders on the grounds that both legal and illegal immigrants "endanger" the country "because they bring terrorism, disease, and advance Mexico's 'longtime goal to open the U.S. border.'" This has led to the inclusion of restrictive measures against immigrants in the "anti-terrorism legislation pushed through Congress by the Bush administration in 2001."[47]

The anti-immigration movement advances several arguments in support of its stance against amnesty for undocumented immigrants in the US. It is argued that guest workers will not return to Mexico so "the temporary amnesty linked to a guest worker program will permanently increase the number of immigrants who remain in the United States." Furthermore, it is believed that "Amnesty for undocumented immigrants rewards the "lawlessness" for their entry into the" United States, whereas "the INS should be strengthened so as to be able to identify and prosecute all undocumented immigrants."

The anti-immigration movement takes the view that "Amnesty will provoke a backlash among White voters because the costs of supporting immigrants' health care and education fall largely to White taxpayers, who, on average, earn higher incomes and therefore pay more in taxes." In addition it is believed that "Any newly legalized Mexican workers will have primary loyalty to Mexico, not to the United States," and that "this 'dual

---

[45] Heidi Beirich, The Anti-Immigrant Movement, Southern Poverty Law Center, http://www.splcenter.org/get-informed/intelligence-files/ideology/anti-immigrant/the-anti-immigrant-movement.

[46] Jean Hardisty. (2002). Corporate Desires vs. Anti-immigration Fervor: The Bush Administration's Dilemma, *Political Research Associates*, http://www.publiceye.org/ark/immigrants/CorporateHardisty.html.

[47] Jean Hardisty. (2002). Corporate Desires vs. Anti-immigration Fervor: The Bush Administration's Dilemma, *Political Research Associates*, http://www.publiceye.org/ark/immigrants/CorporateHardisty.html.

loyalty' presents a threat to U.S. sovereignty because these new residents might place the interests of Mexico ahead of those of the United States."[48]

The anti-immigration movement takes the position that "When the federal government encourages population growth through relaxed immigration policies such as amnesty, it works directly against the interests of a clean and safe environment." This is because "immigrants' 'larger families' and 'lower living standards,'" play a major "role in disproportionately polluting the environment and increasing the U.S. crime rate." Another view it holds is that, "Immigrants take jobs from native U.S. workers, adding to the number of unemployed U.S. workers." Finally, it is believed that "Immigrants slow innovation in technology because they provide low cost manual labor." The view is that, "If employers were forced to hire more costly workers, they would feel increased pressure to develop new technologies to replace those more costly workers and also increase productivity."[49]

These positions taken up by the anti-immigration movement are met by ambivalence on the part of some capitalist supporters of immigration. Thus, for example, in South Carolina, where state law SB20 requiring E-verification of immigrants is being vehemently opposed by immigrants, some sectors take a clear stand one way or the other on the bill, while others tend to waver between the two positions. But, this apparently "neutral" position on immigration taken up by some businesses is opportunistic. Agriculture, construction, the hotel industry, restaurants and food services in South Carolina depend in large measure on immigrant labor.

These businesses do not want to give the impression that they approve of undocumented immigrants, and that they hire them illegally because this "could drive potential customers away and affect their businesses." Thus, "The South Carolina Chamber of Commerce, representing some 18,000 firms with more than 1 million employees, decided not to take a position with regard to SB20." The estimates are that if undocumented immigrants leave South Carolina "the state would lose $1.8 billion in consumer spending, $783 million in production and about 12,000 jobs."

---

[48] Jean Hardisty. (2002). Corporate Desires vs. Anti-immigration Fervor: The Bush Administration's Dilemma, *Political Research Associates*, http://www.publiceye.org/ark/immigrants/CorporateHardisty.html.

[49] Jean Hardisty. (2002). Corporate Desires vs. Anti-immigration Fervor: The Bush Administration's Dilemma, *Political Research Associates*, http://www.publiceye.org/ark/immigrants/CorporateHardisty.html.

However, the Pew Hispanic Center data showed that "the undocumented population in South Carolina fell by 21.4 percent between 2007 and 2010, from 70,000 to 55,000, respectively."[50]

Arguably, it is the interests of the capitalists of "middle-sized companies, which have not invested abroad" that drive anti-immigration sentiments. These capitalists are said to be in the minority, edged on by "their political pit-bulls." The view is that characteristically, "They sell on the U.S. market and maintain highly restrictive hiring practices." Furthermore, "Out of fear of competition from the giant global corporations, they wrap themselves in the American flag and the banners of right-wing populism," and "find a voting base among economically desperate sections of the petty bourgeoisie and elements of the white labor aristocracy."[51]

Furthermore, immigrant workers are said to be faced with a danger very difficult to combat – "the mainstream capitalists," who "have far greater power today and even claim to be anti-racist, [and] to support immigrant rights and deplore "excessive" police brutality."[52] These capitalists are "the bosses who benefit from immigrants and love the low wages forced on them, and the effect this has in depressing wages in general."[53] This situation in which the immigrant struggle is led by "mainstream capitalists" who benefit the most from low wages, has led to the conclusion that "The immigrants' struggle badly needs a leadership based on the working class, not tied to a capitalist system that thrives on racism, class division and super-exploitation."[54]

Simultaneously that the anti-immigration movement has gained steam, however, there are many sections and sectors of US capital that continue to demand immigrant labor. It is estimated that "about 60 percent of the world's almost 100 million migrant workers" were "in developed or industrial countries, and their distribution" was "markedly different from that of native-born workers." Calculations in 2006 were that about 10 percent of the migrants in the industrial countries were employed in the agricultural

---

[50] "S. Carolina business sector divided over anti-immigrant bill," Read more: http://latino.foxnews.com/latino/news/2011/02/24/s-carolina-business-sector-divided-anti-immigrant/#ixzz1dmRtolZb.

[51] "End Anti-Immigrant Attacks!" *Proletarian Revolution*, No. 55 (Fall 1997) http://www.lrp-cofi.org/PR/immigrationPR55.html.

[52] "End Anti-Immigrant Attacks!" *Proletarian Revolution*, No. 55 (Fall 1997) http://www.lrp-cofi.org/PR/immigrationPR55.html.

[53] "End Anti-Immigrant Attacks!" *Proletarian Revolution*, No. 55 (Fall 1997) http://www.lrp-cofi.org/PR/immigrationPR55.html.

[54] "End Anti-Immigrant Attacks!" *Proletarian Revolution*, No. 55 (Fall 1997) http://www.lrp-cofi.org/PR/immigrationPR55.html.

sector, while 40 percent were in industry, and 50 percent were in services. With respect to the native-born, only 3 percent were in agriculture, 25 percent in industry, and 72 percent in services.[55]

The agricultural sector is one of the major employers of immigrant labor in the US. The main reason for this is that Americans are not attracted to the backbreaking work associated with agricultural production. According to Wasem and Collver (2003) "61 percent of farm workers in the United States worked in fruit, nut, or vegetable production," while "42 percent worked in tobacco cultivation."[56] Furthermore, "States in the southeastern United States account for more than half of all H-2A job certifications."[57]

The estimates were that "about 10 to 40 percent of workers in the restaurant business are undocumented." Illegal immigrants are found in the businesses engaged "in food production, information technology, financial services, construction, and other sectors regarded as 'critical infrastructure and key resources,'" which have become targets of the US government agencies enforcing immigration policy.[58]

The Mexicans in states such as California, Nevada, Arizona, Colorado, New Mexico, and Texas are forced to work in the mines, fields, and homes of the capitalists.[59]

Pro-Immigration Mass Movements

Pushback by immigrants has taken many forms including pro-immigration protest rallies and pro-immigration mass movements. The immigrant rights movement surged in 2006 when it peaked on April 10 and May 1 with marches across the US of over an estimated two million people. The marches were spearheaded by Hispanics immigrants namely Chicanos, Mexicanos, and Central Americans, in their struggle for self-determination and full equality in the US.[60] They were supported by labor

---

[55] Philip Martin. (2006). The Economics of Migration: Managing the Flow of International Labor, *Harvard International Review*, July 17.

[56] Ruth Ellen Wasem and Geoffrey K. Collver. (2003). Immigration of Agricultural Guest Workers: Policy, Trends, and Legislative Issues, CRS Report, January 24.

[57] Ruth Ellen Wasem and Geoffrey K. Collver. (2003). Immigration of Agricultural Guest Workers: Policy, Trends, and Legislative Issues, CRS Report, January 24.

[58] *Reason Magazine*. (2011). Obama's Anti-Immigrant Stance, July 12.

[59] Freedom Road Socialist Organization. (2009). "The Immigrant Rights Movement and the Struggle for Full Equality," http://www.frso.org/docs/2009/immrts2009screen.pdf.

[60] Freedom Road Socialist Organization. (2009). "The Immigrant Rights Movement and the Struggle for Full Equality," http://www.frso.org/docs/2009/immrts2009screen.pdf.

organizations such as the Service Employees International Union (SEIU), aided by organizers from the Food Workers, the Needle Trades, AFSCME, and health-care workers.[61] The millions who poured to the streets were opposed "to proposed Republican Congressional legislation (H.R. 4437) that threatened to deport millions, and build a 700-mile-long wall along the U.S.-Mexican border."[62]

The pro-immigrant mass rallies took place in an estimated 142 cities across in the US. In mid-February an ad hoc coalition in Los Angeles called the first major demonstration that "brought out 100,000 people in Chicago, Illinois." Then, "on March 25, between 300,000 and 500,000 people, mostly high school youth, took over the City of Los Angeles, in a massive demonstration and high-school boycott in favor of treating immigrants like human beings, not criminals."[63] On April 9, "an estimated *half a million* people turned out in Dallas, Texas to call for justice for immigrants." On April 10 record-breaking crowds "including over 300,000 people in Phoenix, Arizona; 20,000 in Indianapolis, Indiana; 25,000 in Seattle, Washington; 75,000 in Fort Myers, Florida; 100,000 in San Diego, California; and 10,000 in Omaha, Nebraska," demonstrated in pro-immigration rallies.

Petras (2006)[64] identified the significance of what he termed the "new mass migrant workers movement." He argues that it opened a new chapter in the working class struggle in North and Central America. According to Petras (2006), "It represents the first major upsurge of independent working class struggle in the US after over fifty years of decline, stagnation and retreat by the established trade union confederation." Secondly, it "reveals a new class protagonist as the leading sector in the labor movement, the migrant worker." Thirdly, it "was organized without a big bureaucratic trade union apparatus, and with a minimum budget on the basis of voluntary workers through horizontal communication." Fourthly, "the leadership and strategists of the movement were independent of the two major capitalist parties, especially the deadly embrace of the Democratic Party."

[61] Nancy Spannaus. (2006). Mass Strike Ferment Hits United States in Pro-Immigration Rallies. *Executive Intelligence Review*.
[62] Nancy Spannaus. (2006). Mass Strike Ferment Hits United States in Pro-Immigration Rallies. *Executive Intelligence Review*.
[63] Nancy Spannaus. (2006). Mass Strike Ferment Hits United States in Pro-Immigration Rallies. *Executive Intelligence Review*.
[64] James Petras. (2006). Mesoamerica comes to North America: The dialectics of the Migrant Workers' Movement, The James Petras Website, 05.02.2006, http://petras.lahaine.org/?p=6.

Also, "The movement demonstrates the proper approach to combining race and class politics."[65]

However, the movement faced political obstacles to growth and development. First, from the outside, "numerous employers fired workers who participated in the first wave of mass demonstrations." Secondly, due to the success of the mass movements "numerous traditional Latino politicos, social workers, professional consultants, non-governmental organizations and clerical notables jumped on the bandwagon." These middle class collaborators then became "active in deflecting the movement into the conventional channels of petitioning Congress or supporting the lesser evil Democratic Party politicians," and in "dividing the movement to serve their purpose of gaining a political platform for career advancement." Thirdly, the struggle developed unevenly "within the working class and between regions of the country."[66]

There are many allies in the struggle for immigrant rights in the US.[67] These include "other Latinos" of different nationalities than the Chicanos, Mexicanos, and Central Americans, who enter the US on the East Coast and then spread west, lacking the "connections to the Chicano nation that Mexicanos and Central Americans have." They are primarily Puerto Ricans who are US nationals and, Cubans who receive automatic legal status once they arrive on US soil.[68]

Then, there is the labor movement whose membership includes a growing number of immigrant workers. However, there is ambivalence in the labor movement towards immigration labor. Organized labor feels threatened by the guest worker programs, which the unions believed would "undermine wages and benefits, and the strength of unions."[69] Opposition to the guest worker program by the labor and pro-immigration movements has brought about a convergence of interests of these two social forces. Also, the Service Employees International Union (SEIU), in

---

[65] James Petras. (2006). Mesoamerica comes to North America: The dialectics of the Migrant Workers' Movement, The James Petras Website, 05.02.2006, http://petras.lahaine .org/?p=6.

[66] James Petras. (2006). Mesoamerica comes to North America: The dialectics of the Migrant Workers' Movement, The James Petras Website, 05.02.2006, http://petras.lahaine .org/?p=6.

[67] Freedom Road Socialist Organization. (2009). "The Immigrant Rights Movement and the Struggle for Full Equality," http://www.frso.org/docs/2009/immrts2009screen.pdf.

[68] Freedom Road Socialist Organization. (2009). "The Immigrant Rights Movement and the Struggle for Full Equality," http://www.frso.org/docs/2009/immrts2009screen.pdf.

[69] Freedom Road Socialist Organization. (2009). "The Immigrant Rights Movement and the Struggle for Full Equality," http://www.frso.org/docs/2009/immrts2009screen.pdf.

its attempt to boost its flagging membership by winning over undocumented workers, "broke ranks with the anti-immigration stance of its sister unions some years ago and has condemned" the raids carried out on immigrants by the Obama administration.[70] But, there continues to exist top union leadership who align themselves with the anti-immigration movement, although large sections of union membership are immigrant workers.[71]

Arab and Asian Americans represent a third category of allies in the struggle for immigrant rights. Asians are the second largest group of immigrants in the US other than Latinos, with more than one million undocumented Asian immigrants. Also, there is a growing Arab American population in the US numbering in the millions comprising immigrants and their children. Arabs and Asians in the US are targeted by the proposal to end family reunification immigration, the basis for most Middle East and Asian immigration to the US. Post-September 11, 2001 racial profiling and harassment are aimed at Arabs and Asians, tens of thousands of whom "were made to undergo special registration and more than 16,000 forced into deportation proceedings."[72]

African Americans are identified as a fourth category of allies in the pro-immigration movement. The African American "sector is growing rapidly with immigrants coming from the Caribbean and Africa." Many African Americans believe that "national oppression is at the core of the immigration debate," and realize that "Chicanos and Latinos share many of the same problems (police brutality, poor schools, etc.)," as themselves. Indeed, the evidence of African American support for "immigration reform," is provided by the Polls. Also, the "more progressive members of the Congressional Black Caucus (representing the African American bourgeoisie) have been supportive of immigration reform, and even introduced a bill in 2004 before the mass upsurge."[73]

---

[70] Shikha Dalmika. (1022). "Obama's Anti-Immigrant Stance," Reason Foundation, July 12. http://reason.org/news/show/obamas-anti-immigrant-stance.

[71] Freedom Road Socialist Organization. (2009). "The Immigrant Rights Movement and the Struggle for Full Equality," http://www.frso.org/docs/2009/immrts2009screen.pdf.

[72] Freedom Road Socialist Organization. (2009). "The Immigrant Rights Movement and the Struggle for Full Equality," http://www.frso.org/docs/2009/immrts2009screen.pdf.

[73] Freedom Road Socialist Organization. (2009). "The Immigrant Rights Movement and the Struggle for Full Equality," http://www.frso.org/docs/2009/immrts2009screen.pdf.

Conclusion

A key conclusion to be drawn from this chapter is that lofty ideals such as democracy, human rights, and freedom, are driven by practical considerations of the people with power. They are the ones who would like to be seen as taking the high ground in the cause of humanity, but in reality it is the practical interests of the ruling elites that governs their actions, not human suffering or the human condition. Thus, although the leading neoliberal capitalist states, international organizations and religious men pay much lip service to the freedom of movement of persons, it is the personal interests of the ruling classes that inform their decisions.

This is clearly the case with the separation walls in Israel and the US, the restrictive migration policies in the EU and US, and the anti-immigration mass movements. The ruling elites in the EU and US expended millions of dollars to deny entry to poor people from other countries, rather than use the money to help the poor countries overcome the socio-economic and political conditions, which force their people to emigrate.

CHAPTER NINE

THE EUROPEAN UNION AND MIGRATION: THE AFRICA CONNECTION

Introduction

This chapter critically examines the EU's approach to the migration of Africans into Europe. Its main purpose is to demonstrate that the EU's approach to African migration constitutes a major fault line in the neoliberal approach to the development impact of migration. To this end, it focuses on three distinct aspects of the EU and migration in the context of Africa. First, it critically analyses the EU's "global Europe" and migration strategies. Second, it describes and analyses the EU's approach to African migration outlined in the Joint Africa-European Union Declaration on Migration and Development.[1] Third, the focus shifts to the case of the EU and Libya, specifically to the EU-Libya migration cooperation agreement,[2] and recommendations of the European Parliament to the Council on the negotiations on the EU-Libya Framework Agreement.[3] Fourth, there is a discussion on the situation of migrants during the war that overthrow Colonel Muammar Gaddafi. Finally, there is a descriptive analysis of the mistreatment of migrants in Libya, and the EU's failure to support democracy in that country under the Gaddafi regime.

The principal proposition is that the EU's "global Europe" and migration strategies, the Joint Africa-EU Declaration on Migration and Development (JA-EUDMD), the EU-Libya Migration Cooperation Agreement, and the European Parliament's recommendations to the Council on the negotiations on the EU-Libya Framework Agreement, together constitute a major fault line in the neoliberal approach to the development impact of migration.

The fault line is that although these EU initiatives are designed to stimulate the private flow of finances from migration processes, they are

---

[1] Africa Union and European Union. (2006). Joint Africa-EU Declaration on Migration and Development, Tripoli, 22–23 November, Final Version.

[2] European Union. (2010). European Commission and Libya agree a Migration Cooperation agenda during high-level visit to boost EU-Libya Relations. EUROPA Press Releases, Brussels, 5 October.

[3] European Parliament recommendation of 20 January 2011 to the Council on the negotiations on the EU-Libya Framework Agreement (2010/2268(INI)).

heavily restrictive of migration. They seek to maximize profits from an increase in the global flows of remittances, due to the free movement of people, at the same time that they promote the management of the movement of people. Management is understood in the Braverman sense as a science of control.[4] But, despite the fact that managed migration allows for the arrival in the EU only of the best of the educated elites and skilled workers from Africa, any form of restriction on migration will negatively affect remittances. This is because remittances flow from all classes of migrants, not only from the educated elites and skilled workers. The ability of the financial elites to capture profits from remittances will therefore be reduced if migration is restricted.

The neoliberal approach to migration is therefore an inherently contradictory process one in which migration is encouraged to fuel the imperialist centered model of capital accumulation, while simultaneously it is discouraged in fulfillment of a variety of other interests. In the end nonetheless, the winners in this process are those belonging to the section of capital, which is most dominant under neoliberal capitalism that is finance capital.

It is also argued that the EU could care less about whether its approach to African migration encourages democracy promotion in Africa as the case of its relations with Libya under Gaddafi amply demonstrated. Gaddafi even used the fact that the EU signed a migration cooperation agreement with Libya to bloc North and Sub-Saharan Africans from crossing the Mediterranean Sea into Europe illegally, to threaten the EU to unleash a flood of Africans into Europe if it sided with the forced opposed to his rule.[5]

The problem however is that the EU compromised its democratic ideals by entering into the migration cooperation agreement with the Libyan dictatorship in order to achieve its objectives to limit the arrival of illegal North and Sub-Saharan African migrants in Europe. The EU-Libya migration cooperation agreement therefore created a dilemma for the EU. The EU's "global Europe strategy" is founded on lofty ideals such as democratic governance as a condition for the developing countries to reap any significant economic development benefits from their trade relations with the EU. This is indeed one of the conditions of the EU's economic partnership

---

[4] Harry Braverman. (1974). *Labor and Monopoly Capital: The Degradation of Work in the Twentieth Century.* New York, Monthly Review Press.
[5] Leigh Phillips. (2011). "EU scorns Libya 'blackmail' on migrants." *euobserver.com.* February 21.

agreements (EPA) under negotiation with various blocs of countries in Africa. However, the EU's migration approach in Libya prior to the war is an obvious double standard and a bad example for the promotion of democratic governance in Africa even by the EU's own standards.

It is not uncommon nonetheless for the leading capitalist states to promote dictators and authoritarian regimes in the developing world. The rich capitalist states use these dictators and authoritarian regimes to suppress local populations that oppose the pillage of their countries by foreign capital. History is replete with examples of such treacherous behaviors by European powers in Africa, Latin America, Asia and the Caribbean. Global capital currently spearheaded by finance capital has historically collaborated with dictators in the developing countries in its self-interest. The agenda of finance capital is to maximize profit from the billions of dollars that traverse the globe in the form of remittances, while simultaneously managing the flow of migrants into the European Union and the US.

Two key strategies favored by the global financial elites to maximize profit from remittances through managed migration, are essentially financial liberalization to make it easier for money to traverse the globe, and migration cooperation agreements with dictatorships to control the flow of migrants to the EU and the US. These elites are less concerned with the dangers that financial liberalization poses to the capitalist system. Examples of these dangers are contradictions such as the Wall Street meltdown in 2008 and its aftermath that threatened to break up the entire system. Also, they include the risks of increased money laundering, human and drug trafficking and smuggling, and the financing of so-called terrorist activities, that could result from making it easier for people to remit money by removing all restrictions, and lowering the cost of remittance.

The EU and Migration

This section highlights some salient features of the EU's "Global Europe" strategy, which in essence seeks to secure raw materials for European corporations, open-up markets for them to sell their products, and promote their competitiveness with the emerging market economies. The "global Europe" strategy however has encountered much opposition in different parts of the globe. The EU's migration strategy is also discussed in the context of "global Europe" to expose the double standards in the EU's approach to migration.

The EU's "Global Europe" Strategy

The European Commission launched its "global Europe" strategy in October 2006, which was subsequently endorsed by the European Council. In essence the "global Europe" strategy seeks to restore Europe's leadership position in the globe in terms of opening up new markets to create business opportunities for European firms, and ensuring the EU's appropriate participation in the emerging market economies. The strategy therefore forces open markets in the developing world for EU businesses. It allows EU businesses to gain access to other countries' natural resources, in their broadest sense including agricultural resources, energy resources and minerals.

In 2008, the EU organized a Raw Materials Conference, and launched its Raw Materials Initiative in September and November, respectively. The strategy seeks to reconstruct the EU single market through neoliberal deregulation measures. The focus of the strategy is "on goods, services, investment and government procurement liberalization, competition policy, intellectual property rights enforcement, [and] non-tariff barriers." In addition it concentrates on "obtaining not only market access but also national treatment for European business." The strategy is based on trade negotiations and economic diplomacy, with the use of "multilateral and bilateral trade defense instruments." Indeed, "the EU interprets exports restrictions as subsidies to the local industry."[6]

In the context of its "global Europe" strategy and the new race for raw materials in Africa the EU engaged Libya to gain access to Libyan markets and oil – Libya controls 3 present of the world's oil resources,[7] and to restrain North and Sub-Saharan Africa migrants from entering into the EU. Individual European countries such as Italy and Britain operating within the EU framework have also established bilateral relations with Libya for the same economic and migration control purposes.

However, the "global Europe" strategy has not enjoyed much success in that there is hardly any movement "in any of the EU's negotiating theatres,

---

[6] Maes, Mark. (2008). The EU's Global Europe Strategy: Where is that Strategy Today? Coalition of the Flemish North-South Movement Introductory presentation made at the informal meeting "Building of A Common Platform Between Developing Countries" organized by South Centre in Brussels on 4–5 December.

[7] Maes, Mark. (2008). The EU's Global Europe Strategy: Where is that Strategy Today? Coalition of the Flemish North-South Movement Introductory presentation made at the informal meeting "Building of A Common Platform Between Developing Countries" organized by South Centre in Brussels on 4–5 December.

not in the WTO, not in the ongoing or the newly launched bilateral negotiations. The EPA with the Caribbean is the only success the Commission has to show for quite some time now."[8] The "global Europe" strategy is contradictory in that it conflicts with regional integration, "which has been proclaimed to be a cornerstone of the EU's foreign and trade policy as can be seen from the bi-regional negotiations with the Gulf, MERCOSUR, ACP, ASEAN, the Andean Community (CAN), Central America, [and] the Mediterranean." The EU puts aside its lofty ideals of regional integration by negotiating with single countries in order to push its "global Europe" strategy. By so doing the EU fractures regional integration movements, as is the case in the EPA negotiations in the ACP regions including the Caribbean Forum (CARIFORUM).

The EU's global Europe strategy has ran up against much opposition in different parts of the world, including in Europe. The ACP regions and Latin America economic groupings have been very careful in signing-on to it unquestioningly. Civil society agencies in Europe including "social movements, trade unions and others working on issues such as agriculture, workers' rights, consumer interests, development, environment, women's issues, corporate accountability, climate change, migration, war, etc.," seek dialogue with the EU on its strategy.[9]

Furthermore, the EU launched its renewed "Market Access Strategy" (MAS) in April 2007, which followed on the "global Europe" strategy of 2006. The renewed MAS is intended to tackle barriers to trade and investment. It involves specialized working groups in Brussels and MAS Teams on the ground in key third-country markets to deal with specific trade barriers. The MAS brings together the appropriate EU member-states bodies, local EU delegations in third countries, and businesses to push for the removal of specific trade barriers. It seeks to establish a best practice approach based on the experience of the operators in removing trade barriers. The EU has reported in its *Global Europe Market Access Newsletter Issue 10 – 30 June 2008* that the MAS has brought much success in China, the USA, Argentina, Turkey and Japan, only one year after its implementation.

---

[8] Maes, Mark. (2008). The EU's Global Europe Strategy: Where is that Strategy Today? Coalition of the Flemish North-South Movement Introductory presentation made at the informal meeting "Building of A Common Platform Between Developing Countries" organized by South Centre in Brussels on 4–5 December.

[9] Seattle to Brussels Network. (2008). The new 'Global Europe' strategy of the EU: Serving corporations worldwide and at home A wake-up call to civil society and trade unions in Europe and elsewhere.

The EU's Migration Strategy

The EU employs a double standard migration strategy, which is an integral component of its global Europe approach. According to Brennan (2008), "Fortress Europe, with the free movement of labor within its borders and militarized borders facing the rest of the world has been constructed step by step during the past two decades." Brennan (2008) observed that during this process, "We have witnessed the sustained and deeper criminalization of migrants, not only by right wing extremists, but by government Ministers at the national level as well as by official policy makers at the European level." Brennan (2008) noted that, "Since 9/11, the issue of migration and asylum has been drawn into the debate and policy making on security."[10]

Brennan (2008) goes on to say

> These trends are very visible in the multiplication of detention centers in several EU countries; militarization of the borders (Frontex project);[11] mass raids on migrant centers and churches and summary deportation practices against undocumented migrants; a new attempt to recycle 'guest worker' programs and to popularize 'circular migration' as a response to the perceived, but often denied need of migrant labor in the European economy.[12]

According to Brennan (2008), "While Europe's economy, politics and culture has benefited enormously from decades of migration, European governments and their electorates continue to display a profound ambivalence about immigration." He argues that while the "similarities between European countries should not be overstated, in almost all cases, the issues of labor migration, undocumented migration, asylum and integration have become highly politically contested." And he stated that, "Public and parliamentary debate on these issues are currently dominated by racism, xenophobia and islamaphobia."[13]

---

[10] Brennan, Brid. (2008). Where have all our Human Rights Gone? EU Migration Policy 2008: Response and Resistance. Transnational Institute, Amsterdam, The Netherlands, September.

[11] Frontex is an intelligence-driven agency whose core activity is operations, the first stage of which is risk analysis.

[12] Brennan, Brid. (2008). Where have all our Human Rights Gone? EU Migration Policy 2008: Response and Resistance. Transnational Institute, Amsterdam, The Netherlands, September.

[13] Brennan, Brid. (2008). Where have all our Human Rights Gone? EU Migration Policy 2008: Response and Resistance. Transnational Institute, Amsterdam, The Netherlands, September.

In June 2008 the European Parliament passed the EU Return Directive, an expulsion Directive that allows member-states "to detain undocumented migrants for up to 18 months and impose a five-year ban on their return to the EU." It is estimated that the new Directive will affect 10 million undocumented impoverished migrants and their children. Amnesty International, the ACP countries, the International Federation on Human Rights, the MERCOSUR governments in Latin America, and social movements globally have, all condemned the Directive.

According to Brennan (2008), the EU Migration and Asylum Pact beginning in 2008, which is at the top of the EU's policy agenda, has a notorious feature, namely its "selective discriminatory immigration" policy "which proposes cherry picking the brains and skills of the South and the use of the carrot of development aid to condition and entice Southern governments to implement EU's migration policies." Furthermore, the EU has a virtual "ban on collective regularization, a mechanism which some EU governments (e.g. Spain, Greece) have implemented to respond to the rights of undocumented workers" which Brennan (2008) observed "is particularly worrying."[14]

The essence of the EU's migration strategy is for the EU members to "adopt common agreements on a 'concerted management of migration flows and co-development' as a model of negotiation through which the EU will promote selective immigration, and insist that Southern countries accept its nationals back home as well as those of other countries who have passed through their territory." Since 1993 the EU's migration policy has led to more than 6,700 deaths of migrants and refugees due to "border militarization, asylum laws, detention policies, deportations and carrier sanctions."[15]

There is a linkage between "global Europe" and "Fortress Europe" in the sense that the "global Europe strategy" is "also directly connected to other policies such as the undemocratic Lisbon Treaty, militarization of borders, and promotion and intensification of polices underpinning Fortress Europe." The EU is using aid to promote its geopolitical interest. For example the French Presidency of the EU in 2008 proposed the re-direction of

---

[14]   Brennan, Brid. (2008). Where have all our Human Rights Gone? EU Migration Policy 2008: Response and Resistance. Transnational Institute, Amsterdam, The Netherlands, September.

[15]   Brennan, Brid. (2008). Where have all our Human Rights Gone? EU Migration Policy 2008: Response and Resistance. Transnational Institute, Amsterdam, The Netherlands, September.

the EU's development policy "towards the fight against migration using part of the ODA budget," and France already has a Ministry, "which combines development and migration policy." The use of developmental aid as a tool to fight migration is highly contentious and is opposed by civil society organizations.[16]

In this connection a EU-African Conference on Migration and Development,[17] was established, the first of which was held in 2006 in Rabat, Morocco, and a second in Paris, France. "The Rabat process" brings together the EU and West African states in regional cooperation on migration between countries of origin, transit and destination on a particular migration route. There was a follow-up meeting of the Rabat Euro-African conference on migration and development in Madrid in June 2007 at which it was announced that ECOWAS has adopted a common policy approach to migration and a regional Action Plan on migration. The EU's idea is to promote shared responsibility between countries of origin, transit, and destination in the management of migration between the EU and Africa. The North African countries want the EU to facilitate visas to their citizens for their legitimate temporary entry into the EU, and the EU wants the North African countries to readmit deportees, and participate in the international protection of their migrants.

The Euro-African dialogue on migration in the context of the Rabat process, now takes place at the regional and continental levels in Africa. At the continental level this is done through the dialogue, which was started in 2007 following the Lisbon Summit between the EU and Africa Union. Dialogue on migration at the bilateral level is undertaken between EU member states and individual African countries. At the Paris conference the EU urged the African countries to pursue responsible policies for the prevention and reduction of illegal migration and the fulfillment of readmission obligations.

According to a EUROPA Press release in 2008 the Euro-African dialogue on migration is "only one aspect of global migration policy which also targets better organization of legal migration and promotion of the link between migration and development in the interest of the country of origin." Indeed, a EUROPA Press release in 2008 states, "The global approach

---

[16] Brennan, Brid. (2008). Where have all our Human Rights Gone? EU Migration Policy 2008: Response and Resistance. Transnational Institute, Amsterdam, The Netherlands, September.

[17] euMonitor. (2008). Euro-African Conference in Paris on migration and development: the Commission asks its partners to deliver on their commitments, 25 November.

to migration is now upheld by both Europe and Africa, despite the difference in their situations and their dissimilar experiences and perceptions of migration."[18]

The EU has used its developmental aid to elicit commitments from the African countries through "various cooperation initiatives," to participate in its migration schemes. According to a EUROPA Press release in 2008, "in the past three years" the European Commission, which is acting as the driving force, "has launched over one hundred migration projects in Africa." The press release states that the EC "supports the establishment of information and migration management centers in Africa" in countries such as Mali." Furthermore, the EC "contributes to capacity-building in African countries to help them manage migration" and "promotes increased cooperation, in particular on legal migration, through mobility partnerships and by organizing specific migration and development initiatives." The EC also "focuses on promoting respect for human dignity and the protection of the most vulnerable," according to the press release.

The EU's "migration projects in Africa" are nothing more than the creation of mechanisms to rape Africa of its human resources with the promise of development assistance. The net result of the "migration projects" will be that the professional and skilled classes in Africa trained with taxpayers money from the African countries will end-up working in the EU, while Africa will be left with the unskilled labor force and the problem of acquiring skilled labor to further its development. Such is the modus operandi of the imperialist centered method of capital accumulation in which migrant labor keeps the sea of profits flowing.

Joint Africa-EU Declaration on Migration and Development (JA-EUDMD)

The European Union under the disguise of achievement of the Millennium Development Goals, and development in general cajoled the African countries to sign on to its migration strategy. The key element that enticed the African countries to agree to the EU's migration strategy was the attachment of the word "development" to migration. The African countries were sold the idea that by cooperating with the EU's migration strategy, they could achieve the Millennium Development Goals. This would

---

[18] European Union. (2008). Euro-African Conference in Paris on migration and development: the Commission asks its partners to deliver on their commitments EUROPA Press Release Rapid Brussels, 25 November.

bring about the socio-economic development of the African countries. This argument is supported by the contents of the joint Africa-EU declaration on migration and development.

Through the declaration the African countries agreed to the EU migration policy outlined above. They agreed to participate in a "well-managed migration" process with the EU to "promote closer ties between countries of origin, transit and destination," and to help to meet "existing and future labor needs and contribute to the development of all countries." They also agreed that "well-managed migration" within the wider context of EU-African partnership could lead to the "achievement of the Millennium Development Goals."[19]

Furthermore, the JA-EUDMD commits the African countries to a partnership with the EU on the "origin, transit and destination" of migrants "to better manage migration in a comprehensive, holistic and balanced manner, in a spirit of shared responsibility and cooperation." The commitments to which the African countries have agreed require their political and concrete actions, which are "based on a common understanding of the opportunities and challenges that migration brings and that appropriate policy responses can best be found together."

The key areas for cooperation identified in the JA-EUDMD are first, the consideration of how to link migration and poverty reduction, and "other national development and co-development strategies of African countries," and agreeing that "well-managed migration can have a positive development impact for countries of origin, transit and destination." There is also the view of the need for cooperation on "creating and sustaining societies where citizens, in particular the youth, can build a future," and that the "mechanisms and channels that facilitate circular migration," and "recruitment policies" should "take into account the specific needs of countries of origin and destination."

The JA-EUDMD linked the root causes of migration and refugee flows with poverty eradication and the realization of the MDG and the objectives of NEPAD, improving living conditions and livelihoods of the poorest, and conflict resolution and prevention. It encourages and promotes FDI as an employment generation strategy and deterrence to migration outflows. It addresses the lack of employment as a root cause of migration, which requires better targeted development policies to ensure that "trade,

---

[19] Africa Union and European Union. (2006). Joint Africa-EU Declaration on Migration and Development, Tripoli, 22–23 November, Final Version.

agriculture and fisheries produce a positive impact on the socio-economic situation of African countries." Support for Africa's regional economic cooperation and integration groupings is embraced as an "effective means of ensuring economic growth and combating poverty" on the continent.

Also, the JA-EUDMD supports migratory flows and the freedom of movement of labor within Africa and facilitates Diasporas as sources of "sustainable development of their countries of origin." This requires "building the capacity of Diaspora organizations," support for "Diaspora networks," enabling the highly skilled African Diaspora "to carry out some of their professional activities in their home countries as well in the entire continent without necessarily needing to give up their employment abroad." The migrant-receiving countries are called on, to promote "equal treatment and assistance in the creation and registration of associations by migrant communities."

According to the JA-EUDMD both migrant sending and receiving countries must help to "set up mechanisms, services and effective financial products to facilitate the transfer of remittances, to reduce the costs of these transfers and to make them conducive to development, bearing in mind the private nature of remittances." This is the key agreement because of the billions of dollars that migrants remit on a yearly basis. In essence, therefore, the hub of the EU's approach to migration and development as contained in the JA-EUDMD is all about the money from migration flowing through financial houses and into the private accounts of the financial elites. Migration must be managed but the finalization and liberalization of remittances must, simultaneously be undertaken.

The "mutual recognition of academic qualifications and professional certificates through the conclusion of bilateral agreements or by other means," is identified as priorities for "further cooperation on employment and social policy, which have a strong link with migration and development." Also regarded as a priority for cooperation on migration and development is the issue of unemployment in Africa, and "its attendant consequences of illegal migration, drug abuse, crime and other social repercussions."

Finally, JA-EUDMD involves the strengthening of "African access to European and regional markets." This involves "working towards agreeing Economic Partnership Agreements (EPAs)" as "instruments of development," the promotion of poverty reduction, and the reinforcement of the "economic integration processes in Africa and Africa's integration in the global economy." Also, it entails "redoubling efforts to achieve an EU-Mediterranean Free Trade Area by 2010."

The JA-EUDMD also addresses what it terms the "migration manage-ment challenges." According to the JA-EUDMD these challenges involve "finding concrete solutions to the problems posed by illegal or irregular migratory flows by regulating the influxes of migrants from Africa within the context of genuine partnership that ensures the eradication of pov-erty, unemployment and diseases thereby achieving comprehensive and sustainable development." Both sides agree to the pursuit of a "holistic approach, ensuring a balanced response and concerted action in the area of migration."

The EU pledges to provide "assistance to African countries for the man-agement of both South-South and South-North migratory movements." The EU agreed to develop along with the African countries "regional ini-tiatives appropriate to different migration routes both within Africa and from Africa to Europe." Through this action the EU intends to foster "close links between the respective regional organizations" and to deepen its activities suitable to the managements of South-South and South-North migration.

Also, the JA-EUDMD characterizes the migration management chal-lenges as involving "generating policy coherence at international, regional and national levels." Migration challenges could be met for example by "promoting better integration of the impact of migration into develop-ment policies in respect of developing countries, and developmental aspects into migration strategies." This must be undertaken with the con-sultation of civil society actors at all levels.

In the view of the JA-EUDMD, other management challenges include issues such as "meeting the concerns and interests of countries of origin, transit and destination alike, as well as the migrants themselves." Another migration challenge involves "addressing illegal or irregular migratory flows," as these "are currently taking serious dimensions that can under-mine stability and security and must be adequately addressed through a comprehensive approach." Furthermore, there is the problem of "creating an enabling environment in the countries of origin through good gover-nance and the respect for the rule of law, elimination of corruption, [and] promotion and protection of human rights."[20]

The JA-EUDMD addresses issues concerning peace and security, by which the EU and African countries agree, "that conflict is a root cause of

---

[20] Africa Union and European Union. (2006). Joint Africa-EU Declaration on Migration and Development, Tripoli, 22–23 November, Final Version.

forced displacement." The view is expressed that "displacement caused by conflict has destabilizing effects on national and regional security," which has "adverse consequences for the ability of host nations to provide protection to refugees and security to their own nationals." The EU and African countries agree that the spontaneous, illegal or irregular migration in large numbers negatively impact "national and international stability and security." Also, it affects the countries' "abilities to exercise effective control over their borders." In turn, this creates "tensions between origin, transit and destination countries in Africa and within local host communities."

Thus, there are a number of key security concerns stated in the JA-EUDMD, which engage the attention of the EU and African countries. These include for example, the strengthening of crisis management in Africa. Furthermore, they involve building the Africa's capabilities for conflict prevention, and resolving conflicts peacefully. The engagement of Africa countries in "post-conflict reconstruction, including through implementation of the AU Policy Framework on Post-Conflict Reconstruction and Development with special attention to the situation of women and children," is another key security concern mentioned in the JA-EUDMD. Finally, the EU agrees to provide "logistical support to the African Regional and Sub-Regional mechanisms for conflict prevention and consolidation of stability," and to ensure "the flow of funds in a predictable manner, in support of peacekeeping operations, and as a contribution to post-conflict reconstruction."

The JA-EUDMD also addresses human resources and brain drain issues resulting from migration. In this connection, it seeks to promote "concrete and tailor-made policies and reforms to address skills shortages caused by brain drain." Furthermore, it supports programs that "foster the mobility and temporary return of members of the Diasporas with the necessary skills in their countries of origin, in order to contribute to capacity building."

The JA-EUDMD pledges to develop "common innovative instruments to enable countries of origin to benefit fully from skilled African workers based in host countries." It also promises to strengthen the educational system in Africa, while fashioning them to meet "the needs of each African country." It assures the advance in working conditions of African researchers, teachers, and encourages "the use of local consultants for different development projects." It pledges to encourage "the movement of skilled African labor between host countries and countries of origin through the creation of centers of excellence and partnerships between EU and African institutions." Finally, it promises, "to mitigate the effects of large scale departures of highly skilled African professionals in critical sectors."

The JA-EUDMD covers a number of other issues including the human rights and well being of individual migrants. It concentrates on sharing best practices in order for sending and receiving countries to support each other "in capacity-building so as to better manage migration and asylum." Also, it focuses on information sharing and "exchanging best practices on the broad migration agenda to the fullest degree possible" in a variety of settings. These should be undertaken particularly, "via meetings between the EU and the AU, and AU RECs (Regional Economic Communities), Commission to Commission meetings, Euro-Med Migration Cooperation and bilateral meetings between EU and African states."

Regular migration opportunities for Africans to the EU also gained the attention of the JA-EUDMD. To this effect the need is expressed for the study of "the possibilities of harnessing the benefits of regular migration between countries of origin and countries of destination in order to better manage migration." In the area of illegal or irregular migration the JA-EUDMD pledges to undertake various actions. It intends inter alia, to extend "support for building institutional capacity and developing projects in countries of origin and transit to combat illegal migration, migrant smuggling and trafficking in human beings." Also, it pledges to protect the rights of refugees by effectively protecting "refugees and internally displaced persons." This should be done "including via regional protection, implementation of relevant international and regional conventions relating to the status of refugees, and respect for the principle of non-refoulement."

To finance the migration initiatives contained in the JA-EUDMD the EU promises to implement its commitments. These are "to support the development efforts of countries of origin or transit, and within the wider framework of contributing to the achievement of the Millennium Development Goals (MDGs) and the EU commitment to collectively increase ODA to 0.56 percent of GNI by 2010 and 0.7 percent by 2015, and to allocate at least 50 percent of the agreed increase to Africa." Also, there is agreement for "examining the feasibility of setting up a fund to implement" the measures outlined in the JA-EUDMD. In this connection the EU and AU agreed to establish a "Joint Working Group," which "will report to their respective Councils."

The follow-up mechanism for the JA-EUDMD is understood to "take place in the context of the Joint EU-Africa strategy and joint implementation matrix." This involves "regular expert level troika meetings on migration and development issues," and the exchange of experiences and information on bilateral, regional and continental policies. Also, "mandating the AU and EU Commissions to develop an implementation Roadmap for the Joint Declaration," is considered an important follow-up mechanism, as well as the "EU-Africa Ministerial Conference on Migration and Development," to be held in three years' time "to provide an initial review of migration and development in the context of the overall Africa-EU Dialogue." Finally, follow-up is placed in context of dialogue in the framework of the Global Forum as a part of "the UN High Level Dialogue on Migration and Development, including further work on migration and development within the UN system."

Critique of the Joint Africa-EU Declaration on Migration and Development

This detailed description of the JA-EUDMD is necessary for readers to realize the scope of the EU's plans concerning the migration of Africans into the Europe. The African countries are made to believe that they are equals with the EU. The inferiority complex, from which they are made to suffer, makes some of their leaders feel exalted when they are called on to sign agreements created in the EU. They even feel a greater sense of belonging, acceptance, and arrival when they are allowed to make minor alterations to EU prepared documents, for which they claim ownership. On careful examination, the JA-EUDMD definitely appears to be an agreement in which the African countries are equals to the EU, or belong in the same league as the EU.

In the first instance the EU uses its leverage, as a developed region intended to help poor countries achieve the MDGs, to cajole the African countries to agree to its migration strategy. The JA-EUDMD is a EU initiative designed by rich states for poor African countries, which the latter merely signed possibly for fear of reprisals by the EU if they did not. For example, the EU has been threatening to implement punitive measures against regions that refused to sign its Economic Partnership Agreement. Indeed, the EPA is recognized as a key instrument for the economic development of Africa, which is central to the EU's migration strategy for the continent.

Second, the EU links its development assistance to reduce poverty in the African countries and their achievement of the MDGs. Thus, poverty reduction is central to the EU's migration strategy for Africa. In this connection, the African countries must cooperate with the EU's approach to

managed migration in order to achieve the MDGs and to receive development assistance from the EU.

Third, an explicit stance of the JA-EUDMD is that the cooperation of
the African countries with the EU's migration approach will help the EU to
meet its "existing and future labor needs." The African countries are then
made to share the responsibility for managing the migration of Africans
into Europe to meet the EU's labor needs.

Fourth, the JA-EUDMD opens up Africa to FDI from the EU in order to
achieve the usual sham outcomes – employment generation. This is the
intended role of FDI in the effort to manage migration. African Diasporas
networks are also identified as having a key role to stimulate FDI to bring
about "sustainable development," inclusive of employment generation.

Fifth, the EU is cleverly shifting the burden of its fight to curtail African
migration into the Europe, from the EU to the African countries. The
African countries must share in the management of migration to ensure
the EU satisfies its current and future labor needs. Also, the African countries must look to their Diasporas to facilitate FDI, and the transfer of
knowledge, technology and skills, for their sustainable development. They
must take measures to prevent undesirable African migrants from going to
Europe.

Sixth, the EU links its financial commitments to the MDGs and Overseas
Development Assistance (ODA) to its migration initiatives contained in
the JA-EUDMD. This means that the EU intends to get more for less, by
passing on increasing responsibilities for migration management to the
African countries, but within the confines of the EU's MDGs and ODA
financial commitments. The African countries have to do more for less by
taking on increased responsibilities concerning managing migration to
the satisfaction of the EU, with whatever financial support it received from
the EU through the MDGs and ODA.

The EU and Libya

This section examines the EU-Libya relations on migration under the former Gaddafi regime. That relationship represented a case in point concerning the EU's approach to migration being a fault line of the neoliberal
approach on the development impact of migration. Also, it demonstrates
how the EU watered down the idea of democracy and good governance,
and at the same time compromised its democratic ideals. It examines the
circumstances surrounding the EU's enlistment of the former Libyan

dictatorship through a migration cooperation agreement, in the EU's fight against migrants from North and Sub-Saharan Africa. Also, the section scrutinizes the EU-Libya framework agreement that sought to humanize the Libyan dictatorship "as a step to develop a new relationship for the EU in the Mediterranean region and in Africa" (Negotiations on EU-Libya Cooperation Agreement).

The European Union and Libya Migration Cooperation Agreement[21]

In its attempt to curtail migrants from North and Sub-Saharan Africa entering Europe the EU initiated migration cooperation with Libya (Hamood, 2008). This collaboration involved among other thing the EU's funding of Libya to patrol the Mediterranean Sea, and led Libya to dismantle the UN Center for Refugees in Tripoli (Kopp, 2010). This initial alliance developed into a migration cooperation agreement between the European Commission and Libya (European Union 2010).

The migration cooperation agenda involves inter alia the development in Libya of an efficient system to manage migratory flows, and enhancing Libya's capacity to address smuggling and trafficking in human beings. Also, it involved border management that required a "gap analysis on the current functioning modalities of the Libyan border and immigration services." It sought to strengthen "cooperation between Libya and the neighboring and other transit and origin countries" in border surveillance. Libya has land borders with Tunisia, Algeria, Niger, Chad, Sudan, and Egypt, while the Mediterranean Sea is to the north. It gave support to "the development of Libyan patrolling, search and rescue capacities in its territorial waters and at high sea." It sought to establish "an integrated surveillance system along the Libyan land borders, with focus on the areas prone to irregular migration flows." Also, it explored "concrete possibilities of cooperation between Libyan police, border, migration authorities and agencies and those of the EU Member States as regards the return and readmission of irregular migrants" (European Union 2010).

In 2008 the EU gave €2 000000 to Libya for the prevention of irregular migration at Libya's southern borders with Chad and Niger. The aim was to improve the overall capacity of the Libyan authorities, in particular by assisting them to reform the system in place in Libya to prevent irregular migration into Europe. The EU contributed 1.5 m Euros to strengthen

---

[21] European Union. (2010). European Commission and Libya agree a Migration Cooperation agenda during high-level visit to boost EU-Libya Relations. EUROPA Press Releases, Brussels, 5 October.

border cooperation between Libya and Niger in 2006–2007. Then in 2008–2009 the EU contributed 1 m Euros to strengthen border cooperation between Libya and Algeria. Also, the EU gave Libya €3 500 000 for the management of irregular migration pressures in Libya.

The EU's aim was to assist the Libyan law enforcement authorities to ensure the appropriate registration, reception and treatment, in line with international standards, of irregular migrants apprehended at the southern borders of the country. Also, the EU intended to promote the establishment of a system of assisted voluntary return for stranded migrants willing to return, and resettlement for asylum seekers and migrants in need of international protection. The Italian Ministry of Interior was given the responsibility to manage both of these projects, which were being finalized with Libya, and with other EU member states as partners (European Union 2010), before the overthrow of Gaddafi.

The agreement between the EU and Libya covers broad areas including – regional and pan-African dialogue and cooperation; ensuring effective management of migratory flows; border management; and international protection. In the area of regional and pan-African cooperation it is agreed that there will be an increase in "joint efforts in the development of African countries of origin of migration." The intention is to build on "the serious and substantial efforts of Libya and the European Union as major donors to African countries." The view is that the development support to African migrant sending states by Libya and the EU would create "viable alternatives to migration in these countries." Furthermore, the EU and Libya pledged to "support awareness campaigns" in the "main countries of origin of migrants transiting through North Africa and Libya specifically to alert migrants to the dangers of irregular migration."[22]

Also, the two sides planned to "work together "in the implementation of the 'Declaration of Tripoli on Migration and Development' of 2006, and the EU-Africa Migration, Mobility and Employment Partnership adopted in Lisbon in 2007." Two other areas of cooperation between the two sides in this connection were, first increased dialogue and information exchange on "issue of smuggling of human beings and related illicit traffics reaching Libya from other countries and the EU from Libya." The second area was the establishment of "an informal consultative group" comprising Libyan government officials and representatives of the EU, which would engage

---

[22] European Union. (2010). European Commission and Libya agree a Migration Cooperation agenda during high-level visit to boost EU-Libya Relations. EUROPA Press Releases, Brussels, 5 October.

in information exchange on development policies benefiting Africa and in identifying development projects in Sub-Saharan Africa.[23]

In the area of the effective management of migratory flows the agreement is that the EU would support "the development in Libya of a more efficient system to manage labor migration." This would be done through programs that allowed existing and future migrants the opportunity to maximize their skills. The two sides agreed to enhance the capabilities of Libyan authorities, civil society agencies, and international organizations "to properly launch and implement search and rescue operations aimed at saving lives of migrants in the desert or on high seas and to provide them with the necessary humanitarian assistance."[24]

Libya agreed to treat intercepted irregular or stranded migrants in the country, in a decent manner and to provide them with a proper reception and assistance based on international standards. The focus here is "on migrants belonging to vulnerable categories (like unaccompanied minors, victims of trafficking; pregnant women, and families with small children)." Besides "offering assisted voluntary return home to irregular migrants intercepted," the agreement seeks to enhance "the capacity to address smuggling and trafficking in human beings," in accordance with the "protocols of the 2000 UN Convention on the Trans-national organized Crime, and in view of reinforcing the capabilities of law enforcement officials in charge of the implementation of this legislation."[25]

The agreement on border management involved undertaking of a "gap-analysis on the current functioning modalities of the Libyan border and immigration services, aimed at reinforcing the capacity of the latter to prevent the irregular migration flows from entering Libya from its Southern borders," with Niger and Chad. Also, it addresses the issue of strengthening cooperation between Libya and its neighbors that are other transit and origin countries in "border surveillance" and preventing illegal migrants and smugglers from violating Libyan border. This is done through "the development of joint training, the facilitation of working contacts and the

---

[23] European Union. (2010). European Commission and Libya agree a Migration Cooperation agenda during high-level visit to boost EU-Libya Relations. EUROPA Press Releases, Brussels, 5 October.

[24] European Union. (2010). European Commission and Libya agree a Migration Cooperation agenda during high-level visit to boost EU-Libya Relations. EUROPA Press Releases, Brussels, 5 October.

[25] European Union. (2010). European Commission and Libya agree a Migration Cooperation agenda during high-level visit to boost EU-Libya Relations. EUROPA Press Releases, Brussels, 5 October.

establishment of dedicated communication channels aimed at transmitting early warnings and sensible data."

The EU also pledged to support "the development of Libyan patrolling, search and rescue capacities in its territorial waters and at high sea." It agreed to help establish "an integrated surveillance system along the Libyan land borders, with focus on the areas prone to irregular migration flows." Finally, the agreement on border management involves concrete "cooperation between Libyan police, border, migration authorities and agencies and those of the EU Member States as regards the return and readmission of irregular migrants."[26]

As a part of the agreement on international protection, the EU is supposed to support Libya in its efforts to establish "a protection system able to deal with asylum seekers and refugees in line with international standards and in good cooperation with the competent international organization." Also, the EU is supposed to assist Libya "in screening migrants" to identify genuine cases "in need of international protection," the resettling of some of them in EU member states, and supporting their voluntary return to their country of origin, and "enhancing the reception capacities offered in Libya to asylum seekers and refugees."[27]

The EU-Libya Framework Agreement

The European Parliament's recommendations to the EU Council and Commission on the EU-Libya Framework Agreement spoke to the EU's intentions in Libya. The recommendations acknowledged that Gaddafi was a dictator, albeit in flowery language.[28] It was stated that "the exercise of State power in Libya" was "not anchored in the rule of law or in democratic accountability and has led to arbitrary and unpredictable behavior regarding foreign persons and interests..." However, the European Parliament welcomed the "negotiations between the EU and Libya, as a step to develop a new relationship for the EU in the Mediterranean region and in Africa." The European Parliament considered "cooperation with

---

[26] European Union. (2010). European Commission and Libya agree a Migration Cooperation agenda during high-level visit to boost EU-Libya Relations. EUROPA Press Releases, Brussels, 5 October.

[27] European Union. (2010). European Commission and Libya agree a Migration Cooperation agenda during high-level visit to boost EU-Libya Relations. EUROPA Press Releases, Brussels, 5 October.

[28] European Parliament recommendation of 20 January 2011 to the Council on the negotiations on the EU-Libya Framework Agreement (2010/2268(INI)).

Libya useful in addressing issues such as security and stability, migration, public health, development, trade, climate change, energy and culture."[29] These issues are interlinked especially security, stability, and migration.

The wide-ranging recommendations cover issues such as the EU pressurizing Gaddafi to "ratify and implement the Geneva Convention on Refugees of 1951 and its 1967 Protocol" and for him to cooperate fully "with UNHCR so as to guarantee adequate protection and rights for migrants." The EU Parliament also suggested that the Council and Commission should push Gaddafi to "adopt asylum legislation that recognizes refugees' status and rights accordingly, notably the prohibition of collective expulsion and the principle of 'non-refoulement'." It insisted on the obligations of the Council and the Commission "to ensure full compliance of the EU's external policy with the Charter of Fundamental Rights, particularly its Article 19, which prohibits collective expulsion and grants the principle of 'non-refoulement'." Its preference was that Libya signed "a Memorandum of Understanding granting UNHCR a legal presence in the country, with a mandate to exercise its full range of access and protection activities."

The readmission agreement with Libya is "envisaged for irregular immigrants." This excludes "those who declare themselves asylum-seekers, refugees or persons in need of protection." The readmission agreement "reiterates that the principle of 'non-refoulement' applies to any persons who are at risk of the death penalty, inhumane treatment or torture." It encourages the EU to "offer resettlement to recognized refugees identified by UNHCR in Libya according to the agreed Migration Cooperation Agenda of 4 October 2010." Also, it strengthened the EU's support for UNHCR activities and promoted the Libyan authorities to have "respect for international humanitarian standards for undocumented migrants in the country, including the systematic access of the UNHCR to detention centers."

It was proposed that the EU and expert agencies such as the UNHCR, IOM, ICMPD helped Libya to address the problem of human trafficking in the region. In this connection, special attention is paid to "the protection of women and children, including assistance to integrate legal migrants and to improve conditions for migrants found illegally in the country."

In addition the European Parliament suggested that the EU-Libya Framework Agreement includes the encouragement of Libya to place a

---

[29] European Parliament recommendation of 20 January 2011 to the Council on the negotiations on the EU-Libya Framework Agreement (2010/2268(INI)).

moratorium on the death penalty with a view towards its abolition. The intention was to push Libya to participate "in the Euro-Mediterranean Partnership and the activities and main projects of the Union for the Mediterranean." Also, the EU sought to make it easier for Libyans to be granted Schengen visas and for Europeans to go to Libya, and for the establishment of a "EU Delegation in Tripoli as soon as possible."

These selected issues on migration and others that the EU negotiated with Libya for inclusion in the EU-Libya Framework Agreement were designed to help the EU achieve its imperialist mission in Libya – capture raw materials (oil and natural gas), and manage the flow of African migrants into Europe. These goals are in serious danger due to the EU-US-NATO war in combination with domestic fighters in Libya that swept Gaddafi from office in October 2011. But, on the other hand, it is predictable that the goals would be strengthened in favor of the EU based on the newness of the puppet regime that replaces Gaddafi, installed by US and NATO bombs, finance, arms and ammunitions in conjunction with genuine revolutionary fighters against the Gaddafi dictatorship.

The Libyan War and Migrants

Libya had emerged as a key rendezvous for illegal immigrants from North and Sub-Saharan Africa en-route to Italy in the EU.[30] and Malta via the Mediterranean Sea. The Mediterranean countries of the EU with the exception of France have had a long history of emigration. However, the immigration phenomenon under consideration is a fairly recent development since the late 1980s. The number of foreign residents regular or illegal in Italy mainly from Eastern Europe and non-European countries primarily North Africa reached more than 3 million in 2005 (Lucht 2011). It was estimated in 2000 that 85 percent of the foreign residents in Italy came from non-European countries, and that a majority of these had no documents.

According to Lucht (2011) the number of illegal immigrants in Italy is estimated to vary "between 200,000 and 500,000 at any one time." Lucht (2011) noted that "Most cross the Italian-Slovenian border, following routes used by both independent travelers and human smugglers transporting would-be immigrants from Central and Southern Europe, the Middle East,

---

[30] Hans Lucht. (2011). *Darkness Before Daybreak: African Migrants Living on the Margins in Southern Italy Today*. Berkeley, University of California Press.

the Indian Subcontinent, and elsewhere in Asia." This contrasts with "the sea routes from North Africa," which "are used especially by African immigrants," whom "the Berlusconi administration" in Italy "has carried out highly controversial and widely criticized deportations directly to Libya."[31]

The EU used the Gaddafi regime, whose brutally repressive acts with the full knowledge of the EU, successfully disabled Libya as a transit rout for the African migrants bound for Europe.

Undoubtedly, a hidden dimension of the recent war in Libya that toppled the Gaddafi regime is its impact on the migration of Africans into the EU. The war deterred African migrants from using Libya as a jump-off point to the EU, especially since many of them were accused of being pro-Gaddafi mercenaries. The long-term effect of the war on African migration to the EU will be that the Transitional National Council (TNC) Libya's new provisional government will do the EU's biddings to choke-off the Libya-EU migration route to Africans. This will be one of the payback to the EU for its support to the TNC in the overthrow and murder of Colonel Muammar Gaddafi. The initial impact of the war had been to increase the flow of Africans, Asians, and other migrants into the EU. This is because many of the thousands of migrant workers in Libya entrapped by the war, fled to the EU.

Human Rights Watch's emergencies director Peter Bouckaert pointed out that due to the war, "Thousands upon thousands of foreign workers" were "stuck in Benghazi, after being forced from their factories and losing their possessions."[32] Also, in the early weeks of the war the UN High Commissioner for Refugees estimated that "some 75,000 refugees" fled Libya "to Tunisia and 69,000 to Egypt, with about 40,000 others unable to leave" the country.[33]

According to Amnesty International, tens of thousands of immigrant workers from developing countries in Africa and Asia were stranded in Libya due to the war. Amnesty International pointed out that "30,000 to 150,000 Filipino overseas foreign workers, 60,000 Bangladeshis, 2,000 to 5,000 Nepalese and over one million refugees, asylum-seekers and migrants, mostly from sub-Saharan Africa," were in Libya prior to the war.

---

[31] Hans Lucht. (2011). *Darkness Before Daybreak: African Migrants Living on the Margins in Southern Italy Today*. Berkeley, University of California Press.

[32] Aprille Muscara. (2011). "Libya: Thousands of Foreign Laborers Trapped in Turmoil," Inter-Press Service, Washington, March 3.

[33] Aprille Muscara. (2011). "Libya: Thousands of Foreign Laborers Trapped in Turmoil," Inter-Press Service, Washington, March 3.

Human Rights Watch noted that about "3,500 of these non-Africans – including laborers from Bangladesh, Pakistan, the Philippines, Thailand and Vietnam" were "awaiting departure in two Benghazi camps, with thousands of others in company compounds."[34]

Some of the sub-Saharan African immigrant workers in Libya were being prevented from leaving the country "due to misguided suspicions that they are among the regime contracted mercenaries." They were accused of being imported from "Chad, Ethiopia, Guinea, Kenya and Niger, in addition to the North African countries of Algeria and Tunisia," to fight as Gaddafi's hired guns. According to Muscara (2011), as the African migrants remained marooned "thousands of foreigners from Algeria, Bosnia, Britain, Bulgaria, Canada, China, Croatia, Greece, India, Jordan, Lebanon, Macedonia, Morocco, the Netherlands, Nigeria, South Korea, Syria, Turkey, the U.S., Vietnam" were evacuated by their companies or governments.[35]

The EU and Democracy in Libya

This section focuses on another aspect of the EU's double standard concerning democracy and the rule of law. It considers the mistreatment of the refugees in Libya with the full knowledge of the EU, and the infamous arms deal Britain and Libya entered into in 2004. The EU's behavior concerning the mistreatment of migrants in Libya and the arms deal with Britain further hindered democracy in the country.

The Mistreatment of Refugees in Libya

Closer cooperation between Libya, Italy and the European agency for external border security (Frontex) had registered a decline of irregular migration from Libya to Malta and Italy by 83 percent, by the end of May 2010. The number of boat people arriving at Malta had decreased from approximately 2,700 in 2008 to 1,470 in 2009, while in Italy the decline was from 36,000 to 8,700 in the same period (Kopp 2010). Through its cooperation with Libya the EU has been highly successful in keeping out African migrants from Europe. However, the UNHCR, Commissioner for Human

---

[34] Aprille Muscara. (2011). "Libya: Thousands of Foreign Laborers Trapped in Turmoil," Inter-Press Service, Washington, March 3.

[35] Aprille Muscara. (2011). "Libya: Thousands of Foreign Laborers Trapped in Turmoil," Inter-Press Service, Washington, March 3.

Rights of the Council of Europe and the Vatican expressed deep concerns regarding Italy's illegal record of deporting migrants to Libya. Also, the 2010 Amnesty International annual report criticized Italy's cooperation with Libya, on the basis that the forced return to Libya of refugees picked up at sea amounts to a violation of the international law principle of non-refoulement (Kopp 2010).

Human Rights Watch made a frantic appeal to Libya not to deport 245 Eritrean refugees but to turn them over to the UNHCR, the UN Agency for Refugee in July 2010.[36] Eritreans in increasing numbers are "fleeing the indefinite national military service imposed by the Eritrean government and pervasive arbitrary detention and torture." However, the Gaddafi dictatorship had stripped the UNHCR of its ability to protect refugees and asylum seekers in Libya. It proceeded to not only brutalized the refugees, denying them food and water, transporting them through the desert in overcrowded trucks, but was prepared to send them back to Eritrea knowing full well that they will face torture. This action was in violation of Libya's legal obligations towards refugees. The "Convention against Torture, and the African Refugee Convention forbid Libya, from sending individuals to countries where they face a serious risk of persecution or torture." Furthermore, Libya is "a state party to the International Covenant on Civil and Political Rights (ICCPR), which, under article 13, prohibits arbitrary expulsion and entitles foreigners to an individual decision on their removal/expulsion."[37]

The UNHCR carries out asylum-related activities in Libya, including the registration of asylum-seekers, the screening and profiling of new arrivals, refugee status determination (RSD) and the search for durable solutions. UNHCR also provides vulnerable refugees living in urban areas with limited financial assistance and access to other vital services. Asylum-seekers and refugees in detention who are known to UNHCR are provided with emergency food and basic items such as blankets and mattresses.

The Libyan government told the UN refugee agency that it must close its office and halt its activities in Libya in June 2010.[38] Melissa Fleming, UNHCR chief spokesperson made this disclosure to journalist with the

---

[36] Human Rights Watch. (2010). *Libya: Do Not Deport Eritreans*, 2 July, available at: http://www.unhcr.org/refworld/docid/4d33e42d2.html [accessed 22 February 2011].
[37] Human Rights Watch. (2010). *Libya: Do Not Deport Eritreans*, 2 July, available at: http://www.unhcr.org/refworld/docid/4d33e42d2.html [accessed 22 February 2011].
[38] "UNHCR says ordered to close office in Libya." Geneva, 8 June 2010, http://www.unhcr.org/4c0e79059.html.

hope the closure was temporary as negotiations continued for a solution. According to the UNHCR, "Most of the refugees" it "deals with are Palestinians and Iraqis, with others typically coming from Sudan, Somalia, Eritrea, Liberia and Ethiopia." The EU did little or nothing to prevent the Libyan dictatorship from closing the UNHCR in Tripoli. Also, Gaddafi destroyed the UN shelter for refugees in Tripoli in his bid to please the EU in the anti-immigration fight against the Africans. The EU rewarded Gaddafi handsomely for his actions, which were a gross violation of human rights appropriately condemned by the UN.

Democracy in Libya

The fact that Gaddafi was a dictator did not stop the EU and its individual member countries from doing business with him. For example, Britain and Libya entered into an infamous deal in 2004, at the signing of which British Prime Minister Tony Blair and Colonel Gaddafi shook hands as the best of friends. The Anglo-Dutch Shell oil company entered into a 1$ billion oil exploration contract with Libya.[39] The 2004 deal also served to bring Libya into the international community of states. Then in 2007 British Petroleum (BP) signed a $900 million off shore oil exploration contract. The contract allowed BP operating in Libya for the first time in over 30 years to explore an area of some 54,000 square kilometers primarily for gas, but also in the hope of finding oil.[40] Also, Britain supplied Libya with arms and ammunition, but only cancelled eight arms export licenses for Libya during the 2011 crisis in Libya, when the UN Commission on Human Rights suggested that Britain might be found guilty of "complicity" in the murders of demonstrators by Colonel Gaddafi's regime.

According to the UK based Campaign Against Arms Trade (CAAT), in the third quarter of 2010 equipment approved for export from the UK to Libya "included wall and door breaching projectile launchers, crowd control ammunition, small arms ammunition, tear gas/irritant ammunition, training tear gas/irritant ammunition. Ammunition comprised £3.2 m of the £4.7 m million of military items licensed."[41]

---

[39] Nicola Clark. (2004). "Libya Signs Energy Exploration Deal With Shell." *New York Times Global Edition* Business Day World, March 26.

[40] "Blair hails relations with Libya, $900 million gas deal," Middle East Online. May 5, 2007, http://www.middle-east-online.com/english/?id=20886.

[41] Campaign Against Arms Trade (CAAT). (2011). UK arms sales to Middle East include tear gas and crowd control ammunition to Bahrain and Libya, February 17.

Campaign Against Arms Trade (CAAT) stated that, "Sniper rifles were among the other equipment licensed in 2010." The CAAT noted that

> No requests for licenses were refused in 2010. Libya is a UKTI/DSO (UK Trade and Investment Defence and Security Organization) priority market country, and the UK has made 'high level political interventions' in support of arms sales to Libya. Libya was also invited to attend the UK arms fairs: the Farnborough Airshow in 2010 and Defence and Security Equipment International in 2009. The UK had by far the largest pavilion at Libya's arms fair LibDex in 2010, and was supported by a team from UKTI DSO.[42]

Thus, the EU did not only wanted Libya to protect its borders from North, and Sub-Saharan African migrants, it also provided Libya with the arms to do the job.

The EU's main concern was to get Libya to turn away from its self-confessed terrorist activities as defined by the EU and US. Once Gaddafi declared that Libya would no longer engage in activities classified by the EU and US as terrorist then the EU and US could find ways to use Gaddafi in their self-interest. That understanding was exactly the meaning behind Tony Blair's rendezvous with Gaddafi in 2004, and Condoleezza Rice's (US Secretary of State in the George Bush II Administration) remark that US-Libya relations had entered into a "new phase." The economic interest of the EU does not only concern Libya's oil, but the use of Libya to operate as the EU's policeman with respect to African migrants trying to cross into the EU.

The Arab Spring, which saw the fall of the notorious Ben Ali government in Tunisia, Hosni Mubarak in Egypt, Gaddafi in Libya, and threatening al-Assad in Syria was purportedly unanticipated by the Western powers. The Gaddafi dictatorship ruled Libya for 41 years and suppressed the human rights of Libyans. Until the Arab Spring when the Libyan people took to arms against Gaddafi, the EU had turned a blind eye to Gaddafi's repression of his people, so long as he desisted from attacking Europe. The EU preferred stability albeit erratic under the Libyan dictator rather than to have an uncertain alternative in Libya. However, the EU had no choice but to join-in with the Libyan people in their revolutionary activities that overthrew Gaddafi. But, in that process due to the role of NATO and the US in the war in Libya, the EU and its allies in the US are set to cheat the

---

[42] Campaign Against Arms Trade (CAAT). (2011). UK arms sales to Middle East include tear gas and crowd control ammunition to Bahrain and Libya, February 17.

Libyan people of victory by establishing a puppet regime to replace Gaddafi, from whom they will extract tribute.

Conclusion

The self-interest of the EU ruling elites takes precedence over democracy in the approach that the EU adopts towards African migration into Europe. In a real sense therefore, the neoliberal approach to the development impact of migration is founded on the self-interest of the global financial elites. The promotion of economic development, democracy, and good governance in the underdeveloped countries as espoused by the neoliberal capitalist and their spokespersons in the global institutions and academy take the back seat to the self-interest of the neoliberal global capitalists. The type of capital that is dominant in the capitalist mode of production will determine migration policies in its self-interest. This means that the dominant capitalist must maximize profit from migration arrangements between the rich and poor countries. The theory and practice of migration must channel profits to the capitalist through the extant imperialist centered model of capital accumulation.

CHAPTER TEN

IDEAS FOR A RADICAL APPROACH TO MIGRATION STUDIES

Introduction

This concluding chapter provides a broad outline of a radical alternative framework for the analysis of human migration. It consists of ideas that scholars, political activists, and policymakers should consider in their development of radical approaches to the study of human migration at any specific historical conjuncture in the development of capitalist society. It contains considerations for the treatment of financial capital in the present period of neoliberal capitalism. It presents ideas on redefining the development impact of migration to make it serve the interests of working people.

The main objective of a radical alternative framework for the analysis of human migration, which may be called – *the study of capital accumulation from migration processes*, is to explain how capital accumulation takes place from human migration processes. Current approaches to the study of human migration do not have such a focus. Instead, they concentrate on the range of issues discussed in previous chapters, which serve the interest of the dominant capitalists of the day. The idea behind a radical alternative framework for the analysis of human migration is to deepen understanding of the complex process of capital accumulation, and to know how capital accumulation takes place from human migration processes. The alternative framework is being proposed as a catalyst for radical social transformation that favors working people.

Based on the history of the human experience with migration the premise is that the phenomenon of human migration will continue regardless of the type of class dominated socio-economic system in place in society and that the rulers will profit from it. Specifically, the dominant economic classes under capitalism will always find ways to accumulate wealth from the movement of people. Profit making from human migration is therefore a historically dynamic process and not static or homogenous. As capitalism advances different sections of capital are positioned to receive the bulk of the profit from migration. The same is true today under neoliberal global capitalism dominated by finance capital. The section of capital dominant at any historical conjuncture or period in the evolution of global capitalism will determine the manner in which capital is accumulated from extant migration processes.

Mercantile capital for example profited from the forced and voluntary migrations of millions of people transported as slaves, indentured servants, criminals, and fortune seekers from Africa, Asia, and Europe to the so-called New World also known as the Americas – North and South America and the Caribbean islands, Australia, etc. In line with Eric Williams' thesis on capitalism and slavery, the capital accumulated from that period, which he termed "capitalism-cum-slavery," went to finance the development of industrial capitalism in Europe.[1]

In turn, industrial capital had its heyday in accumulating wealth from migration processes associated with push-pull factors and continues to do so today. The industrialization processes in Europe, Asia, the Americas and Africa required and stimulated rural-urban and international migrations of large amounts of people. Hughes (1968) observed, "All of the industrial nations benefited from the migration of skilled persons, and the so-called countries of European overseas settlement received a massive direct input of labor in the great nineteenth-century migration." Hughes (1968) noted, "The United States alone received 35 million immigrants between 1820 and 1914."[2]

The number of internal and international migrants in the current period of neoliberal capitalism dwarfs those of earlier periods under mercantile and industrial capitalisms. Özden and Schiff (2007) observed however that, "it was not until the 1990s that the world witnessed an upsurge in international migration, particularly in skilled labor migration."[3] The UNDP in its 2009 Human Development Report for example estimated that there were approximately 740 million people who were internal migrants. This number was almost four times as many as the 200 million international migrants, with fewer than 70 million people moving from developing to developed countries.

---

[1] Eric Williams. (1994). *Capitalism and Slavery*. Chapel Hill, The University of North Carolina Press.

[2] J.R.T. Hughes. (1968). "Industrialization: Economic Aspects." International Encyclopedia of the Social Sciences http://www.encyclopedia.com/topic/Industrialization.aspx.

[3] Çağlar Özden Özden and Maurice W. Schiff. (2007). *International Migration, Economic Development and Policy*, Washington, DC and New York, A co-publication of the World Bank and Palgrave Macmillan.

Some Considerations for a Radical Approach

The following features characterize the historical experiences with the accumulation of wealth from migration processes by the ruling classes in capitalist society. First, capital accumulation under mercantile capitalism was founded on forced and voluntary migration. Second, capital accumulation under industrial capitalism depended on mass migration both rural-urban to populate the emerging industrial cities, and international in the direction of expansionary imperial capital. Third, internal and external migration plays a large part in capital accumulation under neoliberal capitalism dominated by financial capital. In the current period the financialization of migration processes – that is the mechanisms through which migration takes place and is sustained, and the socio-economic activities of migrants – is a major means by which migration bolsters capital accumulation. Fourth, the ruling classes that dominate each of these historical periods in the development of capitalist society are the chief beneficiaries of the mass movement of people. Fifth, the ruling classes in each period create the institutional structures to facilitate migration and capital accumulation from migration. Sixth, the migrants themselves, although their movements may result in an improvement of their socio-economic conditions, remain the object of capitalist exploitation in these broad historical periods. Seventh, the challenge is how to effect social transform such that migration really serves the interests of migrants and working people in general rather than those of the dominant capitalist classes.

Given the historical experiences with the accumulation of wealth from migration processes by the ruling classes in capitalist societies, a radical alternative framework for the analysis of human migration must therefore provide guidance on research, study, teaching and practice in the area. It must provide those involved with the tools to undertake analyses of internal, international, and south-south migrations that unravel the different ways in which ruling classes accumulate wealth from migration processes. It must therefore be historical and dialectical in order to identify the principal actors involved and the social, political and economic institutional frameworks that facilitate capital accumulation. Importantly, it must be available for use by existing pro-immigration mass movements, which in the present period for example is under threat of being taken over by sections of capital that openly or clandestinely encourage immigration to enhance their profit margins.

The key point to be belabored in the radical approach is the organization of migrants to resist their exploitation at all levels including against migration agencies and agents, and the capitalist sectors that hire them in the receiving countries. Migrants must be identified for specific roles in the struggle by working peoples to secure revolutionary change in capitalist society. The goal of the radical approach must therefore be to radicalize the relationship between migrants and the capitalist factions in receiving countries and regions that benefit from migration through production and financialization.

An important point for recognition is that dominant forms of capital simultaneously spearhead capitalism's development and globalization. Thus, development takes its shape from the dominant form of capital, which leaves its imprint on capitalist society. Perhaps, this is the reason why capitalist development has turned out to be so elusive in the so-called developing countries. Capitalism is a dynamic phenomenon and as the developing countries begin to join in the scheme of things of the dominant form of capital, the system changes due to the arrival of a new dominant group. This pushes back and stymies capitalist development in the developing countries that operated on the basis of the old version of capitalism. There is concrete historical evidence in support of this observation.

For example, as the developing countries began to receive positive gains from their capitalist industrialization processes launched in the post-World War Two period, the arrival of neoliberal capitalism has brought a halt to that process. The policies of neoliberal capitalism forced the developing countries to de-industrialize and to adopt new rules to join in with finance capital, the current form of dominant capital. The industrialization process in the developing countries was state-led and protectionist. However, neoliberal capitalism forced these countries to pursue "free" market-led approaches, which rapidly piloted their de-industrialization due to their inability to remain competitive with the European and US multinational corporations. Thus, the developing countries are always in a state of playing catch-up with the dominant form of capital. This is one of the central contexts for a radical analysis of migration at any given historical conjuncture of the capitalist system.

Understanding this intrinsic link between capitalism, development and globalization is crucial for the correct study of capital accumulation from migration processes. There is an abundance of literature on migration, but what is lacking are studies that seek to understand how capital is accumulated from migrants – internal, external, regular or irregular. The study of capital accumulation from migration processes will generate knowledge, to the following critical ends.

First, by having an understanding of the different ways in which the capitalists profit from migration the radical forces in the pro-immigration movements that articulate migrants' causes will be able to formulate strategies to push back against those different sections of capital.

Second, by using this knowledge to educate working people and migrants the relationship between migrants and the capitalist factions that benefit from migration could be radicalized. The view here is to change that relationship such that migrant workers will gain the upper hand and the added advantage of joining forces with other workers to transform labor-capital relations in the self-interest of working people.

Third, it will provide useful counter-points to the anti-immigration movements and their activities. Anti-immigration movements and activities constitute the current and future fault lines in the approach to migration identified as *the development impact of migration* by neoliberal capitalism.

Fourth, its political relevance is that the information generated from *the study of capital accumulation from migration processes* could be used to forge links between immigrant and working class movements, for the purposes of direct political action against the capitalist state. Immigrant movements themselves are working class movements, and the knowledge on capital accumulation from migration must be used to show how capital exploits migrants and the domestic or local working classes alike, demonstrating that working people of all varieties, including migrant workers have common causes in their struggles against capitalism. The study of capital accumulation from migration processes therefore has great potential in forging working class unity for political action.

Fifth, there is a need to understand the institutional structures in place, which facilitate capital accumulation from migration processes. Each historical conjuncture of capitalism produces its own complex of social, political, and economic institutional structures to facilitate the smooth operations of the dominant form of capital. Also, as we have seen in the current neoliberal period of global capitalism, existing institutional structures are converted or transformed to serve the interests of the dominant form of capital. The Bretton Woods institutions are cases in point, which have been transformed from performing the original mandates given to them at the time of their formation by the industrial capitalists countries, to serve the interests of financial capital.

Sixth, the dynamic radical approach must constantly be on the lookout for new studies of migration that directly or indirectly provide the underlining theoretical foundations for the dominant form of capital. For instance, a central feature of neoliberal capitalism is the combination of internal, international and south-south migrants with "a growing number of people across the world living and working precariously, usually in a series of short-term jobs, without recourse to stable occupational identities or careers, stable social protection or protective regulations relevant to them" (Standing 2011).

This feature however has led Standing (2011) to mistakenly argue that this category of individuals have emerged as a new class, which he terms the "precariat."[4] The "precariat" of which immigrants constitute a substantial part are seen to be a "class of people" who "could produce new instabilities in society." They are said to be increasingly "frustrated and dangerous because they have no voice, and hence they are vulnerable to the siren calls of extreme political parties." However, while Standing (2011) seems to want to help his "precariat" by integrating them into capitalist society, the dominant capitalists could draw strength from his work.

Viewed from the perspective of Standing (2011) the problem is that immigrants in his "precariat" are seen to be disturbing the social order, whose stability needs to be maintained – a typical conservative position. For this reason immigrants are regarded, as "dangerous" and the state must therefore formulate wages and employment policies to incorporate them for their appeasement. There are some major problems with Standing's (2011) argument concerning the emergence of the "precariat," their possible disrupting role in society, and the solution to appease them.

In the first instance, his argument is in line with the anti-immigration movement in Europe, whose position is that immigrants are the cause of social disintegration in European countries. The maintenance of social cohesion in Europe therefore requires the implementation of measures to restrict immigration, through whatever means necessary fair or foul, democratic or authoritarian.

Second, Standing (2011) is concerned with maintaining the social order rather than transforming it. Because immigrants are "dangerous," the state must formulate and implement wages and employment policies to incorporate them into society. Thus, the immigrants are not to be incorporated because of their contributions to the process of capital accumulation in

---

[4] Guy Standing. (2011). *The Precariat: The New Dangerous Class*, USA, Bloomsbury.

Europe, but because they are a "dangerous" group who would disrupt the society, causing it to disintegrate.

Third, Standing (2011) reinforces the neoliberal position on the development impact of migration, which will become more widespread when the immigrants are incorporated into the society through better employment and wages. The migrants would have a reliable source of income and more knowledge, skills, etc. to remit to their home countries. Financial capital will then have a field day in profits from the increase in remittance that would result from the incorporation of immigrants into society by providing them with better employment that pays them higher wages.

The Treatment of Finance Capital

As mentioned above, neoliberal capitalism is associated with a greater number of internal and south-south migrations rather than with migration from the developing to the developed countries. The greater numbers of internal, international and south-south migrations are due to the fact that people are in closer contact with each other as a result of the improvements in technology, communications, etc. in the global march of capitalism and human progress. This is the context in which the financialization of migration is talking place. It is a mistake to think therefore that the financial hawks in the global financial centers are only concerned with the financialization of migration processes from the developing to the developed countries.

The global financial grid established by the financial elites embraces almost all countries and regions around the world. Thus, all monetary and financial transactions in migration processes are within the reach of the financial elites located in financial centers dispersed around the globe. A key point however is that although financial districts are located in every country and they are linked in a global financial grid, the wealth generated from financialization disproportionately accumulates in the rich countries as evidenced by soaring Wall Street profits. The estimates for 2007 were that the top 1 percent in the US for example controlled 42 percent of financial wealth, while the bottom 80 percent controlled only 7 percent of the financial wealth.

In this connection, the imperialist centered model of capital accumulation represents the methods through which financial capital financializes internal, international and south-south migration processes, captures the resulting wealth generated from interests, fees, etc., and transmits it to the financial centers in the US and Europe. It also involves processes through which wealth is transmitted to the US and Europe for accumulation there from trade, production, services and other economic activities involving immigrants and non-migrants.

The official estimates by the neoliberal international financial institutions were that officially recorded remittance flows alone to developing countries would increase by 6 percent to $325 billion in 2010. Also, remittance flows were projected to increase by 6.2 percent in 2011 and 8.1 percent in 2012 to reach $374 billion in that year. These are indeed huge sums of money from which financial capital could profit. But, it has to be fully within the ambit of financial capital to maximally benefit that sector of capital.

The financialization of migration processes is construed within the framework of "the great financialization," "the financialization of accumulation," and the imperialist centered model of accumulation. It therefore involves the treatment of remittances by migrants under neoliberal capitalism a period exemplified by the "reversion to accumulation by dispossession," "the financialization of accumulation," and the creation of a "permanent mass surplus labor population."

Indeed, what parades today as new directions and thinking in migration and development is nothing more than a return to past ideas. The difference is that the migration and development debate is being revisited at a historical conjuncture dominated by neoliberal capitalism in which finance capital is at the helm. The core thrust of neoliberal capitalism in regards to the development impact of migration is the central role assigned to remittances and Diasporas in the process of capitalist development in the periphery. Thus, the development impact of migration concerns the facilitation of remittances and Diasporas within the framework of the "great financialization" and "the financialization of accumulation," to further the imperialist centered model of accumulation.

In the current period of neoliberal capitalism, different sections of capital profit from migration. Thus, although neoliberal capitalism is dominated by financial capital the productive capitalists who need cheap migrant labor to aid the production process are firm believers in migration, while the financial capitalists in the current era of neoliberal capitalism seek to derive financial benefits from migration. Thus, while the productive capitalists engaged in agriculture and manufacturing, accumulate wealth by hiring cheap migrant labor, the financial capitalists accumulate wealth from the financial processes associated with migration.

And because financial capital is the dominant section of global capital under neoliberal capitalism, it finds ingenious ways made possible by new information communication technologies to create financial instruments to subject migration processes to high finance, through payment of fees for remittances, the use of cell phones inter alia, which they use in turn to create financial instruments such as derivatives for speculation in financial markets. In other words, it takes the necessary steps to bring about the financialization of migration process. Also, the domination of the state and global institutions by finance capital aid the process of financialization of migration through the creation and implementation of the appropriate policies.

The capitalist system of production for market exchange is therefore associated with the financialization of accumulation. In the current period of neoliberal capitalism we are also witnessing the great financialization[5] in which financial capital seeks to subordinate all sections of capital and social relations to its dictates. These processes are subsumed within an imperialist centered model of capital accumulation, itself more a dynamic than static phenomenon whose modus operandi is shaped by the dialectical relations of the form of capital that is dominant. Nonetheless, the end result of financial accumulation, the great financialization, and the financialization of migration is the accumulation of wealth in an imperialist centered model of capital accumulation.

Also, all capitalist do not benefit equally from migration processes and this leads to intra-class conflict over migration. Those who benefit the most from migration encourages it while the others who do not benefit oppose it. The central role of a radical migration theory is to unravel the many ways that the different factions of capital, those that are dominant and those that are not, profit from migration.

Redefining the Development Impact of Migration

In the neoliberal perspective development means the accumulation of capital based on the capitalist mode of production. Technical change and class exploitation lies at the heart of capitalist development. Alternative development is understood as something other than capitalist development – it is the transformation of the capitalist power structures engaged in the processes of capital accumulation based on the capitalist mode of production. It involves the utilization of technical change to improve the

---

[5] Kari Polanyi Levitt. (2008). "The Great Financialization," John Kenneth Galbraith Prize Lecture, June 8, http://karipolanyilevitt.com/documents/The-Great-Financialization .pdf.

socio-economic conditions of working people not merely to accumulate wealth to enrich the classes who are already in control of the wealth nationally and globally. In this context therefore the alternative development impact of migration takes on a different meaning. Capital accumulation through migrant labor must enhance the living conditions of working people globally, and not just a few individuals who own/control the capitalist production system and the social structures erected on it. It involves the transformation of the power structures in the current period of neoliberal capitalism such that the people who produce the wealth will become the principal decision makers in all areas of society. It involves counteracting the imperialist-centered model of capital accumulation and the placement of remittances and other diaspora activities in the service of working people.

Thus, alternative development is considered here in the specific context of the role of migration in bringing about socio-economic development in both sending and receiving countries. Rather than playing a role in the deepening of capitalism globally, there is need for alternative roles for migration in helping to transform the capitalist power structures. This is the principal goal of the alternative development impact of migration under neoliberal capitalism.

BIBLIOGRAPHY

Abbott, E. (1931). "The Problem of Crime and the Foreign Born," in *National Commission on Law Observance and Enforcement: Report on Crime and the Foreign Born*, Washington, D.C., United States Government Printing Office.

Africa Union and European Union. (2006). Joint Africa-EU Declaration on Migration and Development, Tripoli, 22–23 November, Final Version.

Agbesinyale, P.K. (2003). *Ghana's Gold Rush and Regional Development: The Case of Wassa West District*. Dortmund, SPRING Centre.

Agunias, D.R. (2010). *Migration's Middlemen: Regulating Recruitment Agencies in the Philippines-United Arab Emirates Corridor*. Washington, DC: Migration Policy Institute, June.

Agunias. D.R. (2009). Guiding the Invisible Hand: Making Migration Intermediaries Work for Development. United Nations Development Program Human Development Research Paper 2009/22.

Arsenault, C. (2011). "Migrants Decry New US Legislation," *Aljazeera.net*, June 23.

Attaran, A. (2005). An Immeasurable Crisis? A Criticism of the Millennium Development Goals and Why They Cannot Be Measured, *PLoS Medicine* Volume 2, Issue 10 e318 pp. 0955–0961.

Baker, S. (2011). "Immigration Enforcement Against Employers of Undocumented Workers is a 'Cash Cow' for State and Local Agencies!" in *Wolfsdorf Navigating Immigration* January 28.

Banerjee, A.V. and Duflo, E. (2005). "Growth Theory Through the Lens of Development Economics," in Aghion P. and Steven Durlauf, S. ed. (2005). *Handbook of Economic Growth*, Vol. 1 Part A, Elsevier, pp 473–552.

Beirich, H. The Anti-Immigrant Movement, Southern Poverty Law Center, http://www.splcenter.org/get-informed/intelligence-files/ideology/anti-immigrant/the-anti-immigrant-movement.

Benach, J. Muntaner, C. Delclos, C. Menéndez, M. and Ronquillo, C. (2011). "Migration and 'Low-Skilled' Workers in Destination Countries." PLoS Med 8(6): e1001043. doi:10.1371/journal.pmed. 1001043.

Bernanke. B. (2005). The Global Saving Glut and the U.S. Current Account Deficit, Remarks at the Sandridge Lecture, Virginia Association of Economists, Richmond, Virginia, March 10.

Best, L. (1969). "Outline of a Mode of Pure Plantation Economy," *Social and Economic Studies*, Volume 19, No.1.

Bhagwati, J. (2004). *In Defense of Globalization*. New York. Oxford University Press.

Boeke, J.H. (1953). *Economics and the Economic Policies of Dual Societies*, New York, Institute of Pacific Relations.

Bon. A. (2008). "Rethinking ICTs for Development." Conference on Rethinking Development Studies, Institute for Development Studies, University of Cape Coast, Ghana, November 3–6.

Bourguignon, F.J. (2007). "Foreword." In Özden, Ç and M.W. Schiff. (2007). *International Migration, Economic Development and Policy*, Washington, DC and New York: World Bank and Palgrave Macmillan.

Braverman, H. (1974). *Labor and Monopoly Capital: The Degradation of Work in the Twentieth Century*, New York, Monthly Review Press.

Brennan, B. (2008). Where have all our Human Rights Gone? EU Migration Policy 2008: Response and Resistance. Transnational Institute, Amsterdam, The Netherlands, September.

Borjas. G.J. (1989). "Economic Theory and International Migration." *International Migration Review*, Vol. 23, No. 3, Special Silver Anniversary Issue: International Migration an Assessment for the 90's (Autumn), pp. 457–485.

Borjas, G.J. and Hilton, L. (1996). "Immigration and the Welfare State: Immigrant Participation in Means-Tested Entitlement Programs," The Quarterly Journal of Economics, Vol. 111, No. 2, May.

Boyd, R.L. (2002). A "Migration of Despair": Unemployment, the Search for Work, and Migration to Farms During the Great Depression, *Social Science Quarterly*, Volume 83, Number 2, June.

Brinkerhoff, J.M. ed. (2008). *Diasporas and Development: Exploring the Potential*, Lynne Rienner.

Bukharin, N. (1972). *Economic Theory of the Leisure Class*, New York, Monthly Review Press.

Buttrick, J. (1960). "Toward a Theory of Economic Growth: The Neoclassical Contribution," in Hoselitz, B.F., Spengler, J.J., Letiche, J.M., Erskine McKinley, E., Buttrick, J., and Bruton, H.J. ed. *Theories of Economic Growth* (1960), Glencoe, Illinois, The Free Press.

Camarota, S.A. (2004). *The High Cost of Cheap Labor: Illegal Immigration and the Federal Budget*. Center for Immigration Studies Washington, DC, August http://www.cis.org/articles/2004/fiscal.pdf.

Campaign Against Arms Trade. (2011). UK arms sales to Middle East include tear gas and crowd control ammunition to Bahrain and Libya, February 17. http://www. caat.org.uk/press/archive.php?url=20110217prs.

Canterbury, D.C. (2010). *European Bloc Imperialism*. Boston, Brill.

Canterbury. D.C. (2005). *Neoliberal Democratization and New Authoritarianism*. Aldershot, Hampshire, Ashgate Publishers.

Canterbury, D.C. ed. (1998). Guyana Gold Industry: Evolution, Structure, Impacts and Non-Wage Benefits, *Transition* Special Issue 27–28, Institute of Development Studies, University of Guyana.

Caribbean360. (2011). Address at the 100th Session of the Council of IOM December 5, 2011 Palace des Nations. *Caribbean360*, Belleville, St. Michael, Barbados December 30.

Carroll, S. (2010). "Big Names on the List of Companies ICE Fined," *Immigration Chronicles* September 9.

Center for Economic Policy Research. (2000). "Trade and Migration," *European Economic Perspectives 24*, January, pp. 6–8.

Chami, R., Fullenkamp, C., and Jahjah, S. (2005), Are Immigrant Remittance Flows a Source of Capital for Development? *IMF Staff Papers*, Vol. 52, No. 1.

Charnovitz, S. (2002). WTO Norms on International Migration. Paper Prepared for IOM Workshop on Existing International Migration Law Norms, April 30.

Chiang, A.C. (1984). Fundamental Methods of Mathematical Economics 3rd Edition, New York, McGraw-Hill.

Clark, N. (2004). "Libya Signs Energy Exploration Deal With Shell." *New York Times Global Edition* Business Day World, March 26.

Committee on the Elimination of Racial Discrimination (CERD) Immigrant/Migrant Rights Working Group. (2007). Rights of Immigrants and Migrants to the United States: A Critical Look at the US and Its Compliance under the Convention: A Response to the 2007 Periodic Report of the United States of America.

Cortes. P. (2008). "The Effect of Low-Skilled Immigration on U.S. Prices: Evidence from CPI Data," *Journal of Political Economy*, Vol. 116, No. 3, pp. 381–422.

Curry, G.E. (2011). New Migration Needed For African-Americans, *The Seattle Medium* 6/8/2011.

Dalmia, S. (2011). Obama's Anti-Immigrant Stance: Under the guise of immigration enforcement, the White House pushes a pro-union agenda, *Reason Magazine*, July 12.

Davis, T.W.D. (2009). "The MDGs and the Incomplete Relationship between Development and Foreign Aid," Paper presented to the "Meeting the Millennium Development Goals:

Old Problems, New Challenges" Conference 30 November-1 December 2009 Institute for Human Security Latrobe University.

Debroy, B. (2011). What Will Happen to the MDGs? *Indian Express.Com* April 6.

DeGennaro, R.P. (2005). Market Imperfections, Federal Reserve Bank of Atlanta Working Paper Series, Working Paper 2005–12, July.

De Haas, H. (2006). Engaging Diasporas: How Governments and Development agencies can Support Diaspora Involvement in the Development of Origin Countries," International Migration Institute, James Martin 21st Century School University of Oxford, A study for Oxfam Novib.

Development Research Center on Migration, Globalization and Poverty. (2005). "GATS Mode 4: How Trade in Services Can Help Developing Countries," Briefing No. 4, November.

De Wolf, M. and Katherine Klemmer, K. (2010). "Job openings, hires, and separations fall during the recession." *Monthly Labor Review*, May, pp. 36–44.

Dobb, M.M. (1973). *Theories of Value and Distribution Since Adam Smith*, Cambridge, Cambridge University Press.

Domar, E.D. (1946). "Capital Expansion, Rate of Growth and Employment," *Econometrica*, Vol. 14, 1946.

Domar, E.D. (1964). *Essays in the Theory of Economic Growth*, New York, Oxford University Press.

Dovlo, D. (2005). "Taking More Than a Fair Share? The Migration of Health Professionals from Poor to Rich Countries." PLoS Med 2(5): e109. doi:10.1371/journal.pmed.0020109.

Edgeworth, F.Y. (1925). *Papers Relating to Political Economy*, London, Macmillan and Company.

European Commission. (2005). *Communication on "Migration and Development: Some Concrete Recommendations*," September, in Ionescu, D. (2006). Engaging Diasporas as Development Partners for Home and Destination Countries: Challenges for Policymakers, Prepared for IOM the International Organization for Migration, Geneva.

European Parliament. (2011). European Parliament recommendation of 20 January 2011 to the Council on the negotiations on the EU-Libya Framework Agreement (2010/2268(INI)).

EuMonitor. (2008). Euro-African Conference in Paris on migration and development: the Commission asks its partners to deliver on their commitments, 25 November.

European Union. (2010). European Commission and Libya agree a Migration Cooperation agenda during high-level visit to boost EU-Libya Relations. *EUROPA Press Releases*, Brussels, 5 October.

Findlay, R. (1982). "On W. Arthur Lewis' Contribution to Economics," in M. Gersovitz, M., Diaz-Alejandro, C.F., Ranis, G. and Rosenzweig, M.R. (Ed.), *The Theory and Experience of Economic Development: Essays in Honor of Sir W. Arthur Lewis*, London, Allen & Unwin.

Foster, J.B. (2010). "The Financialization of Accumulation," *Monthly Review*, Volume 62, Number 5, October.

Fox News Latino. (2011). "S. Carolina business sector divided over anti-immigrant bill," February 24, http://latino.foxnews.com/latino/news/2011/02/24/s-carolina-business -sector-divided-anti-immigrant/#ixzz1dmRtolZb.

Freedom Road Socialist Organization. (2009). "The Immigrant Rights Movement and the Struggle for Full Equality," http://www.frso.org/docs/2009/immrts 2009 screen.pdf.

Furnivall, J.H. (1939). *Netherlands India: A Study of Plural Economy*, Cambridge, Cambridge University Press.

Furnivall, J.H. (1948). *Colonial Policy and Practice: A Comparative Study of Burma and Netherlands India*, Cambridge, Cambridge University Press.

Girvan, G. (1973). "The Development of Dependency Economics in the Caribbean and Latin America," *Social and Economic Studies*, Vol. 22, No.1.

Goldstein, J.P. (2009). "Introduction: The Political Economy of Financialization," *Review of Radical Political Economics*, Special Issue: The Financialization of Global Capitalism: Analysis, Critiques, and Alternatives, Volume 41, Number 4, Fall.

Greenberg, J. (2011). "Flow of African Migrants Poses Dilemma for Israel," *The Washington Post*, Friday, April 15.

Gueron, J. and Spevacek, A.M. (2008). Diaspora-Development Nexus: The Role of ICT. USAID Knowledge Services Center, August 18.

Hardisty, J. (2002). Corporate Desires vs. Anti-immigration Fervor: The Bush Administration's Dilemma, *Political Research Associates*, http://www.publiceye.org/ark/immigrants/CorporateHardisty.html.

Harris, D.J. (1978). *Capital Accumulation and Income Distribution*, Stanford, Stanford University Press, 1978.

Harris, J.R. and Todaro, M.P. (1970). "Migration, Unemployment and Development: A Two-Sector Analysis," *The American Economic Review*, Vol. 60, No. 1, pp. 126–142.

Harrod, R.F. (1963). *Towards a Dynamic Economics: Some Recent Developments of Economic Theory and Their Application to Policy*, New York, St. Martin Press.

Harrod, R.F. (1939). "An Essay in Dynamic Theory," *Economic Journal*, Vol. 49, 1939.

Hatton, T.J. (2007). "Should we have a WTO for international migration?" *Economic Policy*, Volume 22, Issue 50, April, pages 339–383.

High-level Dialogue on International Migration and Development, UN General Assembly, September 2006 in Ionescu, D. (2006). Engaging Diasporas as Development Partners for Home and Destination Countries: Challenges for Policymakers, Prepared for IOM the International Organization for Migration, Geneva.

Hilferding, R. (1981). *Finance Capital: A Study of the Latest Phase of Capitalist Development*, Edited by Tom Bottomore London, Routledge and Kegan Paul, 1981.

Hughes, J.R.T. (1968). "Industrialization: Economic Aspects." International Encyclopedia of the Social Sciences http://www.encyclopedia.com/topic/Industrialization.aspx.

Hulme, D. (2009). Governing Global Poverty? Global Ambivalence and the Millennium Development Goals," Brooks World Poverty Institute, and Institute for Development Policy and Management University of Manchester, May 6.

Human Rights Watch. (2010). *Libya: Do Not Deport Eritreans*: Allow Access to UN Refugee Agency, 2 July, http://www.unhcr.org/refworld/docid/4d33e42d2.html.

International Labor Organization, Thesaurus, http://www.vocabularyserver.com/ilo/index.php.

International Monetary Fund. (2010). The Fund's Role Regarding Cross-Border Capital Flows, IMF Washington DC: November.

International Organization for Migration, "GATS Mode 4," http://www.iom.int/jahia/Jahia/about-migration/developing-migration-policy/migration-trade/GATS-mode-4.

International Organization for Migration. (2003). IOM's Role in Enhancing Regional Dialogues on Migration, Eighty-Sixth Session, MC/INF/266, November 10.

International Organization for Migration. (2005). International Migration, Development and the Information Society. World Summit on Information Society (WSIS) Concept Paper Geneva 2003-Tunis 2005.

International Organization for Migration et al. (2006). Migration and Development Conference, Final Report 2006, Brussels, A joint initiative: The Government of the Kingdom of Belgium, The International Organization for Migration (IOM), The European Commission, The World Bank, March.

International Organization for Migration et al. (2006). "Migration and the Millennium Development Goals (MDGs) Facts and Myths," in Migration and Development Conference, Final Report 2006, Brussels, A joint initiative: The Government of the Kingdom of Belgium, The International Organization for Migration (IOM), The European Commission, The World Bank, March.

International Organization for Migration. (2005). The Millennium Development Goals and Migration, IOM Migration Research Series, No. 20, Geneva, Switzerland.

Ionescu, D. (2006). Engaging Diasporas as Development Partners for Home and Destination Countries: Challenges for Policymakers, Prepared for IOM the International Organization for Migration, Geneva.

Jalée, P. (1968). *The Pillage of the Third World*. New York, Monthly Review Press.

Jamaica Observer. (2011). "US to protect Caribbean immigrants from bogus lawyers," June 10 http://www.jamaicaobserver.com/news/US-to-protect-Caribbean-immigrants-from-bogus-lawyers_8989104.

Jevons, H.S. (1916). "The Teaching of Economics," *Indian Journal of Economics*, Vol. 1, (1916–1917).

Jevons, S. (1965). *The Theory of Political Economy*, 5th Edition, New York, A.M. Kelley.

Johnson, B., and Sedaca, S. (2004). "Diasporas, Emigrés and Development, Economic Linkages and Programmatic Responses," US Agency for International Development (USAID) and Trade Enhancement for the Services Sector (TESS) project, March.

Jolly, R.A. The Human Development Perspective, http://www.adb.org/Documents/Conference/Poverty_Reduction/chap1.pdf.

Kamndaya, S. (2011). "Mobile Cash Transfer Hailed," *The Citizen* (Dar es Salaam), May 9.

Kay, C. (1989). *Latin American Theories of Development and Underdevelopment*, London, Routledge.

Keynes, J.M. (1935). *The General Theory of Employment, Interest, and Money*, New York, Harcourt and Brace.

Lanzet, P. (2011). "Toothless Tiger," *The European Magazine*, January 14.

Leight, J. (2004). The International Republican Institute: Promulgating Democracy of Another Variety. Washington. Council On Hemispheric Affairs, Memorandum to the Press 04.40, July 15.

Levine, L. (2010). Immigration: The Effects on Low-Skilled and High-Skilled Native-Born Workers, Congressional Research Service (CRS) 7-5700, 95-408, April 13.

Levitt, K. (1992). The State of Development Studies, IDS Occasional Papers No. 92.1, Saint Mary's University, Halifax, Nova Scotia.

Levitt, K.P. (2008). "The Great Financialization," John Kenneth Galbraith Prize Lecture, Progressive Economics Forum, University of British Columbia, Vancouver, Canada, June 8.

Lewis, Sir W.A. (1971). "Socialism and Economic Growth," The Annual Oration, London, London School of Economics.

Lewis, Sir W.A. (1954). "Economic Development With Unlimited Supplies of Labor," *The Manchester School*, Vol. XXII, No. 2, May pp. 139–91.

Lewis, Sir W.A. (1950). "Industrialization of the British West Indies," *Caribbean Economic Review*, Vol. 2, No. 1.

Lewis, Sir W.A. (1955). *The Theory of Economic Growth*, Illinois, Richard D. Irwin.

Lin, H.H. (2011). Determinants of Remittances: Evidence from Tonga, IMF Working Paper, Asia and Pacific Department, WP/11/18, January.

López-Córdova, E. (2006). Globalization, Migration and Development: The Role of Mexican Migrant Remittances, Institute for the Integration of Latin America and the Caribbean (INTAL) and Integration, Trade and Hemispheric Issues Division (ITD), Buenos Aires and Washington, Working Paper 20.

Lowell L., and Gerova, S. (2004). "Diasporas and Economic Development: State of Knowledge," Report to the World Bank, Washington, D.C., Institute for the Study of International Migration, Georgetown.

Lucht, H. (2011). *Darkness Before Daybreak: African Migrants Living on the Margins in Southern Italy Today*. Berkeley, University of California Press.

Maes, M. (2008). The EU's Global Europe Strategy: Where is that Strategy Today? Coalition of the Flemish North-South Movement Introductory presentation made at the informal meeting "Building of A Common Platform Between Developing Countries" organized by South Centre in Brussels on 4–5 December.

Malthus, Rev. T.R. (1951). *Principles of Political Economy, Consider With a View to Their Practical Application*, New York, Augustus M. Kelley.

Mandelbaum, K.M. (1947). *Industrialization of Backward Areas*, Oxford, Basil Blackwell.

Mariani, F. (2010). Migration and Crime: Preliminary Draft. IRES, Université Catholique de Louvain Paris School of Economics IZA, Bonn March 15. http://www.iza.org/conference_files/ LeIlli2010/mariani_f2907.pdf.

Marshall, A. (1910). *Principles of Economics*, London, Macmillan and Company.

Massey, D.M. (1988). "Economic Development and International Migration in Comparative Perspective,"*Population and Development Review*, Vol. 14, Issue, pp. 383–413.

Martin, P. (2006). The Economics of Migration: Managing the Flow of International Labor, *Harvard International Review*, July 17.

Marx, K. (1909). *Capital: A Critique of Political Economy*, Volume I, Chicago, Charles H. Kerr and Company.

Marx, K. and Engels, F. (1998). *The German Ideology*. New York. Prometheus Books.

Menger, C. (1965). *Principles of Economics*, New York, New York University Press.

Middle East Online. (2007). "Blair hails relations with Libya, $900 million gas deal," Middle East Online. May 30, 2007, http://www.middle-east-online.com/english/?id =20886.

Mohamoud, A.A. (2007). The Contribution of African Diaspora to Policy Dialogue, African Diaspora Policy Centre, The Netherlands, October.

Monger, R. (2010). "U.S. Legal Permanent Residents: 2009," *Annual Flow Report 2010*, US Department of Homeland Security, Office of Immigration Statistics, April.

Moses, J.W. (2006). *International Migration: Globalization's Last Frontier*, London, Zed Books.

Muscara, A. (2011). "Libya: Thousands of Foreign Laborers Trapped in Turmoil," *Inter-Press Service*, Washington, March 3.

Myint, H. (1948). *Theories of Welfare Economics*, Cambridge, Harvard University Press.

Myint, H. (1954). "An Interpretation of Economic Backwardness," *Oxford Economic Papers*, Vol. 6, No. 6.

Newland, K., with Patrick, E. (2004). *Beyond Remittances: The Role of Diasporas in Poverty Reduction in their Countries of Origin*, Washington DC: Migration Policy Institute, MPI.

Newland, K. (2011). Migration and Development Policy: What Have We Learned? Washington DC: Migration Policy Institute.

Newland, K. and Tanaka, H. (2010). Mobilizing Diaspora Entrepreneurship for Development Migration Policy Institute and US Agency for International Development, Diasporas and Development Policy Project, October.

Ness, I. (2007). "Forging a Migration Policy for Capital: Labor Shortages and Guest Workers," *New Political Science*, Volume 29, Number 4, December 2007, pp. 429–452.

Niessen, J. (2003). Negotiating the Liberalization of Migration – Is GATS a Vehicle or a Model for Global Migration Governance? *The European Policy Centre (EPC)* Issue Paper No. 6 Issued on 28/10/2003.

Niessen, J. and Yongmi Schibel, Y. (2003). EU and US Approaches to the Management of Immigration: Comparative perspectives. Migration Policy Group Brussels, May.

Niles, B. (2006). Are Guyanese welcome in Barbados? *BBC Caribbean.com* September 7.

Nurkse, R. (1952). "Some Aspects of the Problem of Economic Development," *American Economic Review*, Vol. XLII, No.2.

Nurkse, R. (1953). *Problems of Capital Formation in Underdeveloped Countries*, Oxford, Blackwell, 1953.

O'Brien. K.J. (2008). "Taking steeps towards mobile cash." *The New York Times*, Wednesday, July 2.

Overseas Development Institute. (2001). Economic Theory, Freedom and Human Rights: The Work of Amartya Sen, *ODI Briefing Paper*, November.

Özden, Ç and Schiff. M.W. (2007). *International Migration, Economic Development and Policy*, Washington, DC and New York: World Bank and Palgrave Macmillan.

Peria, M.S.M. (2010). What Drives the Price of Remittances?: New Evidence Using the Remittance Price Worldwide Database, http://blogs.worldbank.org/.

Petras, J. (2007). *Rulers and Ruled n the US Empire: Bankers, Zionists, Militants*, Atlanta, Clarity Press.

Petras, J. (2011). US Working and Middle Class: Solidarity or Competition in the Face of Crisis?" http://petras.lahaine.org/?p=1865.

Petras, J. (2006). Mesoamerica comes to North America: The dialectics of the Migrant Workers' Movement, The James Petras Website, 05.02.2006, http://petras.lahaine .org/?p=6.

Phillips, L. (2011). "EU scorns Libya 'blackmail' on migrants." *euobserver.com*. February 21.

Polaski, S. (2003). Trade and Labor Standards: A Strategy for Developing Countries, Carnegie Endowment for International Peace, Washington, DC.

Pomfret, J. (1999). "A Less Tibetan: Many residents fear Chinese Migration will Dilute Culture." Washington Post Foreign Service, Sunday, October page A31.

Prebisch R. (1950). *The Economic Development of Latin America and Its Principal Problems*, New York, United Nations.

Preobrzhanski, E.A. (1979). *The Crisis of Soviet Industrialization: Selected Essays*, New York, Sharpe.

Proletarian Revolution (1997). "End Anti-Immigrant Attacks!" *Proletarian Revolution*, No. 55, Fall 1997, http://www.lrp-cofi.org/ PR/ immigrationPR55.html.

Razin, A. and Sadka, E. (1996). "Suppressing Resistance to Low-skill Migration." *International Tax and Public Finance*, Vol. 3, No. 3, pp. 413–424.

Razin, A. and Sadka, E. (1995). Resisting Migration: The Problems of Wage Rigidity and the Social Burden, NBER Working Paper No. 4903 Issued in June.

Reddy, S., and Heuty, A. (2004). Achieving the MDGs: A Critique and a Strategy, August 12. http://dspace.cigilibrary.org/jspui/bitstream/123456789/13325/1/Achieving%20the%20 MDGs%20A%20Critique%20and%20a%20Strategy.pdf?1.

Report of the West India Royal Commission (Moyne Commission Report). (1945). Cmd. 6656, London, Her Majesty's Stationary Office.

Ricardo, D. (1980). *Principles of Political Economy and Taxation*, London, George Bell and Sons.

Rosenstein-Rodan, P.N. (1943). "Problems of Industrialization of Eastern and South-Eastern Europe," *Economic Journal*, Vol. 53, No. 210/211.

Ruedin, D. and D'Amato, G. (2011). Improving EU and US Immigration Systems' Capacity for Responding to Global Challenges: Learning from Experiences Social Cohesion Challenges in Europe, Research Report, Background paper, EU-US Immigration Systems 2011/04 European University Institute, Robert Schuman Centre for Advanced Studies, Italy.

Schumpeter, J. (1954). *History of Economic Analysis*, Cambridge, Harvard University Press, 1954.

Sergeant, H. (2008). "Commentary: The facts behind crime and migration." Mail Online, April. http://www.dailymail.co.uk/news/article-560181/Commentary-The-facts-crime -migration.html.

Sherwood, MAJ. J.T. (2008). Building the Wall: The Efficacy of a US-Mexico Border Fence. Thesis presented to the Faculty of the U.S. Army Command and General Staff College in partial fulfillment of the requirements for the degree Master of Military Art and Science, Homeland Security, December.

Singer, H. (1950). "Distribution of Gains Between Investing and Borrowing Countries," *American Economic Review*, Papers and Proceedings.

Sirojudin, S. (2009). "Economic Theories of Emigration." *Journal of Human Behavior in the Social Environment*, 19: 702–712.

Seattle to Brussels Network. (2008). The New 'Global Europe' Strategy of the EU: Serving Corporations Worldwide and at Home A Wake-up Call to Cvil Society and Trade Unions in Europe and Elsewhere.

Seelke, C.R. (2011). Mexico-U.S. Relations: Issues for Congress, Congressional Research Service, 7-5700 RL32724, February 15.

Sen, A. (1973). *On Economic Inequality*, New York, Norton.
Sen, A. (1982). *Poverty and Famines: An Essay on Entitlements and Deprivation*, Oxford, Clarendon Press.
Sen, A. (1982). *On Ethics and Economics*, Oxford, Basil Blackwell.
Sen, A. (2000). *Development as Freedom*. New York, Anchor Books.
Smith, S. (1952). *An Inquiry Into the Nature and Causes of the Wealth of Nations*, London, Encyclopedia Britannica.
Sogge, D. (2010). Millennium Development Goals for the Rich? Transnational Institute (TNI), September.
Spaan, E. (1994). "Taikongs and Calos: The Role of Middlemen and Brokers in Javanese International Migration," *International Migration Review*, Volume XXVIII, No 1, Spring.
Spannaus, N. (2006). Mass Strike Ferment Hits United States in Pro-Immigration Rallies. *Executive Intelligence Review*, http://www.larouchepub.com/other/2006/3316immigr _masstrike.html.
Sraffa, P. (1960). *Production of Commodities by Means of Commodities: Prelude to a Critique of Economic Theory*, Cambridge, Cambridge University Press.
Standing. G. (2011). *The Precariat: The New Dangerous Class*, USA, Bloomsbury.
Stanley, E. (1944).*World Economic Development: Effects of Advanced Industrialized Countries*, Montreal, International Labor Organization.
Sweezy, P.M. (1997). "More (or Less) on Globalization," *Monthly Review* 49, Number 4, September.
Taylor, J.E. (2006). International Migration and Economic Development. International Symposium on International Migration and Development, Population Division, Department of Economic and Social Affairs, United Nations Secretariat, Turin, Italy, 28–30 June. UN/POP/MIG/SYMP/2006/09 26 June.
The Global Commission on International Migration (GCIM), October 2005 in Ionescu, D. (2006). Engaging Diasporas as Development Partners for Home and Destination Countries: Challenges for Policymakers, Prepared for IOM the International Organization for Migration, Geneva.
Third World Network. (2010), Achieving the Millennium Development Goals (MDGs) Requires Fundamental Reforms in the International Financial Architecture, TWN Info Service on Finance and Development, June 15.
Thomas, C.Y. and Hosein, R. (2007). "Caribbean Single Market Economy (CSME) and the Intra-Regional Migration of Nurses: Some Proposed Opportunities," *Global Social Policy*, Vol. 7 No. 3, pp. 316–338.
Thomas, C.Y. (1974). *Dependency and Transformation: The Economics of the Transition to Socialism*, New York, Monthly Review Press.
Toye, J. (1987). *The Dilemmas of Development*, New York, Basil Blackwell.
Ul Haq, M. (1976). *The Poverty Curtain: Choices for the Third World*, New York, Columbia University Press.
Ul Haq, M. (1969). *Reflections on Human Development* (1996), Oxford, Oxford University Press.
United Nations (1949). *Relative Price of Exports and Imports of Underdeveloped Countries*, New York.
United Nations. (1952). *Instability of Exports Proceeds of Underdeveloped Countries*, New York.
United Nations. (2011). Millennium Development Goals (MDGs) Report 2011: We Can End Poverty, United Nations, New York.
United Nations High Commissioner for Refugee. (2010). "UNHCR says ordered to close office in Libya." Geneva, 8 June, http://www.unhcr.org/4c0e79 059.html.
United Nations Research Institute for Social Development. (2010). Combating Poverty and Inequality: Structural Change, Social Policy and Politics, Geneva, Switzerland, UNRISD/2010/4.
Urrutia, C., and Meza, F. (2010). Financial Liberalization, Structural Change, and Real Exchange Rate Appreciations, IMF Working Paper IMF Institute, WP/10/63

Montgomerie, J. (2006). "The Financialization of the American Credit Card Industry," *Competition and Change*, Vol. 10, No. 3, September, 301–319.

US Department of Commerce, Bureau of Economic Analysis (2010), News Release, BEA 10-47, September 30.

U.S. Department of Homeland Security (2010). Yearbook of Immigration Statistics 2009, Office of Immigration Statistics, August.

U.S. Department of Homeland Security, (2010). Computer Linked Applicant Information Management System (CLAIMS), Legal Immigrant Data, Fiscal Years 2007 to 2009.

U.S. Department of Labor, U.S. Bureau of Labor Statistics (2006). Extended Mass Layoffs in 2005, Report 997, September.

U.S. Department of Labor, U.S. Bureau of Labor Statistics (2004). Extended Mass Layoffs in 2003, Report 982, December.

U.S. Department of Labor, U.S. Bureau of Labor Statistics (2003). Extended Mass Layoffs in 2002, Report 971, August.

U.S. Department of Labor Bureau of Labor Statistics (2011). Foreign-Born Workers: Labor Force Characteristics – 2010, News Release, USDL-11-0763, Friday, May 27.

U.S. Department of Labor, Bureau of Labor Statistics (2008). Foreign-Born Workers: Labor Force Characteristics in 2007, USDL 08-0409, March 26.

U.S. Department of Labor U.S. Bureau of Labor Statistics (2010). Extended Mass Layoffs in 2008, Report 1024, June.

U.S. Department of Labor, Bureau of Labor Statistics (2010). Employment and Earnings January 2010, http://www.bls.gov/cps/tables.htm.

U.S. Department of Labor, U.S. Bureau of Labor Statistics (2008). Extended Mass Layoffs in 2006, Report 1004, April.

Van Vechten, C.C. (1941). "The Criminality of the Foreign Born," *Journal of Criminal Law and Criminology* 32, pp. 139–147.

Veltmeyer, H. ed. (2011). *The Critical Development Studies Handbook: Tools for Change*, London and New York, Pluto Press; and Halifax and Winnipeg, Fernwood Publishing.

Walras, L. (1954). *Elements of Pure Economics, or the Theory of Social Wealth*, London, Allen and Unwin.

Wasem, R.E. (2010). Immigration of Foreign Workers: Labor Market Tests and Protections, Congressional Research Service (CRS), 7-5700, RL33977, August 27.

Wasem, R.E. and Collver, G.K. (2003). Immigration of Agricultural Guest Workers: Policy, Trends, and Legislative Issues, CRS Report, January 24.

Whitehead, T. (2011). EU Migrants Commit 500 Crimes a Week in UK, *The Telegraph*, Sunday 17 April.

Williams, E. (1994). *Capitalism and Slavery*. Chapel Hill, The University of North Carolina Press.

World Bank, International Financial Corporation, Remittance Prices Worldwide, http://remittanceprices.worldbank.org/.

World Trade Organization. (2009). "World Trade 2008, Prospects for 2009: WTO Sees 9% Global Trade Decline in 2009 as Recession Strikes," Press Release 554, March 24 (08-0000).

World Trade Organization, "SERVICES: GATS The General Agreement on Trade in Services (GATS): Objectives, Coverage and Disciplines," http://www.wto.org/english/tratop_e/serv_e/gatsqa_e.htm.

Zaidi, K.R. (2010). Harmonizing Trade Liberalization and Migration Policy Through Shared Responsibility: A Comparison of the Impact of Bilateral Trade Agreements and the Gats in Germany and Canada," *Syracuse Journal of International Law and Commerce*, 267, Spring.

Zimmermann, K.F. and de Melo, J. ed. (1999). Migration: The Controversies and the Evidence, published for Center for European Policy Research by Cambridge University Press, London.

NAME INDEX

Sherwood, Major John T. 183
Singer, Hans 37–39
Sirleaf, Ellen Johnson 119
Sirojudin, Siroj 48
Smith, Adam 22–24, 27, 29, 30, 32, 39
Sogge, David 140–142
Soledad Martinez Peria, Maria 106
Spaan, Ernst 158
Spannaus, Nancy 199
Spevacek, Anne Marie 116
Standing, Guy 2, 37, 86, 107, 114, 137, 140,
  163, 212, 223, 229, 231, 234–237
Stanley, Eugene 32, 37
Streeten, P. 38, 39
Sweezy, Paul M. 88, 89

Tanaka, H. 98, 100–102
Taylor, J. Edward 3, 4
Thomas, Clive Y. 22, 24, 28, 38, 139, 164

Tinbergen, J. 39
Todaro, Michael P. 41
Toledo, Alejandro 119
Toye, John 39

ul Haq, Mahbub 148
Urrutia, Carlos 93

Van Vechten, C.C. 192
Veltmeyer, Henry 71

Walras, Leon 32
Wasem, Ruth Ellen 188–190, 198
Whitehead, Tom 193
Wicksell, J.G.K. 39
Williams, Eric 232

Zaidi, Kamaal R. 74
Zimmermann, Klaus F. 75

SUBJECT INDEX